ASAP

ACADEMIC
SKILLS ACHIEVEMENT
PROGRAM

ASAP

ACADEMIC SKILLS ACHIEVEMENT PROGRAM

LINDA K. LINVILLE

IRWIN
MIRROR PRESS

Burr Ridge, Illinois
Boston, Massachusetts
Sydney, Australia

To Don, in partnership

Mirror Press: David R. Helmstadter
                Carla F. Tishler

Marketing manager: Lynn M. Kalanik
Project editor: Ethel Shiell
Production manager: Bob Lange
Designer: Larry J. Cope
Art coordinator: Heather Burbridge
Art studio: Electronic Publishing Service, Inc.
Cover art: Darcy Gerbarg
Compositor: Graphic Composition, Inc.
Typeface: 11/13 Criterion
Printer: Von Hoffmann Press

Library of Congress Cataloging-in-Publication Data

Linville, Linda K.
    ASAP academic skills achievement program / Linda K.
Linville.
        p.   cm.
    Includes bibliographical references and index.
    ISBN 0-256-14219-X
    1. Study skills.   2. Active learning.   3. Career education.
    4. Reading.   5. Life skills.   6. Test-taking skills.   I. Title.
    LB1049.L53   1994
    371.3′028′1−dc20   93−14480

Printed in the United States of America

1 2 3 4 5 6 7 8 9 0 VH 0 9 8 7 6 5 4 3

PREFACE

ASAP means priority. Study skills are a high priority for every student's academic success. Based on my years of teaching experience at Robert Morris College and Broome Community College, I believe students can progress rapidly and effectively when they are able to

- Rely on self-motivation.
- Draw constructively on both their academic knowledge and their work experience.
- Build learning skills progressively.
- Manage stress productively.

In developing the *Academic Skills Achievement Program,* I have striven to create a book for students that integrates these vital factors into an active study skills program.

ASAP makes connections between traditional study skill topics and on-the-job skills sought by employers. In each chapter, students are encouraged to link the mastery of a study skill not only to immediate academic goals, but also to long-term career goals. To actively engage students in the learning process, *ASAP* stresses interactive exercises that draw upon the student's current knowledge and life experience.

SCOPE AND SEQUENCE

ASAP explains, step by step, the essential study skills needed for academic success, giving special emphasis to developing vocabulary, summary writing skills, problem-solving skills, memory skills, organizational patterns, active reading skills, listening skills, note-taking skills, and testing skills. It also emphasizes motivation and attitude, along with time and stress management.

The sequence of topics allows students to build skills logically and progressively. For example, students first learn better concentration skills, then use their improved concentration skills to build better memory skills. All topics are cross-referenced so students can easily review and refine skills from previous chapters. *ASAP* provides students with many opportunities for growth and learning success. The book is organized in 12 chapters grouped into three parts.

Part 1: Developing Success Skills sets the foundation for successfully meeting the challenges of academic life. In Part 1, students learn the importance of developing their own commitment to the learning process, along with a system of organizing their work, strategies for problem solving, and proven guidelines for time management.

Part 2: Developing Active Learning Skills focuses on helping students actively build skills in concentration, memory, reading comprehension, underlining, note taking, self-quizzing, and analytical thinking.

Part 3: Developing Performance Skills coaches students on test-taking skills and effective techniques for preparing reports. In this part, students learn strategies for building self-confidence, controlling test anxiety, studying effectively, analyzing test questions, and using test results to improve future learning.

LEARNING DEVICES

No study skills program is effective unless students become actively involved in the learning process. *ASAP* provides numerous charts, summary boxes, and samples to build and sustain interest and increase understanding. Several chapter features are expressly designed to engage the student in active learning:

THE SKILL THAT GETS THE JOB. Each chapter begins with an actual newspaper job advertisement that highlights the skills to be mastered in the chapter. Students can immediately connect the study skills taught in the chapter to academic success *and* the world of work.

WHAT'S YOUR EXPERIENCE? This brief writing exercise stimulates students to explore and consider their own knowledge and experience as a foundation for learning.

ASAP SKILL FAST FORWARD. These learning objectives help students be effective learners by previewing each chapter's main points and highlighting skills to be mastered.

STRESSBUSTERS. Because stress is an ongoing challenge, upbeat stress reduction tips and techniques help students cope with academic and life pressures.

INFORMATION FILES. To broaden the learning context of each chapter, these feature boxes contain interesting and often humorous facts related to chapter topics. This feature also gives students additional practice in reading and comprehending statistical data and historical and scientific information.

ASAP REWINDS. A question-and-answer summary reviews the major concepts of each chapter. This feature demonstrates the importance of questioning as an active learning technique and also serves as an effective review.

WORD POWER. These exercises develop students' ability to acquire new vocabulary from reading. Students use context and word meaning clues to define new words. Accordingly, vocabulary development becomes an ongoing process integrated with active reading.

TAKE ACTION. These exercises are challenging and practical activities that directly reinforce the learning objectives of each chapter and also encourage students to develop analytical thinking skills, practice writing, and apply study skills consistently.

CHECK YOUR PROGRESS. These checklists are unique self-assessment exercises that close each chapter. Students review their mastery of chapter material and then jot down their own ideas on maintaining newly acquired skills.

INSTRUCTOR'S RESOURCE MANUAL. The manual provides instructors with suggestions for course organization and lesson development, including additional skill reinforcement exercises and suggestions for student activities. Transparency masters suitable for reproduction are provided for the chapters. Suggested answers and solutions are given for all exercises in the text. Test items for each chapter are also included and can be reproduced from the manual.

ACKNOWLEDGMENTS

This textbook represents the collective wisdom and positive efforts of many people, who have my thanks and gratitude. Each student with whom I have learned during 20 years of teaching has contributed to *ASAP*. My family—my husband, children, and mother—has provided invaluable support throughout the development of the book. Publisher David Helmstadter and editors Carla Tishler and Ethel Shiell have immeasurably enriched this effort with their guidance, expertise, and professionalism. The astute comments and suggestions of the following reviewers contributed positively to each phase of this project.

Paul Bittner, Southwestern College of Business, Cincinnati, OH

Betty Brace, Mt. Hood Community College, Portland, OR

Anita Brownstein, Drake School, New York, NY

Maxine Byers, Chemeketa Community College, Salem, OR

Darlene Pabis, Westmoreland County Community College, Youngwood, PA

Margaret Reysen, National College, Albuquerque, NM

Courtney Small, Robert Morris College, Chicago, IL

Dr. Tom Stander, Southern Ohio College, Cincinnati, OH

John Turpin, Phillips Jr. College, Salt Lake City, UT

Dr. Tom Weaver, Central Florida Community College, Ocala, FL

Mel Wyler, Hagerstown Business College, Hagerstown, MD

I am also grateful for the assistance I received from my friends and colleagues Lynn Balunas, Deborah Brooks, Donna Firenze, and Steve Natale. Finally, I wish to thank Ms. Lorena Morante for her generous contribution of journalism materials.

Linda K. Linville

TO THE STUDENT

True or false: School is not part of the real world. False. Learning in school is a job that requires the same skills for success that are necessary in career jobs. When I speak with employers to give references for students, they are interested in more than the student's degree. They are concerned with the individual's

- Attendance and punctuality.
- Organization and time management skills.
- Problem-solving abilities.
- Communication skills.
- Stress management skills.

These are the very same skills that successful students develop.

One of my goals in writing *ASAP* for students is to build a strong connection between study skills and employment skills. As a result, this textbook has a unique format and these special features.

Job advertisements. Each chapter opens with a classified advertisement taken from a major newspaper. The skills listed in the ad are the skills you will master in that chapter. Therefore, as you build study skills, you also lay the foundation for your future career.

Experience checks. Before you read each chapter, draw upon your past experience and knowledge in a brief writing exercise. You will be forming a foundation for more meaningful learning. In school, as on the job, *experience counts.*

Time savers. As you read on, you will notice the picture of a clock placed next to certain chapter headings. This symbol indicates tips that will help you learn more efficiently, save time, and consequently, reduce stress. These time savers can become part of your lifelong work habits from this point on.

Stressbusters. Each chapter also gives you practical tips for managing everyday stress that you can use now and in the future.

Skill builders. In every chapter you will practice specific study strategies and build basic communication skills through a variety of challenging activities. As on the job, you will test your ability to apply your knowledge to real situations and express yourself clearly.

Progress checks. To assure your success in using new strategies, each chapter ends with a self-assessment activity. By completing a brief checklist, you will be able to analyze your strengths and seek solutions to problems you are encountering.

By mastering the skills in *ASAP*, you will be working toward academic success AND the job traits sought by employers. Your future begins on page one. *Good luck*!

Linda K. Linville

CONTENTS

DEVELOPING SUCCESS SKILLS

Meeting the Challenge

THE SKILL THAT GETS THE JOB

Accounting Clerk.
To prepare monthly computerized financial statements for an international company. The successful candidate will be a mature self-starter, willing to take on new challenges. Super opportunity for the right person.

WHAT'S YOUR EXPERIENCE?

Your VCR and coffee maker can be programmed to start automatically, but how can you get off to a good start in school? How do requirements of this school differ from the expectations of your high school? What would you like to learn about becoming a self-starter in school or on a new job? Use the space below to explore your expectations, your knowledge, and any questions you have about this chapter's topic.

_____

_____

_____

_____

_____

_____

_____

_____

_____

_____

_____

_____

In this chapter you will learn to

»»»   *Fulfill your essential course requirements.*

»»»   *Use a daily assignment record and to-do list.*

»»»   *Maintain a unified notebook system.*

»»»   *Build on your experience and current skills.*

»»»   *Master new vocabulary.*

»»»   *Use summarizing to increase your learning.*

MEETING THE CHALLENGE

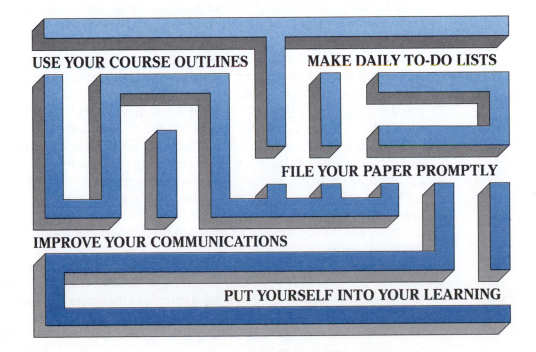

USE YOUR COURSE OUTLINES   MAKE DAILY TO-DO LISTS

FILE YOUR PAPER PROMPTLY

IMPROVE YOUR COMMUNICATIONS

PUT YOURSELF INTO YOUR LEARNING

You've filled out all the papers, chosen your courses and class schedule, and bought your books. What's next? How can you meet your newest and perhaps biggest challenge—college? You already possess the essential requirements to meet your school obligations. You have developed these skills and used them in high school, as part of a team, or on the job. Regardless of the challenge you face, the success strategies are the same.

1. First, you must understand and focus your efforts on the basic requirements expected of you.

2. Next, you must organize your tasks daily and establish a system for handling documents efficiently.

3. Finally, you must involve yourself in the tasks, enriching your performance with your knowledge, experience, and enthusiasm.

When do you get started—tomorrow, before the first exam? Get started NOW with the ideas and practical suggestions in this chapter.

FOCUS YOUR EFFORTS

More than likely, college is not the only focus for your attention. Perhaps you have a part-time job or family responsibilities. Maybe you're a club officer or you're just beginning a new, serious relationship. Regardless of your circumstances, one of your major objectives now should be efficiently handling your school work. Instructors, like employers, evaluate an individual on the quantity and quality of work completed. In many ways, businesspeople follow the same or similar guidelines.

Attend Every Class

Most successful businesses achieve high production levels, in part, by keeping absenteeism to a minimum. If you've worked in retail sales, food service, or even on a class project, you know that the absence of one worker increases others' workloads while decreasing efficiency.

As a student, if you skip a one-hour lecture you are not creating extra work for your classmates, but for yourself. First you will have to borrow lecture notes, then copy and interpret them. Reading your textbook will be more difficult because you did not process the lecture yourself. If you have difficulty with the concepts, approaching the instructor after an absence will be awkward.

Typically courses meet just three or four hours per week, rather than daily. As a result, some students have difficulty maintaining regular attendance and preparing assignments in the interim. Rather than face class without completed homework, you may decide to skip class. Most likely your absences will snowball because each absence will put you further behind, making the next lecture harder to attend. Ultimately you may be forced to drop the course, losing valuable time and possibly money.

Try to avoid making snap judgments about your classes during the first few sessions. Both you and your instructors will need several classes to establish a comfortable rapport. Forming a negative attitude at the outset will make consistent attendance throughout the term very difficult. Make class attendance your first step toward academic success and you'll also develop the most desirable of employee traits—good attendance.

rapport

INFORMATION FILE: MEETING THE CHALLENGE

You're in Good Company . . .
Regardless of your age, your contemporaries are attending school alongside you. Approximately 44 percent of college students are recent high school graduates. Almost 40 percent are 25 to 35 years old, and 16 percent are people who will never stop learning, regardless of their age!

Follow Course Requirements

Employees' duties are usually specified in a job description. After an orientation period, the employee is expected to perform the duties independently. Similarly, instructors distribute a course outline or syllabus during the first week of classes. This document provides basic information about the course requirements and policies such as

- Daily assignments.

- Test dates.

- Grading procedures.

- Attendance policy.

- Make-up policy.

After an explanation session, the instructor expects students to work on assignments independently, following the policies and time schedule provided in the outline. If something is unclear to you when the outline information is presented, discuss it with your instructor. Later on, carefully read the course outline and retain it with your daily study materials. You will be referring to your outlines regularly to follow your instructor's guidelines and to plan your daily study activities.

Keep an Assignment Record

Just as supervisors' instructions vary in detail, so do instructors' course outlines. Some instructors give a detailed, day-by-day listing of assignments. In these courses the instructors will expect you to complete the assignments independently with little or no prompting on their part. Therefore, you must use the outline each day to work on assignments and to keep pace with the instructor. Mark off each assignment as you complete it so you do not overlook any obligations. If your instructor adjusts the assignment schedule, be sure you record the changes accurately. Figure 1–1 shows a typical outline that lists assignments and the student's careful updating.

Other instructors list chapters or topics to be discussed during a certain week without indicating specific assignments. In these cases the instructor usually announces assignments during classes. Many students note these assignments haphazardly by turning down the corners of pages, circling problem numbers, or hastily scribbling directions on a loose piece of paper. Later on, they will have difficulty locating assignments and following directions.

haphazardly

You can make your job easier by developing a consistent system for recording assignments. A simple method is to record the assignment directly in your lecture

FIGURE 1–1   *Recording Daily Assignments*

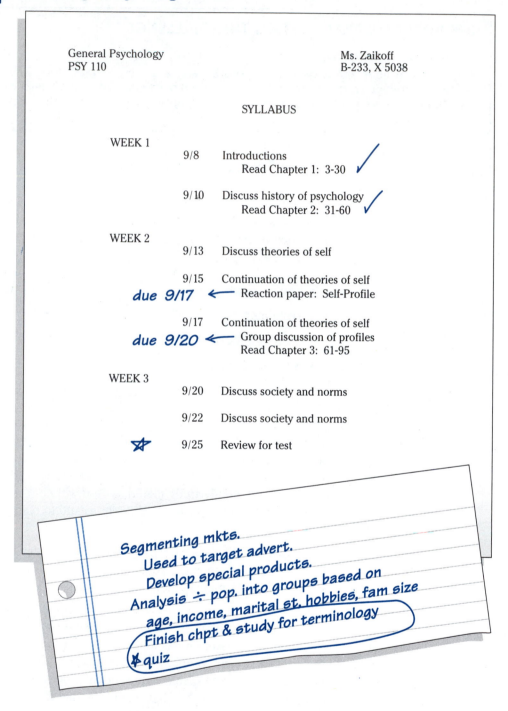

notes. Draw a box around the notation so you can locate it easily later on. This method is shown in Figure 1–1. It works well because you will usually use your lecture notes in preparing homework and in reviewing for the next lecture. Another method is to list all assignments in one place. Some students use a small notebook or create a special section in their large lecture notebook. If you are using a locker on campus, this system provides a quick way to check the books and materials you will need to take home.

INFORMATION FILE: MEETING THE CHALLENGE

Learn Your Degree Alphabet . . .
Have you ever wondered what all those college degree abbreviations mean? Here are some common degrees and their abbreviations. If you are working toward a degree, can you find yours? Is there a degree you aspire to?

A.A.	Associate of Arts	E.E.	Electrical Engineer
A.S.	Associate of Science	M.B.A.	Master of Business Administration
A.A.S.	Associate of Applied Science	M.C.S.	Master of Computer Science
B.A.	Bachelor of Arts	M.Ed.	Master of Education
B.S.	Bachelor of Science	M.S.W.	Master of Social Work
B.N.	Bachelor of Nursing	Ph.D.	Doctor of Philosophy
D.D.	Doctor of Divinity		

At first, the pace of college work can seem slow and unstructured, but within a few short days, assignments and exams begin to mount up. Some students have "survived" high school courses doing little or no work outside the classroom. In college this is not possible. Your instructors will cover more material at a faster pace because they expect you to practice and review skills and concepts outside class. Keep pace with your instructors from the very first day by using an assignment record and your course outlines.

ORGANIZE YOUR EFFORTS

Business and industry are continually seeking ways to make their operations more productive, not by increasing employees' assignments but by increasing employee efficiency. You can increase your efficiency and consequently your productivity by using two simple management tools:

1. Daily to-do lists will channel your efforts to the important tasks.

2. A streamlined system for filing documents will eliminate clutter and duplication of efforts.

Use a To-Do List

Everyone from executives to clerks uses to-do lists to guide their daily activities at work and in their personal lives. This management tip was worth $25,000 to Charles Schwab, a steel magnate. He paid the fee to a consultant who simply handed him a blank sheet of paper and a pencil with directions to keep a prioritized list. Schwab felt his money was very well spent because the technique worked so well for him and his managers. Similar success can be yours if you use written goals and objectives to guide your daily activities.

Perhaps you have tried using to-do lists before, but they didn't work for you. If you avoid some common pitfalls, you can develop an effective, personalized system that will help you to coordinate all aspects of your life. In the following examples, see if you can spot the reasons to-do lists don't work for these students.

Cheryl works full time, volunteers with a scout troop, and takes two night classes each semester. She has a to-do list at work on her desk, a study schedule on the refrigerator, and a third list clipped to her scouts' handbook.

Dwayne is a full-time student and works as an assistant manager in a retail store on weekends. He keeps a single list in a small notebook. Sometimes his list contains 25 items, including daily routine chores as well as midterm exams for his college courses. He reviews his list just before his bimonthly meeting with the store manager.

hindered

To make their to-do lists work, these students will need to follow two basic principles: simplicity and consistency. Both students have made the process more complicated than necessary and consequently have hindered their ability to follow through on the tasks listed. The following guidelines will help you develop an effective listing system that is both easy and dependable.

- **Keep just one list that integrates all aspects of your life.** Figure 1–2 shows Cheryl's revised to-do list. With just one list she is able to coordinate an errand for scouts with accomplishing a work-related errand. Remember to include important obligations such as paying bills, keeping upcoming appointments, and completing current assignments. If you can't find time for personal interests like exercising or writing to friends, make them priorities on your to-do list.

- **Record your lists in a bound format so they are always accessible.** A small spiral notebook, an hourly appointment calendar, or a special section in your lecture notebook are convenient locations. Develop your own style, but avoid Cheryl's scraps of paper or small calendars with one-inch grids. Your daily life as a student is much too busy to squeeze onto fragments of paper.

- **Develop a comprehensive list by compiling it at the same time each day and using your important documents.** Choose a time that works best for your personal style—after classes, before bed, while eating breakfast. Use the following documents to create a complete list of tasks for the upcoming day:

  Yesterday's list. Did you leave tasks uncompleted? Should they be carried over to the new list? Notice how Cheryl's second list in Figure 1–2 is built from her previous one.

  exasperation

  Course outlines. List any immediate assignments and exams. Also be aware of upcoming projects. You can avoid the exasperation of last-minute preparations by adding project tasks to your to-do list well in advance of the project submission date. Cheryl's second list includes a topic search for an upcoming term paper due in one month.

FIGURE 1–2   *Integrated To-Do Lists*

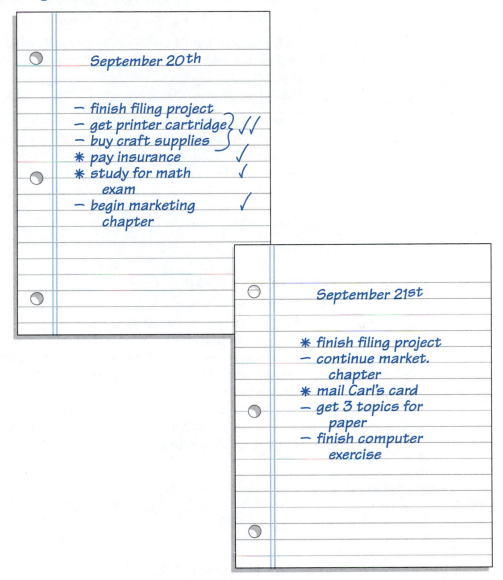

Calendar. Check your calendar for appointments and personal obligations such as family birthdays.

- **Keep your list streamlined.** Since Dwayne balances the cash drawer nightly at work, he need not list it as an objective for the day. Routine tasks will quickly clutter your list and could cause you to miss a priority task.

- **Designate a few priority items each day.** Choose a simple method for designating priorities—numbers, letters, or like Cheryl, asterisks. In Figure 1–2, Cheryl has indicated two tasks as most important: paying her auto insurance and studying for a math exam. When a friend calls to switch carpooling days, Cheryl declines because she knows the insurance payment is her priority after work. Keep your priorities to a minimum. A list comprised of 75 percent priorities leaves little room for flexibility.

- **Refer to your list throughout the day, adjusting your plans when necessary.** Because Dwayne reviews his list just twice a month, he is not on top of things daily. Check off objectives as you complete them so you can easily see the work that remains.

- **Reward yourself for a job well done before you begin your next list.** Even if you still have much to accomplish, enjoy a relaxing break. Visit with friends, watch a favorite television program, escape with a novel, or pump up your body with exercise. Then begin your new list with a fresh outlook.

Make your efforts count with a daily to-do list for all the important activities of your life.

CONTROL THE PAPER FLOW

In business, people spend a great deal of time following what they call the paper trail—the numerous documents and materials produced during daily transactions. Probably you already have a sizable paper trail yourself—that mound of textbooks, notebooks, and orientation papers. Now is the time to devise a paper management system that will allow you to access your documents and materials quickly. Maybe by nature you are organized and can easily handle the flow of documents. Or do you see yourself in the misguided paper handlers depicted in Figure 1–3? Use the following suggestions to avoid the problems of the Stacker, the Stuffer, and the Systematizer. Develop a management system that is

- Unified.
- Accessible.
- Complete.

Use One Notebook System

As a college student, a notebook system is a must. You can reduce loss of valuable papers and filing errors by using a notebook that provides security and flexibility.

The most versatile type is a three-ring notebook, which can hold lecture notes, handouts, and returned assignments for all your courses. To make organization of documents easier, use indexed divider sheets between materials for each course, and purchase a small, lightweight hole punch that can be carried in the notebook. Three-ring notebooks do have their disadvantages, however. They can be bulky and the loose-leaf paper can tear, requiring reinforcement.

Another option is a large spiral-ring notebook with multiple sections. This type should be equipped with divider pockets so you can file loose documents immediately. The possibility of losing documents is a bit higher with this system, but with diligence you can retain and retrieve documents efficiently.

Two common notebook systems do not work well. Many students like using a separate notebook and folder for each course. However, each folder and notebook increases the chance of confusion and error. If you have a series of notebooks and

| FIGURE 1–3 | *Misguided Paper Handlers* |

THE STACKER creates mounds of documents on his desk, the kitchen counter, in his locker. He frantically shuffles through a stack he is convinced holds an important paper. Later he discovers it on top of the television.

folders, reduce your chances of error by placing all of them in a large three-ring notebook. Sometimes students use a single tablet or writing pad for note taking. This choice does not work well because pages tear easily and it is difficult to separate work for different courses. If you are using pads or tablets, save them for composing papers and planning projects. Invest in one of the systems described here for efficient results.

FIGURE 1–3   (continued)

THE STUFFER relies on her pockets as a filing system. She stuffs review sheets for economics in her algebra book and scribbles her math problems on the back of her phone bill, which she shoves in her purse to pay later in the day.

Process Documents Quickly

Any system is only as efficient as the person using it. Have you ever sat staring at a photocopied article trying to decide where you received it? Have you frantically searched for a handout that you received just an hour before? As you receive or create documents, label them clearly and file them logically. Your homework, tests, and handouts should be clearly marked with the course and the date, and if necessary, the topic. In addition, concisely label all your computer disks and list the

FIGURE 1–3   *(concluded)*

THE SYSTEMATIZER has made organizing his papers his lifetime work. He has a folder and notebook for everything, and backups too. But things are so complicated that he continually makes mistakes and wastes time.

documents they contain. If you do not, you could find yourself sitting for hours peering at a computer screen searching for that one important piece of information.

When you have finished with your documents, be sure to file them away logically. You should have a separate storage spot, such as a division in your three-ring notebook or an individual pocket folder, for each course. If you are using pocket folders, simply put the most recent document on top for easy access. In your three-ring notebook, insert the papers with related information. This will be

INFORMATION FILE: MEETING THE CHALLENGE

Wishing You Good Luck . . .
Have people been wishing you good luck in school? Do you feel lucky when you have a special charm? You may be surprised to learn how it became part of our culture.

Rabbit's foot. In ancient cultures, the rabbit itself was considered a symbol of prosperity because it reproduced so rapidly. Eventually just the foot of this happy rodent was associated with good fortune.

Horseshoe. Peasants long ago believed that iron ore warded off evil. Their folklore also taught that witches rode brooms because they feared horses. These two powerful "facts" were combined in the symbol of a horseshoe.

Knocking on wood. This ritual can be traced to the religious beliefs of American Indians and some ancient tribes of Europe. They believed the gods of sky and lightning lived in trees. When a mortal touched the wood of the tree, they made contact with the god.

Crossing your fingers. The pagans of long ago used crosses in their religion because they believed that good, generous spirits resided in the intersection of the two arms. That belief led to a practice of two people forming a cross with their fingers to create good luck for both. Ultimately the practice of crossing one's own fingers evolved. *Now don't break a mirror, or cross a black cat's path, or see the evil eye!*

easy if you have clearly labeled the document. The time to be your most organized is on your busiest days. When rushed, most people begin to stack or stuff papers in an attempt to save time. However, their piles quickly grow, and refiling the papers becomes an insurmountable task. Organize and file your papers daily for increased productivity.

insurmountable

Keep Complete Records

Within just a few weeks you will see that you are accumulating a large amount of paper. As your files and notebook become heavier and larger, you may be tempted to clear out everything. Stop! Many of your academic materials will be needed throughout the term and some throughout your school career and beyond. Toss and you may be at a loss. You don't, however, need to carry all your papers with you every day. As you complete chapters and exams, store those documents at home. If necessary, reorganize the materials, then bind them together and put them in a safe place. When midterms or finals come around, you'll be ready to review with all your previous exercises, handouts, and quizzes.

Figure 1–4 lists recommended time lines for retaining academic documents. Are you surprised by some of the time periods? Your papers and projects are valuable resources for future assignments. You won't be able to simply recycle a five-page paper, but it could become the foundation for an in-depth research project in a higher level course. Why should you hang on to all those official documents? You should keep a full record of your school activities because your academic record will always be of interest to potential employers and other schools. With this information at your fingertips, you can easily construct detailed résumés and job application letters. Your print copies of important documents are also a safeguard against computer errors and loss. Have the right materials for each job you undertake by maintaining complete files throughout your school career.

FIGURE 1–4	*Document Time Lines*

DOCUMENT	TIME LINE
Tests and quizzes	Until final course grade is received
Papers and projects	Throughout schooling
Semester grade reports	Throughout schooling
Grade transcript	Lifetime
Entrance exam scores	Lifetime
Financial aid agreements	Lifetime
Yearly college catalogs	Lifetime

PERSONALIZE YOUR LEARNING

Some of the tools you need for achievement are not external objects. Along with your books and supplies, you must add your personal involvement to the challenge of learning. Think about an activity in which you have been deeply involved. Did time seem to fly by? Did learning seem to happen almost effortlessly? Have you retained much of that experience long since? In the same way, "put yourself" into your college learning, and your work will become easier and more rewarding.

Build On Your Experience

Practical Knowledge.   One of your greatest assets is your own knowledge and experience. As you read this passage, you bring a storehouse of knowledge on many topics: music, economics, chemistry, literature, physics. Do you doubt that you have knowledge in physics because you've never had a course on the subject? If you can maneuver a car smoothly around a sharp curve or play a game of pool, you understand some basic physics principles. Such basic knowledge can become the foundation for the expertise you will gain in your college courses. Every chapter of this textbook begins with an exercise to establish your current knowledge and determine what new information you would like to learn. In all your courses, search for a link between your past experience and the new concepts being presented. Let's see how well you can link these typical college topics to yourself:

- World War I.

- Subconscious mind.

- Computer databases.

- Overhead.

- Blood pressure.

Did you link World War I to your own knowledge of the Gulf War? The two conflicts share some basic elements: the issue of territorial boundaries, the establishment of allied forces. What were your thoughts about overhead? Did cost-saving measures at work come to mind or your own new school expenses?

Values. Along with basic practical knowledge, you also hold many opinions and values that can become part of your personalized learning. As you encounter new ideas and procedures, evaluate them against your current beliefs and expertise. Challenge yourself with tough questions such as these:

> Should advertising aimed at the subconscious be strictly regulated?

> What safeguards should be placed on computer databases to ensure personal privacy?

Jot your thoughts and reactions down in the margins of your book or lecture notes. Don't make snap judgments; allow your thinking to develop as you gain more knowledge about the issue. As you formulate and logically support your own opinions, you will feel yourself growing intellectually and personally. You will have many opportunities to explain your ideas: in class discussions, through papers, and informally with classmates and friends. Don't miss these opportunities to grow and enjoy YOURSELF.

EXPAND AND USE YOUR VOCABULARY

The best support you can have when explaining your ideas is a strong, broad vocabulary. Most people have vainly searched for the right words to express their ideas or have remained outside a conversation because they were unfamiliar with the vocabulary being used. Such situations can leave smart, capable people feeling inadequate and powerless. If you're thinking that learning vocabulary takes work, you're right. Your work, however, will improve your grades now and your communication skills for the rest of your life.

Your powerful vocabulary can be found right in your textbooks and daily lectures. You simply have to seek out the unfamiliar words rather than gloss over them. Once you've targeted a word, you can formulate an informal definition using word parts and context clues. Probably you are already using these strategies without realizing it. Let's try a quick example. The word is *regressive*.

> The psychologist said the 10-year-old girl displayed *regressive* behavior, rather than mature behavior. Her speech and play patterns were similar to those of a five-year-old.

How did you define *regressive—backward* or *declining*? Use these steps as you define new words.

FOUR STEPS FOR LEARNING A NEW WORD

CREATE   Your own definition based on word part meanings and context clues.

TRY   Your definition in the original context.

CONFIRM Your definition with your dictionary.

USE   The word in your writing and conversations.

Create Your Own Definition

Analyze Word Parts.   The term **word parts** refers to the smaller components within a word that contribute to the total meaning. There are three types of word components: the root, prefixes, and suffixes.

> **Root.**   This is the major part of a word and provides its central meaning. For example, *gress* used in a word means step or go.
>
> **Prefix.**   This type of word part is added before the root and contributes its own meaning. The prefix *re* can mean back or again. Thus, *regress* means to go backward.
>
> **Suffix.**   This component is added to the end of a word and modifies the overall meaning. When *ive* is added to regress, it contributes the meaning *tending to.*

Once you know the meaning of each part, you can add them together to get the total meaning.

re	+ gress	+ive	= regressive
back	+ go	+ tending to	= tending to go backward

Learning a stem, a prefix, or a suffix does more than unlock the meaning of that one word. That small bit of knowledge can unlock multiple words as you can see in these examples.

re   *re*pel, *re*flex, *re*active, *re*placement, *re*possess

gress   ag*gress*ion, pro*gress*, di*gress*, con*gress*, e*gress*

ive   select*ive*, predict*ive*, provocat*ive*, prerogat*ive*

Figure 1–5 lists common word parts and their meanings. Use this list as your reference when you define new words. As a bonus, the word parts will also become part of your vocabulary.

Add Context Clues.   **Context clues** come from the group of sentences that immediately surround the word you are defining. Three types of context clues can be very helpful: direct definitions, examples, and opposites.

1. Very often the writer uses a synonym, a word with the same meaning, or a brief phrase to define the word right in the sentence. In the preceding sentence, the term *synonym* is directly defined in the sentence and is marked by commas. Now that's very convenient!

2. Examples used in the context also provide good clues to meaning. The context of *regressive* gives examples that clearly add up to the definition of backward: speech and play patterns similar to those of a five-year-old.

3. Some clues provide a meaning opposite to the word. In the example, *mature* provides a clue opposite to the actual meaning of the word. Watch carefully for opposite clues because they require you to reverse your thinking.

FIGURE 1–5	**Word Parts**

NUMBER

bi-	both, two
di-	two
tri-	three
quino-	five
pent-	five
sex-	six
sept-	seven
octo-	eight
nona-	nine
dec-	ten
omni-	all
semi-	half, partial
poly-	many

QUALITY

-al	related to
-ance/ence	state or quality of
-ant/ent	related to
-ion	act of
-ity	state or quality of
-ive	tending to
-ment	state or quality of
-ness	state or quality of
-ous	full of

TIME

ante-	before
chrono-	time
post-	after
pre-	before
pro-	before
re-	again
neo-	new
retro-	past

COMPARISON

hetero-	different
homo-	same
macro-	large
micro-	small
syn/sym-	similar

RELATIONSHIP

a-	without
anti-	against
co-	together
col/com/con-	joint

ACTION

-ate	to act
-ify	to make
-ize	to make

NEGATION

contra-	against
de-	reverse
ex-	former
in/im/il/ir-	not
non-	not
mis-	bad, wrong
un-	reverse, not

GENERAL DESCRIPTION

bene-	well
phobia-	fear
therm-	heat
mort-	death

PLACEMENT

ex-	away from
hypo-	below
hyper-	above
intra-	within
inter-	between
sub-	below

PEOPLE

-ar/er/or	one who does
-ist	one who does

STRESSBUSTER

If nothing feels the same, put some familiar comfort back into your life. Put on that old sweatshirt and take out a favorite picture album or your high school yearbook. Better yet, call up one of your favorite faces in those books.

Check in Context

tentative

Once you have arrived at a tentative definition, be sure you substitute it into the context to confirm its accuracy. Let's double-check our definition of regressive.

The psychologist said the 10-year-old girl displayed backward behavior. She had speech and play patterns similar to those of a five-year-old.

A perfect fit.

STRESSBUSTER

Would you like an audience that *always* listens and *never* tells? To relieve tension, write your thoughts and feelings in a journal. It takes just a few minutes and the results are terrific.

Double-Check with a Dictionary

Usually you will want to confirm your tentative definition in a good dictionary. And of course, you can turn to your dictionary if you are unable to use word parts and context clues to establish an informal definition. When using the dictionary, remember to read all the definitions given to find the one that best fits your context. Some dictionaries list the most common definition first, but others begin with the oldest definition.

Use Your Word

adage

Are you thinking that you've gone through these steps before, only to forget the definition later on? The adage "use it or lose it" certainly applies to your vocabulary. When you take the time to define a word, also take the time to use the word in your own communications—in class discussions, at work, in your compositions. With continued use, your new word will become an established part of your working vocabulary.

Your ASAP textbook has been designed to get your vocabulary expansion started with a vocabulary exercise in each chapter. When you've completed Chapter 12, you will have 120 new words in your vocabulary. What would be your grand total if you added just 50 words from each of your other courses?

BRAINSTORM AND WRITE THREE-C SUMMARIES

redundant

As your involvement and your learning increase, you will want to condense information to improve your communication of ideas. You probably have become impatient with writers who are redundant and never make a clear point. Developing your summarizing skills will avoid the pitfalls repetitious and unfocused communicators fall into. A **summary** is a brief presentation of all major points using limited explanations and examples. For a summary to be successful, it should be

- Correct.
- Concise.
- Clear.

These easy steps will help you meet each of the Cs.

- **Brainstorm to get started.** Don't rush into writing a complete summary. Take a few minutes to organize your facts and ideas. If you can't get started, don't stare at a blank sheet of paper—brainstorm. Brainstorming is the process of recording your spontaneous thoughts about a topic without editing the ideas or your wording. In effect, brainstorming helps writers to overcome their own doubts and the blank sheet of paper staring at

FIGURE 1–6   *Brainstorming and Planning*

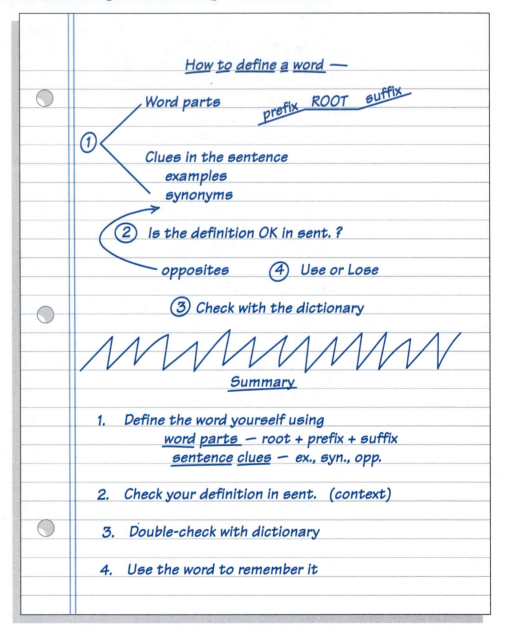

them. Figure 1–6 illustrates brainstorming on a topic discussed earlier in the chapter. Notice the free flow of ideas and even drawings the student has generated. Your brainstorming will be most effective if you record your ideas very quickly so you have little time to be critical. Once you have recorded all your thoughts, you can analyze them in the next phase.

• **Select the information you will include in your summary.** Place it in a logical sequence. Figure 1–6 shows how the student progressed from brainstorming to a brief plan for writing.

- **Use your plan to write a first draft.** Then evaluate it by applying the three Cs.

  Correct. Double-check that all significant concepts are accurate and none have been omitted.

  Concise. Include explanations, descriptions, and examples if they are critical for understanding. The length of your summaries will vary depending on the material and your purpose.

  Clear. Use simple language and define technical terms if they must be used.

criteria

- **Edit your draft where necessary and make a final copy.** The following summary is based on information given earlier in the chapter. Do you think it meets the three-C criteria?

HOW TO INCREASE YOUR VOCABULARY

If you want to increase your vocabulary, look for new words in your classes, your assignments, even at work. When you find a word, try to arrive at your own definition before going to the dictionary. Analyze each part of the word and combine those meanings to develop a specific definition for your new word. Then study the sentences surrounding the word for additional clues to the meaning of the word. Take your tentative definition and place it into the original sentence so you can check its logic. If you are satisfied, then confirm your definition with the dictionary. Once you have a solid definition, begin to use your word in daily communication. Quickly your word will become a permanent part of your vocabulary.

This summary does more than fulfill the three-C criteria. It also carries the unique stamp of the person who selected the ideas, ordered them, and crafted the explanation. That's personalized learning. Throughout your ASAP text, you will encounter many exercises that challenge you to summarize important concepts and procedures. Take summarizing beyond the exercises of this class, and use it to personalize your learning in all your courses.

THE ASAP REWIND «««

How can I get off to a good start in school?

Focus your attention on your requirements. Be sure that you attend every class, follow your course outlines, and keep track of your assignments.

How can I work more efficiently?

Organize your efforts and your materials. Try these tips: Use one notebook system; file and keep important papers; and use a daily to-do list.

How can I make school more interesting?	**Add YOURSELF to your studies.** Use these strategies to make your studies more meaningful: Build on your knowledge and experience; and form your own opinions.
How can I communicate better?	**Expand your vocabulary and write more often.** Improve your skills with these strategies: Define and use new words; and write three-C summaries.

 WORD POWER

Exercise 1

Directions: Begin to expand your vocabulary by mastering these words from the chapter. Define each word using your word meaning techniques: word parts, context clues, and dictionary. Then use each word in an original sentence. Use the following example as a guide. The word is *interim*, which was used on page 4.

Typically courses meet just three or four hours per week, rather than daily. As a result, some students have difficulty maintaining regular attendance and preparing assignments in the *interim*.

1. **Analyze word parts and context clues.**

    Inter usually means between as in interrupt. The context is referring to the days the students have off between scheduled classes.

2. **Formulate your definition.**

    Interim means a time between other events, a gap in the action.

3. **Check it in the context.**

    As a result, some students have difficulty maintaining regular attendance and preparing assignments in the time between.

4. **Check your dictionary.**

    Yes!

5. **Put your word to work.**

    I had not seen David in five years. In the interim he had become a successful attorney.

rapport _____

_____

_____

haphazardly _____

_____

_____

hindered _____

_____

_____

exasperation _____

_____

_____

depicted _____

_____

_____

insurmountable _____

_____

_____

tentative _____

_____

_____

adage _____

_____

_____

redundant _____

_____

_____

criteria _____

_____

_____

Exercise 2

Directions: You have been asked by your admissions counselor to speak to prospective students about managing a typical course load. Based on this chapter, develop three points you would present to the students. Prepare your talk in brief paragraphs, using examples to explain your ideas.

_____

_____

_____

_____

_____

_____

_____

_____

Exercise 3

Directions: One of your classmates has begun to use a to-do list at your suggestion. Figure 1–7 gives a sample list. What advice would you give your friend for improving the list? Make at least three specific suggestions in a brief note.

_____

_____

_____

_____

_____

_____

FIGURE 1–7	*Sample To-Do List*

Read account. assign.
Take back books
Attend. market. class
Double-check bus. m.
Start account. prob.
Attend comput. lab. cl.
Library
Test
Revise composition

Exercise 4

Directions: Personalize your education. For each of your courses, write a paragraph in which you discuss the following.

1. **The purpose of the course.** Why is it part of your college program? What skills and knowledge can you gain from this study?

2. **Your experience base.** What experience do you have in this area? (Remember, your experience can be from everyday situations as well as school.) How would you rate your skill level in this area? Your enthusiasm for the subject?

3. **Your future plans.** How important is this course to your education? Is it a foundation course that will be followed by more advanced courses? Will this subject and its skills be an important part of your professional career? Is this a subject you should understand in order to be a responsible voter?

Course 1

_____

_____

_____

_____

_____

_____

Course 2

_____

_____

_____

_____

_____

_____

Course 3

_____

_____

_____

_____

_____

_____

Course 4

_____

_____

_____

_____

_____

Course 5

_____

_____

_____

_____

_____

_____

CHECK YOUR PROGRESS

Directions: Put the principles of productive learning into action! After one week, complete this checklist to evaluate your progress. Then use the space that follows to write about your growth.

PROGRESS CHECKLIST: Meeting the Challenge

Yes   Usually   No

___ ___ ___   1. I attend all my classes and consult my course outlines for course requirements.

___ ___ ___   2. I keep an accurate record of my daily assignments.

___ ___ ___   3. I use a daily to-do list to coordinate the responsibilities from all aspects of my life.

___ ___ ___   4. I use one notebook system to file my papers.

___ ___ ___   5. I involve myself in the learning process by referring to my experiences and by forming opinions.

___ ___ ___   6. I am adding new words to my vocabulary by defining and using them.

___ ___ ___   7. I make summaries of important information to increase my learning and improve my communications.

A. Discuss the first week of your program and how well you have been able to focus your efforts and adjust to the pace of classes.

B. Identify those areas in which you think you can improve in the coming weeks. Be sure to focus on any obstacles you have experienced and how you might overcome them.

Image Check.   Take a few lines to think about how new goals can change you. How does it feel to be in this program? Do you think of yourself differently? Do you think others do? What will completing your goals mean to you and your self-image? Figure 1–8 provides a sample student analysis to guide you this first time. Read it before you begin. Notice that the student has written informally. This exercise is for YOU. It's not a composition task. Remember to brainstorm if you can't get started.

FIGURE 1–8   *Sample Student Analysis*

My first week went pretty good. I went to all my classes and got all the outlines. My notebook is working great.

Some of the stuff on the outlines is confusing and the assignments are very long. I don't seem to finish much on my to-do list. I think the outlines will make more sense later on. I know I have to get used to studying again and set more time aside for assignments.

Sometimes I feel great about college. A lot of the time I'm uncertain, but I'm still proud of myself. My parents are ecstatic that I'm in college. They put too much pressure on me.

CHAPTER

2

Using Your Resources

THE SKILL THAT GETS THE JOB

Travel Agent.
With developed industry connections and the ability to contribute to a team effort. Join a great team, enjoy the great benefits.

WHAT'S YOUR EXPERIENCE?

Your job on a team probably won't bring you a $5 million contract like a professional baseball player. Then why be a team player? How can you use people and resources to be productive and to solve problems? Explore your experience, your skills, and your knowledge about this chapter's topics in the space below.

_____

_____

_____

_____

_____

_____

_____

_____

_____

_____

_____

_____

_____

_____

In this chapter you will learn to

»»» **Build a school support network.**

»»» **Use the facilities and services of your school.**

»»» **Develop effective questioning techniques.**

»»» **Solve problems logically.**

USING YOUR RESOURCES

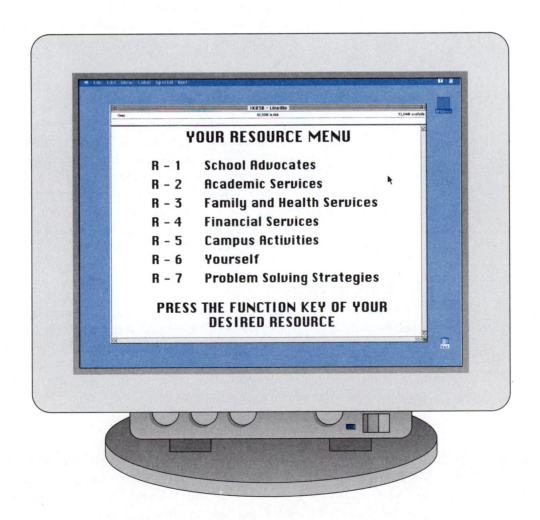

collaborate

innovation

Recently industries have begun to organize their employees into interactive teams. Rather than work on isolated, repetitive tasks, employees collaborate in groups to create and produce a complete product from the first stages of design to the final quality check. This team concept is gaining in popularity because companies have found it improves efficiency, productivity, and worker morale. Actually, the basis for this personnel innovation is quite simple: the potential of one individual increases when combined with the potential of others. By sharing resources, people increase their productivity and creativity.

People often think of the typical student as a solitary figure, sitting in a corner of a library surrounded only by books. Some highly self-reliant students feel they must do everything on their own. Because they limit their resources to themselves, they often struggle with difficult assignments or cope alone with personal needs. As a result, their stress builds, compounding their isolation and frustration. The successful student most often has created a network of people and resources that makes learning more interesting and problems easier to solve. In this chapter you will begin to build your own team and learn effective steps for solving problems.

RESOURCE 1: CAMPUS ADVOCATES

advocate

Perhaps during orientation sessions you have met some of the people who will be on your school team. Many schools match an incoming student with two advocates, an upper-division student and a faculty advisor. These people can be resources for you throughout your college days. If you've already met with them but did not get their full names and phone numbers, see your admissions counselor to locate them again.

Peers

An upper-class advocate, sometimes called "big sister" or "big brother" can be invaluable to you. She or he can provide you with information and tips based on experience and offer a sympathetic ear. Your student handbook will spell out parking regulations, but a student advocate might know of a free lot just beyond the college property. Accounting I is listed as a four-credit course in the college catalog, but an advocate can tell you the real story about homework and quizzes in the course. Student advocates are usually volunteers, so they *want* to help. Be sure to use yours as part of your support network.

Academic Advisor

mentor

Some schools also match an incoming student with a faculty member who will be an advisor or mentor. Your advisor will meet with you periodically to discuss your academic progress and to help you plan your program of study. She or he can give you invaluable advice about adding or deleting courses or changing majors. You might even need her or his approval to make such changes. Most advisors keep regular office hours or make appointments as needed.

RESOURCE 2: CAMPUS SERVICES

Your school is more than a set of buildings filled with classrooms. It's a dynamic community of people providing services, activities, and facilities for you. You have, in a sense, purchased these services with your tuition dollars. Make the most of your purchase and new, exciting opportunities by familiarizing yourself with your

INFORMATION FILE: NETWORKING

United We Stand . . .

In 1990 Americans participated in over 22,000 nonprofit organizations. People worked together to promote everything from fan clubs to church groups to cultural societies. Networking through nonprofit groups has grown by more than 50 percent since 1980.

Lending a Helping Hand . . .

They are in shelters for the homeless, hospital nurseries, and crisis centers. Who are they? The 98 million volunteers who devote their time and energies to charitable causes.

Step by Step . . .

Students from York, England, set a new standard for cooperation. 1,189 participants were tied together at the ankles, forming a human centipede. They were able to walk a distance of 98 feet without anyone falling. Their cooperative effort gained them a place in the *Guinness Book of World Records.*

Have a Friend for Dinner . . .

Animals network too by forming symbiotic relationships that bring benefits to both. For example, the little oxpecker bird dines with the huge Cape buffalo. The bird feasts on ticks and bugs from the buffalo's hide and drinks moisture from his nose while the buffalo enjoys having the pests removed from his body.

campus resources. Begin now so you can use them confidently when needed. Consult your student handbook and orientation materials, but also tap the knowledge of your student or faculty advocate. Use the following checklist to guide your explorations.

Academic Services

Do you panic or groan when a paper is assigned in a course? You can probably make the project easier and better by tapping into your school's academic services. If you are not confident of your writing style, maybe your school offers writing assistance. You don't have to gaze at shelves of books, searching for your topic. Your librarian can point you to key topics to research in a traditional card catalog or possibly with a state-of-the-art computer program. If you want a quiet spot to think while you brainstorm, most schools provide study areas too. Then, when you're ready to produce a final copy, check if you can use a typewriter or a word processor on campus. Now you can see that with your school's academic services, that paper won't be so bad after all. Check into these services so you can make learning easier every day.

- **Tutoring.** Does your school help match students with tutors? Is there a fee? How do you apply for assistance?

- **Writing assistance.** Can you find help when writing a paper? Will you meet with a campus professional or a student volunteer? Do you need an appointment or are drop-in times available?

- **Library services.** Where is the library located? Can you participate in orientation services? Is this library linked with other institutions for interlibrary loans? Does the staff offer workshops in research techniques?

- **Equipment usage.** Are computer terminals and typewriters available for your use outside of specific courses? Where are photocopiers located?

- **Study areas.** What campus buildings provide study areas? Does the college have a policy concerning the use of empty classrooms for study groups?

Family and Health Services

If all you had to do was attend classes and complete assignments, school would be a breeze. If you're like most students, however, you are meeting financial responsibilities along with social obligations and your daily personal needs. Because you have a great deal to manage, most schools offer help in finding jobs and answering your family and health needs. Let your school help take the pressure off when you need advice or assistance in these important areas of your life.

- **Health services.** Can you see a professional on campus for a medical question, or does your school use a community referral system? Are workshops available on topics such as dieting, sexuality, and parenting?

- **Child care.** Does your school provide child care? Is it a full-service facility? What age children are served?

- **Personal counseling.** Are counselors available to discuss problems or concerns that might be difficult to discuss with family and friends? Does your school offer a referral service to community agencies? Are all services confidential?

- **Career counseling.** Can your school assist you in making career choices? Does the institution offer job placement after graduation and a job bank of current part-time positions?

Financial Services

Enrolling in school means new financial considerations and, most likely, stress. Some students are making their own day-to-day and monthly money decisions for the first time. Other students are adjusting to a reduced income because they have given up full-time employment. Everyone must cope with new expenses: books, computer disks, commuting costs. Check into financial services at your school. You might qualify for educational funding, and a campus professional might help you develop a realistic budget that will save you money and ease your stress.

- **Financial assistance.** What campus office can you visit for information on financial aid? Can you meet with a specialist to learn about securing grants and scholarships as well as loans?

- **Budget planning.** Does your school offer workshops on how to develop a budget and stick to it? Can they make community referrals for services such as bill consolidation? Are all services confidential?

RESOURCE 3: CLASSROOM SUPPORT

As you use your campus resources, you will gain a sense of personal confidence and accomplishment. However, your team is not complete. Some of your most important resources are in your classes. Begin now to establish relationships with your classmates and your instructors. They can help you as you learn and as you cope with problems—clarifying a difficult algebra solution, choosing a project topic, improving your test performance. At first your classes might seem impersonal, very different from your high school classes. Over time that will change as you, your classmates, and your instructors interact and form supportive relationships.

Classmates

In each of your classes find another student who will discuss the lesson, loan you lecture notes, or give you the specifics of a homework assignment. Once you've made that first contact in a room of strangers, you will become more comfortable with yourself and the learning process. Perhaps you can simply choose a classmate you already know and like. If not, observe your classmates for a few days. Then chat with someone you think is conscientious and friendly. At the beginning of a semester, other students are also looking for a friendly face, so friendships are easily made. All it will take to connect is a casual question or comment. If you ask "Did you understand problem 12?" or remark "Am I glad we don't have homework over the weekend," you'll soon be in the middle of a conversation. If you are compatible, exchange phone numbers and decide on some times you can get together on campus.

Your new "buddy system" will be especially important when you are absent from class. You can call your classmate and get caught up on the missed assignment and arrange to borrow lecture notes the next day. With some help and extra work on your part, you should be able to compensate for the time you missed.

Teachers

peer
ambivalent

Just as you form peer relationships as part of your team, you should also form relationships with your instructors. Often students are ambivalent about approaching an instructor with their questions and needs. They worry that their questions will be foolish or that it is inappropriate to ask for help. Usually instructors are willing to help and are patient with students who demonstrate that they are making an effort. How do you think most instructors would respond to this student's request for help at the end of class?

What did you do last class? I was absent.

Probably this student will meet with a vague or abrupt response from the teacher because it seems that the student wants an entire lecture capsulized on the spot. How do you think most instructors would respond to this next request?

Could I see you about Wednesday's homework? I borrowed notes from Frank, and I've completed half the assignment, but I don't understand the last formula.

This student has made good use of his class contact and is establishing a positive relationship with his instructor. With some effort you can do the same. Usually instructors establish open office hours that are listed on their course outlines and often outside their office. During these times no appointment is necessary. As in business, always make an appointment for unscheduled hours.

RESOURCE 4: ENRICHMENT ACTIVITIES

In addition to providing support people and services, schools also provide students with opportunities to relax, compete, and enrich themselves outside the classroom and in the community. Some students never consider extracurricular activities, assuming that they won't have time or that there aren't any interesting activities. Before you make an uninformed judgment, learn about the opportunities on your campus. Read your student handbook and pick up the campus newspaper. Take some time to visit the student center and check out bulletin boards. Soon you will be "in the know," and you may be surprised by what you've learned. Which of these resources interest you?

- **Newspaper.** Is there a campus newspaper? How often is it published, and where is it distributed? How can you contribute information?

- **Clubs.** What clubs are offered in your areas of interest? Who is the contact person for additional information?

- **Performing arts/sports events.** What events, such as plays, concerts, and ball games does the college sponsor? Can you use student identification for free or reduced admission?

intramural
- **Sports.** Are intramural games organized in sports you enjoy? Do gymnasiums, weight rooms, and pools provide open hours for students?

- **Community projects.** Does your school network with volunteer community projects? Where would you enjoy lending your talents and your services—a youth hotline, a community ecology campaign, a cross-cultural event?

RESOURCE 5: YOURSELF

No chapter discussing team relationships would be complete without discussing its most vital member, YOU. Once the team is assembled, what are your responsibilities? To be a contributing team player, you should be informed and ready to help others.

Being Informed

When people are uninformed, they cannot contribute effectively to the group. Ideas and comments pass them by, and they avoid tasks because they lack the necessary background. Very quickly, these people find themselves on the fringes of the group with the action occurring beyond their influence. How can you keep informed and be a team player? Ask questions. Often people lack essential information because they hesitate to ask questions. Questions are a natural part of learning and interacting in group situations. As a place of learning, you'll find college a comfortable environment for inquiry and discussion. If you sometimes feel awkward asking questions, try these tips for effective questions:

- **Listen carefully *before* you ask your question.** You may hear just the information you need.

- **Rehearse your question in your head.** That brief practice could help you avoid a great deal of awkwardness.

- **Use specific language to avoid confusion.** Replace vague words such as *thing* with specific terms—*computer terminal, ledger.* Which of these questions will get results?

  Can this thing be adjusted better?

  Can my computer monitor be adjusted for brightness?

Much confusion can also result from the overuse of pronouns, those words you use as substitutes for nouns: *it, he, she, they.* Can you interpret this question? "Both brothers want tutors, but Paul says he doesn't want to work with him, so can I be assigned to him?" Because the speaker does not clearly identify each brother but instead uses the pronouns *he* and *him,* you cannot determine which brother the speaker would like for his assignment.

Skill in posing questions develops over time. Keep trying, keep learning.

Assisting Others

As others help you to acquire information and skills, you have an obligation to assist them too. When your schedule is packed and your to-do list is full, it's easy to decide you don't have the time or energy for others. However, your efforts to help someone else can help you too. When you help a classmate understand a topic, you are also reviewing and confirming your own knowledge. When you give someone a ride, you gain companionship and a source of help for the future. As you exchange favors, a reciprocity is established that you can depend on when you must solve a challenging problem. That kind of support is well worth your time and effort.

reciprocity

Solving Problems Systematically

Even with the best plans, the most diligent students sometimes encounter difficult situations. If you have a support network and a plan of action when problems arise, you can contain the difficulty, reduce your stress, and save valuable time and resources. Follow the steps shown in the summary box on page 38 to cope with problems effectively.

1. **Recognize that a problem exists.** Problems come in two sizes. Short-term situations are usually easily identified because they require quick fixes.

> **PHASES OF PROBLEM SOLVING**
> RECOGNIZE   The problem situation and your feelings.
> ANALYZE   Possible causes and possible solutions.
> PLAN   Each step to reach your solution.
> ACT   Upon each step of your plan.

You can see the steps of problem solving in action below, as used by a famous problem solver, detective Sherlock Holmes.

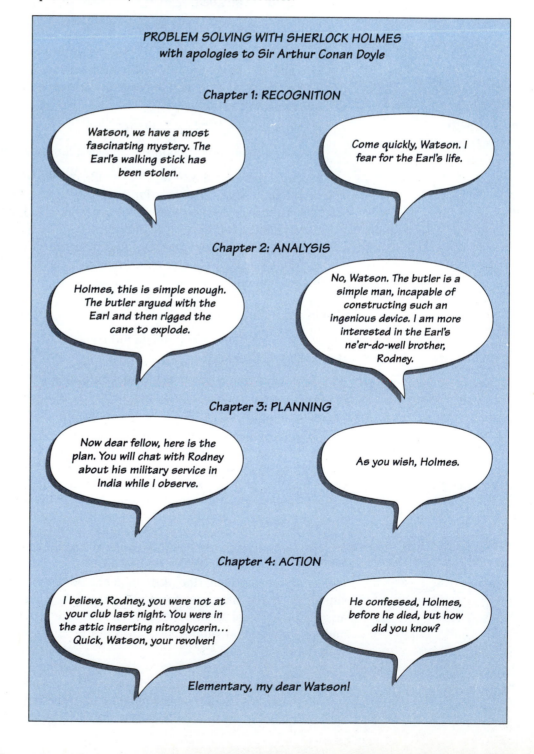

At 7:30 A.M., Eric gets into his car to drive to an 8 o'clock class for a major exam, but his car won't start.

What should be Eric's first concern, fixing the car or finding a ride to school? Most students would decide to focus on quickly finding transportation to school. Eric's problem with the car might be easily solved with a battery boost, or he might face a long-term problem that requires careful analysis and planning. In this case Eric has an immediate need to find a fast solution.

Problems that involve major aspects of your life such as career goals and personal relationships often require long-term solutions. Sometimes people deny that larger problems exist because the problem feels overwhelming. If you are experiencing one or more of these conditions, you are probably facing a significant problem that should not be ignored:

- The quality of your work has declined.
- You are having financial difficulty.
- Stress is negatively affecting your eating and sleeping patterns.
- You usually feel irritable or depressed.

magnitude

Rarely do problems of this magnitude solve themselves. Once you have recognized the difficulty, you must move forward to seek a solution.

2. **Express your feelings about your situation.** What do you think Eric felt when his car wouldn't start? Would he waste valuable time if he "let it all out" by yelling or jumping up and down? When feelings build up, they can cloud concentration and judgment. If Eric took a second to feel his anger and possibly his fear, he would be able to avoid panic. Then he could address his problem logically.

   You can use several approaches to cope with the emotions that arise from serious problems.

   Talk with your network of school associates, family, and friends to relieve some of your stress and gain their insights.

   Write about your problem and the feelings it creates. You will find this process soothing and helpful in identifying possible solutions.

   Seek the help of a professional with whom you are comfortable talking.

3. **Clearly identify the causes of your problem.** The best way to correct a problem is to eliminate some or all of the causes. Therefore, you must carefully analyze all factors contributing to the situation. Read how a student works with a classmate to solve a pressing problem that affects her school work, her job, and her stress level.

One day, Jenny asks Luis, who is working with an accounting tutor, how she can get one too. Jenny complains that the instructor "never explains a thing" and that his exams are "too hard." She admits that she has passed only one test and has failed most quizzes. Luis agrees to help her, and they talk over a cup of coffee. Luis asks Jenny why she frequently misses Friday classes. Jenny explains that her boss is scheduling her to work early on Fridays because they are short-handed. He has increased her work hours from 25 to 32. In addition to missing class, Jenny is having difficulty keeping up with her assignments.

Is the difficulty in the accounting class Jenny's only problem? Will a tutor alone improve her grades? Like many people, Jenny has identified factors outside her control as the source of her problem. Be sure you examine factors you control as well. When analyzing the cause of a problem, don't get stuck blaming yourself or others. Instead, focus on your responsibility for change.

4. **Explore all the possible solutions for correcting the problem.** How many possible solutions do Jenny and Luis discuss?

> Since Jenny has failed her midterm, Luis suggests that she drop the course. Jenny considers quitting her job, since she has never enjoyed it. She still believes a tutor will help her pass the course. Luis thinks Jenny should speak with the instructor before she makes any big decisions.

feasibility

5. **Next, carefully evaluate the feasibility of each possible solution.** These guidelines can be used to evaluate each proposed solution:

    • The solution creates a minimum of new problems.
    • The solution is reasonable within the context of your lifestyle and obligations.

    Often a final solution is a compromise. How does Jenny create a compromise?

> Jenny rejects the solution of dropping the course because she does not want to lose her investment of time and money. Even though she feels embarrassed, Jenny agrees that speaking with the instructor will give her a better idea of what she must accomplish in the course. Because she is self-supporting, Jenny knows she cannot quit her job, but she worries about losing income or being fired if she refuses to work the additional hours. Luis remembers an article in the school paper about an upcoming budget workshop. Jenny reasons that if she follows a better budget, the loss of some income will not be so difficult. She plans to attend the workshop and to speak with her boss. She decides to ask her boss to shift her extra hours to Thursday afternoons and to limit her to approximately 28 hours per week. Luis makes plans to take Jenny to the tutoring office the next day.

    Did you notice how Jenny used many resources from her school network, including her classmate, the course instructor, and the tutoring and financial services?

6. **Devise a plan of action to carry out each phase of your solution.** With a clear idea of her needs and responsibilities, Jenny writes out this plan of action:

    | Tuesday | *make appointment with accounting instructor |
    | | *visit the tutoring office with Luis |
    | | *sign up for budget workshop |
    | Thursday | *discuss an adjusted work schedule with boss |

INFORMATION FILE: NETWORKING

The Elementary Origins of Mr. Holmes . . .
Sherlock Holmes was created by Sir Arthur Conan Doyle, who had a small medical practice in England at the end of the 19th century. He began writing his mysteries while waiting for patients to arrive. Doyle based the character of Holmes on a real person, one of his medical professors who was famous for his brilliant diagnoses. Case closed, Watson.

Notice that Jenny has written a very specific plan so she is committed to act promptly and directly. Each step of her plan will become a priority item on her to-do list for that day. As Jenny proceeds with her plan, she might alter a step of her solution or even decide to delete a step. Although a specific plan is important, you also need to remain flexible so your solution is feasible within your current context.

That's how problems get solved, with day-by-day effort and the help of others. At the conclusion of each chapter in this book, you will have an opportunity to solve problems as they arise. With the help of your support network, address these challenges promptly, honestly, and logically.

THE ASAP REWIND «« ««

How can I get the most from school?

Become familiar with and use your school's resources. You can learn better and enjoy school more by taking advantage of these resources:
1. Campus advocates.
2. Campus services.
3. Teachers and classmates.
4. Enrichment activities.
5. Yourself.

How can I solve problems when they arise?

Use your campus resources and these steps to systematically solve your problems.
1. Recognize the problem and your feelings.
2. Analyze the causes of the problem and possible solutions.
3. Write a practical plan using the best solution.
4. Act upon each step of your plan, using your to-do list.

Exercise 1

Directions: Remember, a broad vocabulary is one of your best resources. Add these words from the chapter to your vocabulary. Define each word using your word meaning techniques: word parts, context, and dictionary. Then use it in an original sentence.

collaborate _____

_____

_____

innovation _____

_____

_____

advocate (noun) _____

_____

_____

mentor _____

_____

_____

peer _____

_____

_____

ambivalent _____

_____

_____

intramural _____

_____

_____

reciprocity _____

_____

_____

magnitude _____

_____

_____

feasibility _____

_____

_____

Exercise 2

Directions: Membership on a team also brings with it a specialized vocabulary, often called *jargon*. You can improve your team position by learning these terms commonly used in college. Define them by consulting your dictionary or school catalog. If you still need help, ASK SOMEONE.

audit _____

bursar _____

cum laude _____

curriculum _____

dean's list _____

grade point average _____

postsecondary _____

prerequisite _____

registrar _____

transcript _____

TAKE ACTION

Exercise 3

Directions: Build your school team by investigating all the resources available to you. Fill in the network data sheet below. For each resource, provide the name of a contact person or a description of the service and a phone number or a location. You can use the questions in this chapter as an additional guide or the orientation materials you have received. This project might require more than one day to complete. Use your to-do list to accomplish part of this project each day, pacing yourself according to the deadline given by your instructor.

> ### EXAMPLES:
> Library services
>
> *The library is located in the MacKay Building. Orientation tours are given Tuesday and Thursday afternoons by appointment. Mr. Tomassi will be conducting a research class during the fifth week of the term. Sign-up is required.*
>
> Classroom support
>
> *1. Introduction to Computers—Dan Pringle, 555–4429*

Student advocate _____

_____

_____

Faculty advisor _____

_____

_____

Tutoring _____

_____

_____

Writing assistance _____

_____

_____

Library services _____

_____

_____

Equipment usage/study areas _____

_____

_____

Health services _____

_____

_____

Child care _____

_____

_____

Personal counseling _____

_____

_____

Career counseling _____

_____

_____

Enrichment activities

Newspaper _____

_____

_____

Organization 1 _____

_____

_____

Organization 2 _____

_____

_____

Classroom support

    1. _____

    2. _____

    3. _____

    4. _____

    5. _____

If during your investigations, you discover other helpful services at your school, list that information here. Be sure you share your knowledge with your classmates.

_____

_____

_____

Exercise 4

Directions: Read the following problem concerning worker tardiness. In a paragraph, identify the problem and analyze its causes. In a second paragraph, discuss the possible solutions and formulate the best solutions into a plan of action for the workers. Be specific. If you're stumped, don't give up—BRAINSTORM.

Ten workers in a small office have been trying to resolve the problem of tardiness. In the last month, the office manager recorded 15 cases of tardiness, 10 of them at the beginning of the day. At the staff's bimonthly meeting, the manager instituted a new policy. He decided that people would be given a point for each late arrival. After two points, the person would lose a half day of personal time. He assigned the receptionist, usually first in the office, to issue points. Due to car trouble she was late herself two mornings. She did not record the tardies because "they were unavoidable." When this became general knowledge, everyone in the office was upset. At the next meeting the office manager ended the point system.

_____

_____

_____

_____

_____

_____

_____

_____

_____

_____

_____

_____

CHECK YOUR PROGRESS

Directions: Put this chapter's principles into action! After one week, complete this checklist to evaluate your progress. Then use the space that follows to write about your growth.

PROGRESS CHECKLIST: Using Your Resources

Yes	Usually	No		
___	___	___	**1.**	I have familiarized myself with the services and facilities of the school.
___	___	___	**2.**	I am developing a network of classmates and instructors who can assist me.
___	___	___	**3.**	I am learning about campus activities.
___	___	___	**4.**	I solve problems systematically with the help of my support network.

A. Identify the aspects of your college environment that are now comfortable for you and discuss how you can use them to further your learning and development.

B. Describe any needs that are not currently being met by your own resources and those of the school. Explore ways that you can fulfill those needs.

Plan a Visit with Your Instructor. Take some time to talk with your teacher. You can let her or him know your achievements. You can tap into your instructor's resources if you'd like some help. All you have to do is ask.

_____

_____

_____

_____

_____

_____

_____

_____

_____

_____

Managing Your Time and Health

exemplify

WHAT'S YOUR EXPERIENCE?

There's much free advice on the topics of time and health: "You can't buy good health." "Time is money." Such sayings, however, give just part of the picture. How do you think time and health are related? What role do they play in a successful life? How would you rate your health habits and your use of time? Use the space below to explore your knowledge and skill and to ask any questions you have about this chapter's topics.

_____

_____

_____

_____

_____

_____

_____

_____

_____

_____

_____

_____

In this chapter you will learn to

»»»   **Establish healthful eating, sleeping, and exercise patterns.**

»»»   **Manage stress.**

»»»   **Set high-yield goals.**

»»»   **Follow a routine schedule.**

»»»   **Use a project schedule.**

MANAGING YOUR TIME AND HEALTH

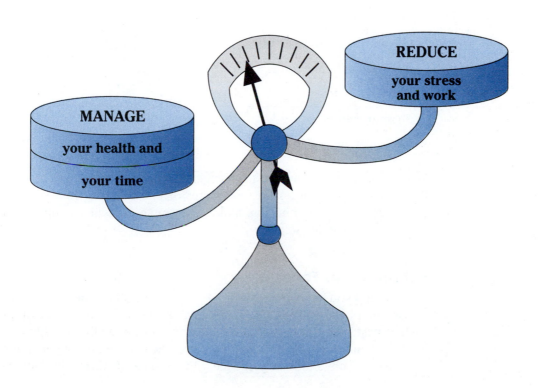

Do you know these people?

> The businessman who recently received a promotion. He works 70 hours a week, eating take-out pastries and deli sandwiches between meetings. Now and then he relieves his stress with a little cocaine. He says it makes him sharper.

> The young mother who has returned to her full-time job. She also puts in long hours. After the children are in bed, she is too exhausted to exercise and too keyed up to sleep. She sees her doctor for medication.

> The student who recently graduated from high school and is juggling a job and college classes. He has no time for afternoon sports with his old friends, so on weekends he relaxes at a bar, drinking until closing time.

Keeping balance in your life as you assume new responsibilities can be difficult. Some people, like those in the examples, find themselves in a negative cycle. As their work increases, they neglect aspects of their daily lives and stress builds. The stress makes work more difficult, and the cycle repeats itself. If unchecked, the cycle could lead to health problems. Now is a good time to take control of your responsibilities, your lifestyle, and your time.

Where should you start? Most people would point to their responsibilities first, but this can lead to unhealthy patterns, as we saw in the examples. Instead, try to focus first on the quality of your daily life so that you relieve stress and energize yourself for your obligations. Although many factors could be included in lifestyle, this chapter examines those that directly affect your health and morale.

MAINTAIN HEALTHFUL EATING HABITS

The following are not for sale:

More energy.

Greater concentration.

Stronger teeth and gums.

Firmer muscles.

Sharper eyesight.

Greater resistance to illness.

You can gain these physical advantages from healthful eating. To eat well, you don't have to shop at health food stores or ban desserts from your table. With some background on nutrition and a few simple guidelines, you can build your body and your ability to perform.

Eat Nutritious Foods

What should you put on your plate? Most of our nutrition should come from foods rich in complex carbohydrates and low-fat proteins. The nutrients found in foods such as pasta, fruit, and yogurt are necessary for generating energy, manufacturing blood, and building bones and muscles. Scientists also believe a diet high in complex carbohydrates may reduce your chance of developing some forms of

Evaluation Request

 **IRWIN**

After reviewing this book, please take a minute to give us your opinion. We appreciate your comments.

Title: LINVILLE ACADEMIC SKILLS ACH PROG
Book No.: 00-4415-01   0-256-14219-X   Qty: 1

CAT	REFER	DATE	ST	SCH	PROF	SRC	O/L
00	874502	12/30/93	34	445	005	1	

Is this book suitable for your course(s)?

Yes _____

No _____

If yes, do you plan to adopt this book?

Yes _____ Class size? _____

No _____

MONROE COLLEGE BRONX
        PROF ALEX EPHREM
DP OF COMP SCI/CHAIRMAN
29 EAST FORDHAM ROAD
BRONX NY 10468

Please identify some of the features that caused you to select this text for your course(s).

a.) _____

b.) _____

c.) _____

If you have chosen not to adopt this text, please explain any deficiencies you may have encountered:

Content _____ Comprehension Level/Too High _____

Presentation _____ Comprehension Level/Too Low _____

Comments: _____
_____
_____

What book(s) are you now using in your course?
_____
_____

Why did you choose this book?
_____
_____

If you have not yet adopted a textbook for your course, what is your decision date? _____

Can we quote your comments?   Yes ☐   No ☐

Your comments are appreciated.

Please write: **Faculty Services**
   RICHARD D. IRWIN, INC.
   1333 Burr Ridge Parkway
   Burr Ridge, IL 60521

Or Call: **Faculty Services**
   (800)-323-4560 (Continental U.S.)
   (708)-789-4000 (Outside U.S.)

Would you be willing to discuss this questionnaire with us? If so, please indicate your phone number. _____

Fold, moisten and mail.

Meeting your needs is our business. You can help us meet these needs by sharing your opinions with us. This *IRWIN* text has been sent to you with our compliments. We hope you'll share in our enthusiasm over this excellent text. Please share your opinions with us.

 Times Mirror
Books

NO POSTAGE
NECESSARY
IF MAILED
IN THE
UNITED STATES

BUSINESS REPLY MAIL

FIRST CLASS   PERMIT NO. 17   HOMEWOOD, IL

POSTAGE WILL BE PAID BY ADDRESSEE

FACULTY SERVICES
RICHARD D. IRWIN, INC.
1333 Burr Ridge Parkway
Burr Ridge, IL 60521-0085

| FIGURE 3–1 | *A Nutritious Diet* |

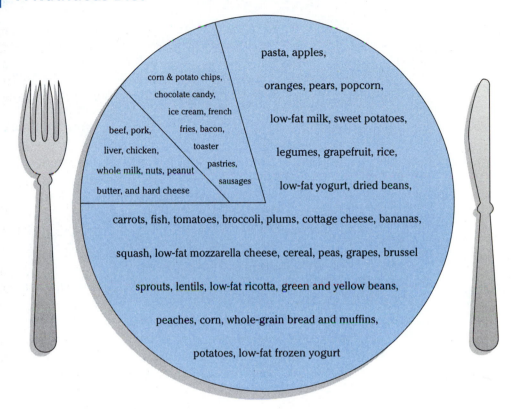

corn & potato chips,
chocolate candy,
ice cream, french
fries, bacon,
toaster
pastries,
sausages

beef, pork,
liver, chicken,
whole milk, nuts, peanut
butter, and hard cheese

pasta, apples,
oranges, pears, popcorn,
low-fat milk, sweet potatoes,
legumes, grapefruit, rice,
low-fat yogurt, dried beans,

carrots, fish, tomatoes, broccoli, plums, cottage cheese, bananas,
squash, low-fat mozzarella cheese, cereal, peas, grapes, brussel
sprouts, lentils, low-fat ricotta, green and yellow beans,
peaches, corn, whole-grain bread and muffins,
potatoes, low-fat frozen yogurt

| FIGURE 3–2 | *Healthful Snack Options* |

TRADE IN YOUR	TRY OUT
Candy-coated chocolates	Fresh grapes or cherries
Ice cream sandwich	Frozen yogurt on a stick
Party mix snacks	Precut veggies from your grocer
Cheese curls	Low-fat cheese tidbits
Taco chips	Popcorn with taco seasoning
Toaster pastries	Whole-grain muffins

contributory

cancer. Other low-fat proteins and complex carbohydrates are listed in Figure 3–1. Notice that in this diagram meats, eggs, and processed foods are small parts of the total diet. Nutritionists recommend that most Americans reduce their intake of these foods because they contain high levels of cholesterol, fat, sugar, or salt, which are contributory factors to heart disease and high blood pressure. Can you still have a roast beef dinner on Sunday? Sure you can, if during the week you have chosen a salad instead of a hamburger and cereal instead of eggs. For healthful snacks, try the suggestions in Figure 3–2.

NEVER SAY DIET

Many people consciously reduce their intake of food to lose weight. They are "on a diet" to reach their optimum weight and shape. Doctors, however, recommend that people maintain their weight within a range typically spanning 8 to 12 pounds. Most often, diets are recommended for people who exceed their weight range by 20 percent or more because they are at greater risk of developing diabetes, heart disease, and high blood pressure. If you are concerned about your weight or are a frequent dieter, visit with your school's health professional for an objective assessment of your weight. You may be surprised to learn that your current weight is well within an acceptable range. To improve your body shape, you may need simply to decrease your consumption of fattening foods and increase your exercise.

Eat Regularly

Are three meals each day a must? Not necessarily, but you should avoid depriving your body of nutrition for long periods of time. If you never eat breakfast, you should definitely plan a midmorning snack of healthy foods. If your lunch hour is too brief for a hearty lunch, eat lightly at midday and enjoy a nutritious snack on your afternoon break. Avoid casual snacking while studying or socializing because you'll ruin your appetite for a full, balanced meal later.

Eat Sensible Portions

Do you have to count calories? No, meals and snacks should be enjoyed, not entered in a ledger. Simply monitor your intake of food to avoid dramatic increases or decreases. Such swings in your total consumption can actually cause your body to store up more fat than would normally be stored with consistent eating. Be alert for stress that might trigger extreme eating patterns. Anxiety, boredom, and depression are often related to major shifts in eating. If you find that a swing in your food consumption continues for more than several days, use your problem-solving skills to relieve the underlying stress.

EXERCISE REGULARLY

Exercising can make the difference between feeling okay and feeling terrific. An investment of just two hours a week could make that difference. If you are already enjoying the benefits of an exercise program, the time management tips in the next section of this chapter will help you maintain your exercise program while meeting your new responsibilities. If in the past you've begun an exercise program but didn't keep it up, use these tips to give exercising another try.

Choose Interesting Activities

An aerobics class won't bring you much satisfaction if you don't enjoy indoor or group activities. A better alternative might be a walking program so you can enjoy nature and time to yourself while getting the benefits of exercising.

Choose Activities that Fit Your Lifestyle

For inexpensive, convenient programs, check into activities offered by your school. You might be able to enjoy an exercise program with classmates immediately after your classes. Sometimes programs are also offered by high schools and community groups.

Exercise Safely

These safety guidelines are common to most exercise programs:

- **Check out** your fitness with a doctor.
- **Use** the proper equipment.
- **Warm up** with stretching exercises.
- **Build** your momentum.
- **Cool down** with reduced activity and stretching.

Vary Your Activities

Fitness experts recommend that you alternate among several activities, as in this schedule:

Day 1: Walking

Day 2: Exercise video

Day 3: Laps at the pool

Often people want to know which exercise will yield the greatest health benefits. Any exercise that is performed correctly and regularly will increase your physical fitness. Activities such as tennis, softball, and weight lifting will increase your flexibility and muscle strength while decreasing your body fat. Continuous activities sustained for 20 to 30 minutes, such as jogging, swimming, and aerobic dance, can increase general fitness, strengthen the heart and lungs, and improve blood circulation. Most important is to become involved in an activity. Get out your tennis racket, put on walking shoes, or check out that aerobic dance class. As you become involved, you will set new goals for yourself and your body. Put your first exercise goal on tomorrow's to-do list. What will it be?

GET REGULAR SLEEP

If you have had a good workout during the day, most likely you'll be able to sleep well that evening. During your sleep cycle, your body rejuvenates itself not just for the next day's physical activities but for upcoming mental work as well. Many students attempt to operate with minimal sleep as a way to squeeze more into their day. In an interview with *Time* magazine, Dr. Charles Pollak of Cornell University Hospital described the serious consequences of sleep deprivation: "People who don't get enough sleep can't think, they can't make the appropriate judgments, they can't maintain long attention spans." Adequate sleep, then, is critical for academic performance. To maintain your body's health and to get the most from each day, you should receive *sufficient uninterrupted* sleep in a *consistent* pattern.

deprivation

INFORMATION FILE: LIFE IN THE 90s

Eye Openers . . .

- You spend one third of your life asleep.

- Drinking heavily every weekend doubles the risk of death.

- In the average American home, the television is on approximately 50 hours a week.

The Fine Print . . .

If sugar is not listed with the ingredients of a food item, then it's sugar free, right? Maybe not. Sugar in food comes in many forms, using many technical names. Whether it's dextrose, sucrose, corn sweetener, or fructose, it's SUGAR.

Pill Poppers . . .

Your body produces its own natural opiates called endorphins that are released during vigorous exercise and as an aid to the healing process. Endorphins are responsible for the "high" experienced by runners. Some researchers speculate that endorphins are also released when a person helps another—producing that good-all-over feeling.

- **Sufficient.** The average person requires approximately eight hours of sleep. If you are sleeping less than the average, decide if you are satisfied with your overall health and your ability to concentrate and to handle stress. If you're not, you probably should increase your nightly sleep time. Some peoples' bodies do require more than the average hours of sleep. Others, however, sleep 10 or more hours a night in reaction to excessive stress in their lives. If you think you are sleeping more than is necessary to revitalize your body, see your doctor for a checkup and to discuss the stress in your life.

- **Consistent.** Recent research indicates that a consistent sleep routine is also important. Yo-yo sleep patterns—5 hours one night, 12 the next—can be very disruptive to your bodily cycles. Try to vary your nightly sleep time by no more than two hours. For some people this might mean taping late-night talk shows and saying good night to visitors by 11 P.M.

- **Uninterrupted.** According to one survey, only one person in three wakes feeling refreshed. Disruptions to your sleep can affect the quality of rest you receive and even your learning. Studies with people whose sleep was interrupted show reduced learning in comparison with people who enjoyed unbroken sleep. If you have difficulty sleeping through the night, eliminate any afternoon naps and disruptive physical factors such as noise and improper ventilation.

AVOID HARMFUL SUBSTANCES

Lack of sleep, a poor test grade, and peer pressure are stresses that send most people looking for quick relief. Drugs, alcohol, and tobacco are short-term solutions to stress that have serious long-term consequences. Their use can result in

Addiction.

Health complications.

Legal or social problems.

If these dependencies are not part of your lifestyle, you can continue your healthful patterns in college by

- Choosing friends with similar values and interests.
- Monitoring your stress level.
- Using your support network to solve problems.

If harmful substances have become a regular part of your lifestyle, college can be your opportunity for a fresh start. Some practical steps can lead the way to a substance-free lifestyle:

self-recrimination

1. **Focus on the future, not the past.** Self-recrimination will only add stress.

2. **Let others help.** Enlist the help of a caring campus professional and your family and friends. They can help you make the right decisions and reduce stress.

3. **Build new friendships and new patterns.** If necessary, end relationships and activities that you associate with substance use, and replace them with new friendships and new activities that are sources of enjoyment.

4. **Keep trying.** Changing habits, especially those involving physical dependency, is difficult. Often people require several attempts to alter their habits. With patience, help, and perseverance you can build a healthful lifestyle.

DEVELOP A SAFE APPROACH TO SEX

One final health concern should be discussed. As adults, each of us must address the very important issues related to sexuality. College is a time when many people find their views of sexuality challenged in new ways. Sometimes people become confused and act without making fully informed decisions. To make safe decisions, you should consider your own feelings, health factors, and society's norms.

1. Male or female, you can say no. If you do not feel ready for sexual intimacy, then wait.

2. No individual has the right to force you into sexual intimacy. In turn, you are obligated, often by law, to respect the wishes of others.

3. If you are sexually active, but not ready to have a child, both you and your partner have an obligation to take protective measures. Consult with your campus health professional for options that are open to you.

> ### STRESSBUSTER
>
> Leave your Timex behind and you'll unwind. On the weekends don't wear your watch. You'll begin to move at your own pace instead of the clock's tick-tock. Have someone call you if you must prepare for a specific appointment.

4. If you are sexually active, each time you are intimate, you have a responsibility to yourself and others to be aware of sexually transmitted diseases and contraceptives.

Sexually Transmitted Diseases

AIDS.   You are vulnerable to the virus that causes AIDS if you come in contact with infected blood, semen, or vaginal fluids during intercourse or petting. Using condoms provides some protection from contact with these fluids. People with multiple partners are at the greatest risk. AIDS can be contracted by anyone who is sexually active, regardless of his or her lifestyle.

STD.   You should also be concerned with other forms of sexually transmitted diseases. Sexual intimacy can result in a number of bacterial and viral infections such as herpes and gonorrhea. These diseases are usually treatable, but some can cause serious health problems if unchecked.

Protection.
- Avoid all casual encounters and limit your partners.
- Know your partner and his or her sexual background.
- Never have sex without using a condom.
- See your doctor if you have any health concerns.

Resources.   Check with these groups if you need more information or advice.

Your campus health service.

Family planning clinic.

Decide now what actions are safe and sensible as you socialize and develop new relationships.

MANAGE STRESS

Has your stress been building as you read this chapter? Stress can result from a wide range of factors, but not all stress is counterproductive. Challenges and changes motivate you to achieve and grow. Stress becomes detrimental when it builds from several sources and goes unabated. Then stress can affect your health, your ability to work, and your relationships. New students face stress from many sources:

unabated

INFORMATION FILE: LIFE IN THE 90s

Time for a Holiday . . .

On a typical day, you have approximately 200 negative thoughts. When you're depressed, the figure triples to 600. (Where are your endorphins when you need them?) When you have those 600 depressing thoughts, tell your instructor or your boss that you need to celebrate one of these holidays:

Boy Scouts Day	On or near February 8, Boy Scouts' founding day.
Girl Scouts Day	On or near March 12, Girl Scouts' founding day.
Aviation Day	August 19, the birthday of Orville Wright.
Midsummer's Day	June 21, the longest day of the year.
Eliza Doolittle Day	May 20, to encourage the proper use of language.

Course requirements.

New associates.

Altered schedules.

New living circumstances.

Changed financial status.

Sometimes you are aware of your stress right away—maybe when you have to deliver a speech or when you meet a new date. Then you might experience the stress as sweaty palms or a racing heart. Other times stress builds from responsibilities—your job, bills, family obligations. Then you might become preoccupied with worry, unable to sleep, or very irritable. Even positive situations such as vacations and Christmas can be sources of stress because you set expectations for the occasion and often expectations are placed on you. Maybe you become keyed up and forgetful as you prepare for that special event.

If you maintain good eating, sleeping, and exercise patterns, you can minimize much of the stress you are experiencing. In addition, you should be sure to set aside time for relaxation. The people described at the beginning of the chapter found themselves in unhealthy lifestyles, in part because they traded recreational time for more work time. Problems become overwhelming when people don't take a break from their problems and responsibilities. Then stress builds unnecessarily. Take a few minutes to identify the major areas of stress in your life.

Stress Points

_____

_____

_____

Now identify a way in which you can escape each pressure for at least 30 minutes. For example, if you listed caring for your children as a source of stress, perhaps someone can watch them at least once a week.

Escape Routes

_____

_____

_____

Now that you have a path from the pressure, be sure that you don't head toward another source of stress. Use your time to enjoy yourself in an activity that brings you pleasure and fosters your positive self-image. List three activities that are relaxing and reduce stress for you.

Relaxing Activities

_____

_____

_____

If you are interested in trying something new, consider stress-reducing activities such as yoga, meditation, or relaxation exercises. School libraries and counseling centers are excellent sources for books, tapes, and videos on these subjects. Whether you choose new activities or a favorite pastime, use recreation time to control your stress and gain new perspective on your responsibilities.

Usually people associate negative thought patterns with major areas of stress. For example, stressed parents might feel guilty that they are so busy with school work and have less time for their children. The message to themselves becomes "I am an inadequate parent." In fact, parents who are also students provide their children with positive role models for school attendance, homework, and goal setting. From that perspective, the inner message can become "I am a positive role model for my children, and I am giving them skills for their future." What negative "tapes" play in your head when you confront a major stress point? How can you erase that negative thinking? In the space below create a positive statement for each of your major stress points. If you get stuck, ask other people for their perspective.

Positive Thought Tape

_____

_____

_____

_____

_____

_____

> ### STRESSBUSTER
>
> Need inspiration, new goals? Read a biography of someone you admire—a sports hero, political leader, an artist. Follow in their footsteps.

When you establish a healthful, positive lifestyle, each day begins with the most important priority, YOU. With that clear focus, you are ready to set your goals and establish a time management plan.

SET YOUR GOALS

When people set goals that span months and build over a year or years, they begin to shape time rather than allowing time to take its own direction. By continuing your studies, you have set in motion the first stages of a life goal. Perhaps your plans are tentative because you are still exploring your talents and the job market. Your classes and your interactions with instructors will aid you in narrowing your career path. Keep in mind that your campus counseling and placement centers are excellent resources for exploring career options.

Whether your goal is clearly established or developing, now is the time to set the academic standards that will make your career and life goals possible. Specific academic standards for each semester will help you make both long-term decisions, such as applying for an internship program, and daily decisions, such as declining a weekend invitation just before final exams. People without clearly defined goals are ruled by time and the whim of the moment. Ultimately they will have little or nothing to show for their time.

Play by the Rules

Some standards have already been set by your institution. Unlike high schools, colleges usually require students to maintain a C average. Just passing courses is not acceptable in several ways. Theoretically a student could pass all the required courses but not graduate because his or her average was below a C. A grade of D is usually not acceptable in prerequisite courses or for transfer to another college.

theoretically

Develop Personal Goals

Is a C average the logical goal to set? No. Students need to consider more than their averages when setting academic goals. Aiming for the bare minimum does not give the student any safety margin. Take the case of Josh. In his first semester he contented himself with earning a C in each of his four classes. He reasoned that a solid C average wasn't so bad. However, the next term he found his courses more difficult, and he finished with three Cs and one D. Unexpectedly his average had slipped below the standards set by his school. In his third term, Josh found himself under great pressure to earn Bs so he could restore his average to a C level. Josh worked very hard but didn't feel as if he was getting ahead. Many institutions give students just two terms to raise an insufficient average to the C level. Don't settle for getting by, which can create unnecessary stress. Use these guidelines to set high-yield goals above the minimum level.

Challenge Yourself beyond Your Immediate Performance Level.   What final grade point average would satisfy you? What average would make you proud? Set your goals so you are building confidence in your ability to compete with yourself as well as with others.

Be Sure Your Goals Are Realistic.   Setting unrealistically high standards can create stress and unnecessarily put you in a self-imposed losing situation. Three factors commonly affect goal fulfillment:

- Responsibility level.

- Past performances.

norms
- Norms or general success levels.

Consider these factors as you evaluate this new student's semester goal.

Philip is carrying 12 credits and has set his academic goal as all As. He works 28 hours per week and is the father of one small child. He graduated from high school seven years ago with a 74 average. Philip is unaware that only a small percentage of students earn an A average.

Certainly Philip's goals are admirable, but he has probably created a losing situation for himself. Instead, he could set his semester goal as a high B average. If he attained that goal, then an A average would be a realistic standard in future semesters.

Specify Your Goals in Writing One Term at a Time.   Like the tasks of a to-do list, goals specified in writing are more often completed successfully. Sometimes, people avoid committing themselves to specific goals because they fear failure. However, the uncertainty of drifting along creates its own anxiety. Take control of time by writing firm, realistic semester goals.

MAKE TIME MANAGEMENT EASIER

For students and professionals alike, time is associated with stress. One reason time is so difficult to manage is that we deal with it on so many different levels, from units as indefinite as a lifetime to the fleeting length of a second. Whether we're turning the page of a calendar, writing the date of a new year, or reflecting at the end of a day, we so often say, "Where did the time go?" This section of the chapter will give you tools for managing your months, weeks, and special projects.

compilation

amend

Use the Calendar Approach   In establishing semester goals, you have a tool to guide you throughout the term. A calendar can provide you with a month-by-month compilation of all that should be accomplished in your courses and your personal life as well. If you are using an appointment book for your to-do lists, you can also use it as a calendar. If you need a separate calendar, be sure to choose one that is handy to carry and large enough to list multiple events on one day. As you fill in dates, use a pencil so you can easily amend your record. For an up-to-date, complete listing in your calendar, follow these steps:

1. **Record all your personal events and obligations.** Daniel Gill, a CEO for Bausch and Lomb, calls this process the block-out technique. Be sure to include

    Birthdays.

    Appointments.

    Meetings for activities.

    Important deadlines.

    Holidays.

2. **List important events from your school catalog and course outlines.** Record on your calendar

    Campus holidays.

    Exam periods.

    Quizzes and test dates.

    If your instructor has listed exams and quizzes by the week rather than on a specific day, place that information across several days with a question mark. You will find it helpful to number the college weeks directly on your calendar.

3. **Continue to record obligations as they arise.** Keep your calendar with you so you can write down the facts accurately the first time. When you have all your obligations recorded, you will see patterns emerge. In just a glance you will know if it is sensible to have out-of-town guests on a particular weekend. Most likely midterm week will be very busy, as is shown in Figure 3–3. Papers and projects are often due several weeks before the end of the term. With dates mapped out on your calendar, you can avoid overcommitting yourself or making appointments that you won't be able to keep.

Develop a Weekly Routine

When you hear the word *routine,* do you think of a boring rut? Peter Drucker, author of *The Effective Executive,* maintains that managers who make decisions under pressure invariably ignore the most important tasks. A weekly routine can remove that minute-to-minute pressure and give you the freedom to enjoy an unscheduled movie with friends without sacrificing your responsibilities. Use these steps to build a well-rounded routine.

1. **Reserve Times for Obligations that Cannot Easily Be Rearranged.**

    • **Classes.** Make every class every day a priority.

    • **Work.** Also give priority ranking in your schedule to work hours. However, carefully consider your total work hours in relation to the study demands of college. As a rule of thumb, study experts recommend the following formula: for every class hour, students should spend two hours in independent preparation. With that ratio, the hours mount up quickly. The total for a typical full-time load of 15 credit hours would be 15 class

FIGURE 3–3			**Monthly Calendar at Midterm**			

OCTOBER						
WK. SUNDAY	MONDAY	TUESDAY	WEDNESDAY	THURSDAY	FRIDAY	SATURDAY
						1
5 2	3 Mom & Dad's anniv.	4 Microecon. test ? Comp. Graph. test	5	6	7 Bus. Writ. critique	8 Home—coming weekend
6 9 Homecoming	10	11	12 Earth Sci Chpt. test	13	14 Finite M. test	15 Amy's birthday
7 16	17	18	19	20	21 Bus. Writ. letters	22 Dance ??? on campus
	☆ ☆ Begin midterm review/study					
8 23	24 Midterm: Finite M.	25	26 Midterm: Earth Sci.	27 Midterm: Microecon	28	29
9 30	31 ☆ ☆ Begin Bus. Writ.proj. ?	Midterm for Comp. Graph, Bus. Writ.				

hours + 30 hours preparation = 45 total academic hours. The conclusion is obvious. FULL-TIME COLLEGE IS A FULL-TIME JOB. For this reason learning experts recommend that full-time students work a maximum of 20 hours per week. If your personal circumstances require that you work more hours, consider a lighter academic load, at least for your first semester.

• **Commuting.** Be sure you include each trip you make on a regular basis to work, classes, and your home. Take into consideration rush-hour traffic and the time it takes to park your car and walk to your destination. Over a week these hours add up.

STRESSBUSTER

If you stare at the ceiling at night, don't despair. TRY a warm shower or bath, soothing music, relaxation techniques. AVOID exercise immediately before bed, afternoon naps, caffeine after 4 P.M.

2. **Reserve Daily Times to Maintain a Healthful Lifestyle.**   Make a commitment on paper to regular meals, sleep, exercise and recreation. Figure 3–4 shows all the elements of a balanced lifestyle woven into one person's routine. Notice that the student alters his or her sleep pattern on the weekend, but the variation is not so great that the sleep cycle will be affected far into the next week.

3. **Schedule Daily Study and Review Times.**   Designate specific study times so that you can review and prepare for each subject PRIOR to the next class session. Be sure that you allot a sufficient amount of study time for each subject. At the beginning of a term you can use the two-hour study formula and then adjust the hours as you progress in your classes. In Figure 3–5, the student has allotted the greatest study time to microeconomics because that is the most challenging subject. Schedule your study during times when your concentration will be the sharpest. Be sure to avoid setting unrealistic expectations. For example, in Figure 3–5 the student has not scheduled study after work on Tuesday evening. To maximize concentration in the evening, the student has alternated study sessions with exercise and chores.

4. **Schedule Times for Domestic and Personal Obligations.**   Buying groceries and washing the laundry simply must be done. An empty fridge at 8 A.M. makes it difficult to get in the groove for the rest of the day. Placing these essentials in your daily routine will assure that they get done, and you're sure to impress your family and friends when they visit!

5. **Leave Flexible Time in Each Day and Provide a Block of Time that Does Not Include School Work.**   If you pack every moment of the day, your routine is sure to fall apart. If you can wake up and get ready for classes in 15 minutes, allow a half hour. Instead of just 30 minutes for dinner, make it an hour. Andrew Grove, a CEO for Intel Corporation, calls this building air pockets in his schedule. In the sample schedule of Figure 3–5, liberal time allotments have been set for travel and meals. Other air pockets are placed at midday and in the evening.

    Another way to take the pressure off your schedule is to create a sizable block of time that does not include school work at all. For each person the ideal time will differ, but most people like to take a weekend block just for themselves. The student using the sample schedule has reserved Friday evening and a small span of time on Saturday because many work hours are also scheduled on the weekend.

6. **Set Aside a Half Hour on the Weekend for Previewing and Planning the Upcoming Week.**   Consult your calendar, assignment, record, and last to-do list to map out the week ahead. Read how weekly planning helped one student.

FIGURE 3–4   **Steps 1 and 2 for Building a Weekly Schedule**

HR	MONDAY	TUESDAY	WEDNESDAY	THURSDAY	FRIDAY	SATURDAY	SUNDAY
6-7	S	L	E	E	P	Sleep	Sleep
7-8			Breakfast / Grooming / Travel				
8-9	Earth Science Class		Earth Science Class		Earth Science Class		Breakfast
9-10		Business		Business		Breakfast	
10-11		Writing Class		Writing Class			
11-12	Computer Graphics Class		Computer Graphics Class		Computer Graphics Class		
12-1		Micro-	lunch	Micro-			Lunch
1-2		economics Class		economics Class		Travel / Work	Travel / Work
2-3	Finite Math Class		Finite Math Class	Earth Science	Finite Math Class		
3-4				Lab			
4-5			Travel				
5-6	Relax dinner	Work	Relax dinner	Relax dinner	Work		Travel dinner
6-7		(dinner)			(dinner)	(dinner)	
7-8							
8-9	Exercise		Exercise	Exercise			
9-10		Travel relax			Evening out	Evening out	
10-11	S	L	E E	P			Sleep

When Rick checked his calendar on Sunday, he was reminded of an extended field trip scheduled for Wednesday afternoon. By planning ahead, he had plenty of time to find a co-worker willing to trade work hours. With minor adjustments, his routine schedule ran smoothly during the following week.

Plan ahead, and you'll save time and reduce your stress.

7. **Adjust Your Routine Schedule after You Have Used It for Two Weeks.** The full sample schedule is mapped out in Figure 3–6. This plan, like most ideas on paper, will need adjustment when put into action. As patterns emerge over several weeks, you will be able to spot weaknesses in your routine schedule, and you can adjust them to suit your needs.

FIGURE 3–5   *Steps 3–6 for Building a Weekly Schedule*

WEEKLY SCHEDULE

HR	MONDAY	TUESDAY	WEDNESDAY	THURSDAY	FRIDAY	SATURDAY	SUNDAY
6-7							
7-8							
8-9		Study Comp. gr. in lab		Study Comp. gr. in lab			Personal time
9-10	Study earth sci.		Study earth sci.		Study earth sci.	Chores & personal	
10-11	Study bus. writ.		Study microecon.		Study microecon.	time	Study earth sci.
11-12		Study bus. writ.		Study microecon.			Study bus. writ.
12-1							
1-2	Study microecon.		Study Comp. gr. in lab		Study Comp. gr. in lab		
2-3		Study microecon.					
3-4	Study finite math	Study earth sci.	Study finite math		Study finite math		
4-5							
5-6							
6-7	Study bus. writ.		Study finite math	Study earth sci.			Chores
7-8	Chores		Chores	Study finite math			Study finite planning
8-9							Study Comp. gr.
9-10	Study finite math		Study bus. writ.	Study microecon.	Personal time	Personal time	Study microecon.
10-11					↓	↓	

Business and industry operate from standardized procedures or routines to produce consistent quality in their services and products. Your routine schedule is your set of standard procedures. Use it to produce consistent quality in your academics, on the job, and in your personal life.

Follow a Project Schedule

Very busy times make it difficult to keep to a routine. Setting early start dates for projects on your calendar can prevent some of the problem. However, people often find it difficult to actually get a project underway. They feel overwhelmed by the task and don't know where to begin. Establishing a project schedule can make

FIGURE 3–6	*Completed Weekly Schedule*

WEEKLY SCHEDULE

HR	MONDAY	TUESDAY	WEDNESDAY	THURSDAY	FRIDAY	SATURDAY	SUNDAY
6-7	S	L	E	E	P	Sleep	Sleep
7-8			Breakfast / Grooming / Travel				
8-9	Earth Science Class	Study Comp. gr.	Earth Science Class	Study Comp. gr.	Earth Science Class		Breakfast / Personal
9-10	Study earth sci.	(in lab) Business	Study earth sci.	(in lab) Business	Study earth sci.	Breakfast Chores	time
10-11	Study bus. writ.	Writing Class	Study microecon.	Writing Class	Study microecon.	& personal	Study earth sci.
11-12	Computer Graphics Class	Study bus. writ.	Computer Graphics Class	Study microecon.	Computer Graphics Class	time	Study bus. writ.
12-1			Lunch			Travel	Lunch / travel
1-2	Study micro econ.	economics Class	Study Comp. gr.	economics Class	Study Comp. gr.	Work	Work
2-3	Finite Math Class	Study microecon.	Finite Math Class	Earth Science	Finite Math Class		
3-4	Study finite math	Study earth sci.	Study finite math	Lab	Study finite math		
4-5			travel				
5-6	Relax dinner	Work	relax dinner	relax dinner	Work		travel / dinner
6-7	Study bus. writ.	(dinner)	Study finite math	Study earth sci.	(dinner)	(dinner)	Chores
7-8	Chores		Chores	Study finite math			Study finite / planning
8-9	Exercise		Exercise	Exercise			Study Comp. gr.
9-10	Study finite math	Travel relax	Study bus. writ.	Study microecon.	Personal	Personal	Study microecon.
10-11			S L E E P		time	time	Sleep

daunting   the job less daunting by breaking it into small steps that can be accomplished in a day. Let's say you have set aside three weeks to prepare a six-page paper for your marketing class. You would begin your project schedule with some general target dates such as these.

Week 1: Choose topic and begin research.

Week 2: Complete research and write rough draft.

Week 3: Write and produce final draft.

Now each of these major phases can be broken down into smaller, daily tasks such as this one for the very first day:

Generate three topics for marketing paper.

Notice that the step is easy but specific. The goal is not *some topics* but *three topics*. Be sure that you write the task on your to-do list and that you carry over unfinished work to the next day's list. Based on the progress you make each day, you may find it necessary to adjust your target dates. Sometimes, despite the best planning and efforts, deadlines are missed. If you realize that you will be unable to meet a deadline, contact the instructor immediately so that he or she is aware of your problem and your plan to solve it quickly.

The challenges of each semester are many. Using time and stress management strategies, you can maintain a healthful, productive lifestyle.

THE ASAP REWIND «««

How can I keep up my energy level when I am so busy?

If you maintain a healthful lifestyle, you can maintain a high energy level.   Follow these guidelines for good health:
1.   Eat nutritious foods daily.
2.   Exercise approximately two hours each week.
3.   Get regular sleep every day.

Should I be concerned about drugs and sexually transmitted diseases?

These issues should concern every adult.   For a long, enjoyable life, consider these cautions:
1.   Avoid using drugs, tobacco, or alcohol to relieve stress.
2.   Know the risks of being sexually active, and develop a safe, personalized approach.

How can I manage the stress I am experiencing?

You can manage and even reduce some of your stress through your lifestyle and special stress-reducing activities.   Manage your stress by maintaining your health, enjoying relaxing activities, forming positive thoughts, and using relaxation exercises.

What kind of goals should I set in school?

You should develop high-yield goals that will focus your efforts.   Be sure that your goals are challenging, realistic, and specific.

How can I manage my time and all of my responsibilities?

Develop a time-management plan that includes your personal needs as well as your responsibilities.   Your management plan should include a calendar record, a weekly schedule, and a project schedule.

Exercise 1

Directions: Did you spot new words while reading the chapter? Add yours to this list and to your vocabulary. Define each of the following words using your word meaning techniques: word parts, context, and dictionary. Then use each in an original sentence.

exemplify _____

_____

_____

contributory _____

_____

_____

deprivation _____

_____

_____

self-recrimination _____

_____

_____

unabated _____

_____

_____

theoretically _____

_____

_____

norms _____

_____

_____

compilation _____

_____

_____

amend _____

_____

_____

daunting _____

_____

_____

TAKE ACTION

Exercise 2

Directions: Help your classmate Chris develop a project schedule. She must prepare a written and an oral review of a magazine article for her economics class. The assignment is due in four weeks. Establish target dates for major phases of the assignment. Then list the tasks necessary to meet that *first* target date.

_____

_____

_____

_____

_____

_____

Exercise 3

Directions: Establish in writing your academic goal for this semester. Briefly explain how this goal is both challenging and realistic for you.

_____

_____

_____

Exercise 4

Directions: Begin managing each month of the semester with your calendar. Use your course outlines, college catalog, and personal date book to log in your responsibilities and holidays. Be sure to establish start dates for any lengthy projects. Ask your instructor for blank calendar pages if you do not have a suitable calendar.

Exercise 5

Directions: Follow the seven steps for developing a weekly routine to customize your own schedule. Use the accompanying weekly schedule form. NOTE: Your use of a weekly routine schedule will also be evaluated in the next chapter since a minimum of two weeks is necessary for in-depth analysis.

WEEKLY SCHEDULE							
HR	**MONDAY**	**TUESDAY**	**WEDNESDAY**	**THURSDAY**	**FRIDAY**	**SATURDAY**	**SUNDAY**

CHECK YOUR PROGRESS

Directions: Put time and health management into action! At the end of one week, use the checklist below to evaluate your progress. Then use the space that follows to write about your growth.

PROGRESS CHECKLIST: Managing Your Time and Health

Yes   Usually   No

___   ___   ___   **1.**   I am maintaining regular eating, sleeping, and exercise patterns.

___   ___   ___   **2.**   I am using recreation and relaxation to manage stress.

___   ___   ___   **3.**   I have established my semester goal, and I use it to guide my decisions about time usage.

___   ___   ___   **4.**   I promptly update my calendar and consult it for my weekly planning.

___   ___   ___   **5.**   I am using a weekly routine based on the seven steps of this chapter.

A.   Examine those areas of your lifestyle that you feel promote good health. Evaluate how well you have been able to maintain these activities while managing your new responsibilities. How has your time management plan helped you to accomplish both?

B.   Identify those areas of your lifestyle that you'd like to improve. Discuss ways you can fit those objectives into your routine schedule.

Escape Reality.   Take a few lines to describe your dream lifestyle. Anything goes because it never hurts to dream.

_____

_____

_____

_____

_____

_____

_____

_____

_____

_____

DEVELOPING ACTIVE
LEARNING SKILLS

Building Concentration

THE SKILL THAT GETS THE JOB

Full-time Medical Secretary. For busy doctor's office. Must be experienced with excellent word–processing skills and attention to detail. Keyboard test required.

WHAT'S YOUR EXPERIENCE?

When people say "Concentrate!" they usually are not talking about frozen orange juice. How would you define *concentration*? How would you rate your current concentration abilities? What would you like to learn about this very important skill? Use the space below to explore your skill, your knowledge, and your questions about this chapter's topic.

_____

_____

_____

_____

_____

_____

_____

_____

_____

_____

_____

In this chapter you will learn to

»»»   *Develop a positive, active approach toward your studies.*

»»»   *Utilize your goals and objectives to extend concentration.*

»»»   *Manage stress that distracts from concentration.*

»»»   *Control your study environment.*

»»»   *Use breaks to renew concentration.*

BUILDING CONCENTRATION

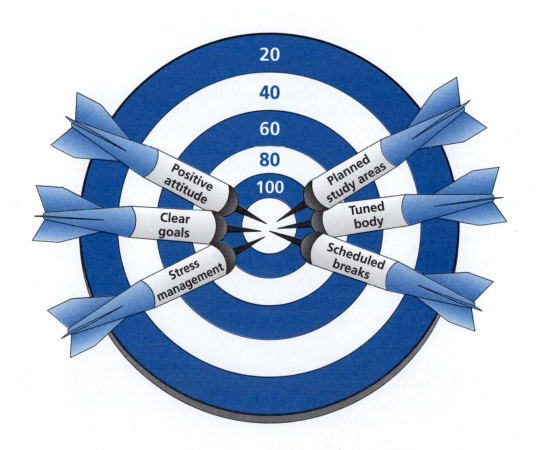

This chapter is your opportunity to unlock your learning potential. How? Through heightened concentration. Actually, you've already taken the first steps to building a greater attention span. Many of the skills and strategies you've developed in Chapters 1 through 3 are your foundation for effective concentration. Now, in this chapter, you can refine those skills and learn practical tips for maintaining a high level of concentration.

CONCENTRATION AND ATTENTION

Some tasks can be completed with minimal attention. You can run down a familiar flight of stairs or turn on the ignition of your car with little mental effort because these are tasks you have already mastered. You cannot, however, acquire new information unless you are mentally focused to receive and process the data. When your concentration is incomplete, your ability to listen, read, or recite is affected. On the job, concentration is critical to quality productivity. As a supervisor, how would you evaluate a worker who performs like this?

> Gretchen, a customer service representative, assists clients in resolving their complaints, usually through phone conversations. She takes a call from a customer whose latest shipment of merchandise is incorrect. After the customer has spoken for several minutes, Gretchen asks the client to repeat the terms of the order. Impatiently the customer repeats the basic information. Several days later the representative calls the customer again to ask for the same information.

Would you evaluate Gretchen as disorganized, inefficient, unmotivated, or lacking in concentration skills? Often, insufficient concentration is a very real problem. People have difficulty concentrating when they have not established a positive mental set or have not controlled physical factors.

ESTABLISH A POSITIVE MENTAL SET

orchestrate

A positive mental set means preparing your mind to accomplish a specific task. An air traffic controller must focus his or her mind to orchestrate the movements of jumbo jets carrying hundreds of passengers. A bookkeeper must be alert to the placement of each figure to avoid errors of thousands of dollars. A nurse must double-check that dosages of medicine are accurate for each patient. As a student, your mind must be actively engaged to absorb all the information received during lectures and study sessions. Three factors affect your mental set in any situation: your attitude, your goals, and your stress level.

Have a Can-Do Attitude

Successful students and professionals achieve remarkable concentration because they begin with a desire to concentrate and achieve. Some students approach a task with the main objective of finishing. During a lecture they concentrate on the clock. They hastily read course material during television commercials. Such attitudes make real concentration impossible. After a lecture or a reading session, the student will have accomplished little beyond producing a list of excuses for poor performance.

Negative feelings usually underlie a poor attitude about an activity or course. Do these statements sound familiar?

INFORMATION FILE: CONCENTRATION

People's potential to achieve seems limitless when they combine skill and concentration. Read on for some remarkable achievements.

Thinking on Your Feet . . .
Leslie Silva balanced on one foot for 45 hours, 25 minutes without support of any type.

Too Close *(and Fast)* **for Comfort . . .**
Gerry Harley shaved 235 men in 60 minutes with a straight-edge razor, drawing blood only once. *But how much blood did he draw?*

A 13-letter Word Meaning ATTENTION . . .
Roy Dean holds the record for the fastest crossword puzzle solution. He completed a *New York Times* puzzle in 3 minutes, 45 seconds.

Not Getting Older but Better . . .
William Walker crossed the South Boulder Canyon on a tightrope for a distance of 320 feet. The drop below was 125 feet. It was Mr. Walker's 82nd birthday.

I did terribly in my senior history class; I can't possibly do any better in this course.

The instructor keeps piling on the work in there. I'll never get it done.

I hate literature, but they tell me I have to take it. Well, they can't make me like it.

I can't stand the teacher in earth science. I don't like the way she does the labs. I don't even know what this week's lab assignment is.

Negative feelings are certainly understandable, but hanging on to them won't get you anywhere. The instructor and the class will go on, and you and your negative feelings will be left right where you are. You can minimize such feelings so you are able to concentrate and progress with your work. Once you make progress, negative feelings often begin to subside. Here are some suggestions for turning around negative feelings:

- **Poor past performance.** Don't assume you'll do poorly this time. Many of the factors that contributed to problems in the past—the instructor, the class, the text—are now different. You can learn from your last experience too. Decide what you can do differently to make this class a success, and then take action.

- **Heavy workload.** You've already learned some tips to conquer this problem: Allot extra study hours to this course in your routine schedule and break assignments into smaller, more manageable tasks. You can work with another classmate to make it easier to understand the

procrastinate

material. Sometimes workloads become unmanageable because students procrastinate. If that's your tendency, be sure you are using a to-do list every day to keep you in control of the workload.

- **Disliked subject.** If you find yourself in a required course that you dislike very much, you should look at the larger picture and the academic plans you have made. What are the benefits of satisfactorily completing that course? You might be able to move on to other courses you enjoy; continue your program of study as planned; and maintain an acceptable G.P.A.

- **Personality conflict.** Often you will not be able to change instructors. In such cases, you should shift your focus away from the source of your negative feelings. Center your concentration on the course content and your personal achievement rather than on the instructor. Team up with a student whose company you enjoy and who has less negative feelings about the class. You may learn more by working with a classmate than during the lectures.

Approach each subject in college with a renewed, positive attitude. As a result, your concentration will be stronger, more focused, and geared toward achieving your goals.

Work Toward Your Goals

Your goals are an essential part of your mental set because they generate motivation and drive. In turn these powerful forces enhance your concentration. In Chapter 3, you developed your semester goal. Do you think your current level of concentration in classes and in study sessions is sufficient to reach that goal? Be sure you use your semester goals to motivate yourself when you are bored or stuck in a pattern of procrastination. You can also set goals in specific courses to establish motivation. Read how one student focused his attention by setting a specific goal for a difficult course.

Calvin has done low C work on his weekly quizzes and his first test in Introduction to Business. He knows he can do better, but his mind often wanders during lectures and when he reads the textbook. Calvin sets this goal for the course:

I want to raise my course average to a B. By reading the textbook more closely, I think I can raise my quiz average to a high B.

Select one course in which you feel your motivation and concentration are low. Gain focus now by establishing a goal for that course. Remember, your goal should be challenging, realistic, and written in specific terms. Begin your drive to success today.

Use Your To-Do List

As we saw in earlier chapters, using a to-do list to plan your day and prioritize activities is one of the best ways to focus your attention. Your list will help you handle your obligations one at a time instead of haphazardly dividing your attention among several duties. Marking off items as you complete them also provides

> GOALS → MOTIVATION → DRIVE → CONCENTRATION →
> ACHIEVEMENT

you with motivation to focus on the next task. Just be careful that you do not rush through activities to move quickly through your to-do list. If you do that, you are focusing on completion instead of achieving excellence in the task itself. If a to-do list has not become a regular part of your routine, master the process today by rereading Chapter 1.

Control Your Stress Sources

Even when you are highly motivated, random thoughts, often stress related, will interfere with your focus. Sometimes it's a minor responsibility: "I have to order take-out dinner before I leave." Other times, you might find yourself trying to resolve a major problem while listening to a lecture or reading an assignment: "What if the new landlord raises the rent?" And, of course, unexpected events can block your concentration.

Respond to Unexpected Distractions.   A flat tire or a misplaced set of keys will certainly disrupt your routine and your concentration. However, you don't need to lose control of your entire day. Once you have resolved the problem, you can restore your equilibrium by focusing on your to-do list. If necessary, eliminate the nonessential tasks for the day and focus on just your prioritized items. You'll keep your stress to a minimum and your concentration sharp.

equilibrium

impromptu

Some unscheduled events, especially social interruptions, can occur with irritating frequency. Phone calls and impromptu visits can disrupt your routine and seriously decrease your ability to concentrate. In his article, "How Top Managers Manage Their Time," Eric Calonius concludes, "Perhaps taking No lessons is the real key to time management." Learn to say "no" to interruptions. Let your friends and family know that you must concentrate on your work and that you can't be disturbed during study times. If you find it difficult to deliver such messages in person, place a note on your door or tape one for a telephone answering machine. Then arrange to spend time with your family and friends during your breaks, flexible times, and weekend free blocks.

Manage Your Daily Responsibilities.   A routine schedule is one of the best tools to reduce stress. Has your weekly schedule helped you concentrate on each task and freed you from worrying that you are neglecting other responsibilities? Later in this chapter you will evaluate the routine schedule you designed. Analyze how and why it has been effective, and see if you can improve it. The time you spend building an effective routine will pay off in reduced stress and improved concentration.

Reserve Special Times to Resolve Ongoing Problems.   Have you ever solved a complex personal problem while at work or in the classroom? Probably not. Most often people just worry about their problems while they work or study. Their anxiety is counterproductive because it breaks concentration and adds to the existing stress. When you face a problem, set aside a logical time to deal with it. Read how Carol separates her family responsibilities from the demands of school.

INFORMATION FILE: CONCENTRATION

Ergonomics R Us . . .

A new field of study called ergonomics examines how technology and environment impact people as they work. At one university, scientists aren't using humans in their studies but a high-tech, life-size doll named Jack. Jack is equipped with sophisticated software to analyze the human factors involved when operating airplane control panels. With Jack's help, researchers measure how well panel lights will be detected by pilots and how much pressure is needed to press a button or throw a switch. Soon they will be measuring information overload by tracking brain waves. *Don't you think Jack should visit your class and measure the hardness of the seats and the distraction level of that wall clock?*

Carol and her family adjusted well to Carol's new school routine. On certain days, though, when the children were sick or midterm exams were approaching, Carol could not concentrate and was worried and irritable all the time. She decided she had to separate the responsibilities of her life. Now, when the instructor closes the door at the start of class, Carol visualizes her family problems being locked outside the door. When she comes home, she keeps her school worries "locked" in her book bag until it's time to study.

If you are fulfilling several roles at one time and find your worries overlapping, try visualizing separations between your responsibilities. Be creative. How can you create some "space" for yourself?

Problems and stress are a common part of life, especially the lives of students who are managing new lifestyles. Do not fall into the trap of believing that the person across the hall or in the next row is stress free. Beneath a composed manner or a cheerful laugh, each individual is coping with stress and unresolved problems. It is futile to declare "I just can't concentrate until my problems are solved" because the responsibilities of school and life are ongoing. For consistent concentration, keep stress under control by using a weekly schedule and problem-solving strategies.

futile

ELIMINATE NEGATIVE EXTERNAL FACTORS

Stress can also be created by other external factors that affect concentration. These external factors are familiar to most people, but they are often ignored. Every day we attempt to carry out our jobs with poor lighting, excessive noise, and weary bodies. Such factors can be classified in two categories: environmental factors and physical factors.

Maintain a Healthy Body

As you learned in the previous chapter, your concentration is greatly reduced by inadequate sleep, erratic eating patterns, and inactivity. Your routine schedule, if properly designed, should account for most of these needs. Here are a few additional tips to give you that extra concentration edge on difficult days.

Choose the right snacks. When your mind seems muddled in the late afternoon, try a snack of yogurt and fruit. In a recent study, participants who ate these foods did significantly better on tests that measured memory, arithmetic reasoning, reading speed, and attention span. Beware of eating candy bars for a quick burst of energy from sugar. Sugar highs only last for a brief period of time. Once the high

| FIGURE 4–1 | | **Study Environment Evaluation Form** | | |

FACTORS	HOME	CAMPUS SPOTS	CLASSES	COMMENTS
Low level of distractions				
Comfortable temperature				
Good line of vision and light				
Comfortable and useful work area				
Equipped with necessary materials				

precipitously

is gone, your energy drops precipitously—maybe just as you begin a big essay question on a test. Chocolate candy bars won't produce a quick burst of energy at all. The high fat content in chocolate causes the digestive process to slow down. You may not get any energy reward until *after* the test.

lethargic

When you become lethargic during lectures or while studying, don't assume you need more sleep. You might need more exercise. On a study break or between classes, try a short, brisk walk. Get your blood pumping simply by avoiding the elevator and entering the next building by the farthest door.

Don't use caffeine to replace sleep or exercise. When you have your morning cup of coffee, you do become more alert and the *symptoms* of fatigue are relieved. However, excessive caffeine can create nervousness and decrease your concentration. Remember that there is also caffeine in cola products, some citrus soft drinks, chocolate, and tea. Tea can provide you with a mild jump-start and has approximately half the caffeine content of drip-brewed coffee.

Control Your Learning Environments

In or out of class, environmental factors play an important part in your ability to concentrate. Although some factors—noisy students in the hall, for example—might be beyond your control, you can control many aspects of your study areas. Each study environment should be arranged to provide you with these benefits:

- Reasonable comfort.
- All materials necessary for the task.
- Freedom from distractions.

Take a moment to evaluate the quality of these factors in each of your learning environments by using Figure 4–1. Place a + or a − in each corresponding box and note the specific problem in that learning environment. Wherever there is a deficiency in a learning environment, take steps now to improve it.

In Your Classes.
- If you're unable to concentrate in your classes, check for these typical sources of distractions: doors, windows, and noisy classmates. Don't stick around them; find a seat that allows you to focus on the instructor.
- Usually seats in the center of the room provide the best opportunity to see and hear any activities at the front of the room.

STRESSBUSTER

Cold hands, warm heart? No, cold hands—lots of stress. If you warm your hands, you can reduce some of the stress effects throughout your body. Visualize that you are holding something soft and warm. Then touch your cheeks (one of the warmest parts of your body) and imagine the heat is being transferred to your hands. End by locking your fingers together and gently squeezing them briefly.

- In your chosen area of the room, try out several spots to find a desk that fits your body size and is comfortable for writing.
- Today's "climate controlled" rooms are sometimes out of control. Don't try to take notes while shivering or sweating. Dress in light layers so you can be comfortable in any of your classes.
- Be prepared to concentrate and learn *before* class begins. Have with you the necessary books, materials, and equipment such as a calculator or computer disks. Get out your pen and notebook and be ready to participate.

Because most new information is presented during lecture, your ability to concentrate in each classroom is crucial. Make those changes today.

Campus Study Areas.   Avoid studying in these popular campus spots:

Student center.	Courtyards and picnic areas.
Cafeteria.	Library reading rooms.
Smoking lounges.	

Usually these spots are very comfortable, but they also have high levels of distraction. Use these enjoyable spots to relax and meet friends on your study breaks, but not for serious studying. Search for a library spot away from the action of the circulation desk and the reference room. Look for a study carrel or table in the middle of the book stacks. Empty classrooms can make great study spots too. Check out the rooms near your classes. Avoid shuttling back and forth between classes, your home, and your campus study spots. You'll waste time and you won't become settled anywhere.

Some students never establish campus study spots, because they use the blocks of time between classes solely for socializing. Those times between classes are ideal for reviewing your day's lecture notes and for beginning homework assignments. A quick 10-minute review of your notes can dramatically reduce forgetting, and an early start on your homework will boost your morale. Put your free time and a campus study spot to good use. Then you'll feel relaxed when you take a break to socialize.

Home Study Area.   Choose a study spot that is comfortable but has minimal distractions. These locations usually do not work well for study because you cannot maintain concentration in them:

Kitchen table. Too much traffic passes through most kitchens as family members or roommates get snacks and meals.

THE SOUND OF MUSIC

Students often protest that a traditional study area is too quiet and confining. They simply must have music playing. However, loud, blaring music will severely hamper your concentration. Some people say they just block out the music, but do they? Have you ever been reading and then realize you are not processing information but reciting the lyrics of the song on your radio? How much time have you lost? At what point did you cease to comprehend the material or begin to form misconceptions? You can avoid such lapses in concentration if you use music as a pleasing background sound. The best type of background music is instrumental because lyrics do not interfere with your thinking. If you are accustomed to listening to your favorite type of music at very high levels, turn the volume down by small increments over several days until the music forms a pleasant background. Even after you have established a comfortable level of background music, you will need to monitor your ability to concentrate because it will vary with the type of work you are doing and the circumstances of your day. Do whatever it takes to maintain concentration—turn down the volume, change the type of music, turn it off completely.

increments

TV room. Your mind cannot totally block out the sound and visual images of television. Consequently, your concentration on your studies is seriously reduced.

Your bed. Because your mind and body are conditioned to associate your bed with sleep, you will probably feel less alert and more fatigued when studying there.

- Equip your study area with a writing surface, a good light, and a comfortable chair. Don't have a desk? You can use a dinette table, a door on two sawhorses or a sturdy card table.

- Try to keep your study area neat. You won't be distracted by the clutter, and the orderliness will create a get-down-to-business atmosphere.

- Make your study spot appealing. Inspire yourself with a poster of someone you admire; reduce your stress with a tranquil picture from nature; bring life to your study area with a blooming plant.

- Don't keep distracting items, such as video games, photo albums, catalogs, and of course, the telephone, in your study area.

- Stock your areas with pencils and pens, paper, a good desk dictionary, and highlighters if you use them. Assemble all your materials *before* you begin to study.

USE ACTIVE LEARNING STRATEGIES

Would you agree with the following answers to these questions?

What do you do during a class lecture?
I sit and listen.

ACTIVE LEARNING

During Lecture   • Participate in discussions.
                         • Paraphrase the instructor's words.
                         • Take notes.
                         • Relate the information to yourself.
                         • Ask questions when you don't understand.

While Reading   • Read for a purpose, not just to cover 21 pages.
                         • Underline important and interesting information.
                         • Relate the ideas and facts to your own experience.
                         • Summarize and recite your learning.
                         • Ask questions.

What do you when you have a textbook assignment?
I read all the pages assigned.

These are typical student responses, and they reflect a passive approach to learning. After a few weeks of sitting, listening, and pushing your eyes across a page, you are sure to lose concentration and motivation. Make your learning easier and better by using active learning strategies in the classroom and while doing homework. You've heard some of the suggestions in the box, "Active Learning," before. In Chapter 1 you learned how to draw on your wealth of experience to enrich your learning, and you discovered the value of summarizing for increased understanding. Other strategies, such as underlining, will be explained in detail in later chapters, but don't wait until then to put them to work. Experiment with underlining and reciting now. You might be surprised by your skill, and you'll be sure to improve your concentration. Later, you'll build on these first experiments with active learning.

USE BREAKS TO RESTORE CONCENTRATION

The rewards of active learning are great, but after a lengthy session you'll find your attention span becoming shorter. You need time away from your studies to refresh your mind and body. Breaks varying in length from 10 minutes to a half hour seem to work well without dramatically reducing study time, but students hesitate to take breaks because they fear that they will not return to their work. They reason that the safest approach is to work nonstop until all their work is completed. However, with each passing hour the work quality decreases because concentration is reduced by fatigue and lowered motivation.

Schedule Breaks into Your Weekly Routine

To avoid such diminishing returns, be sure your routine schedule provides periodic break times. Don't deny yourself a favorite television program. Arrange your work so that the program is a break between study sessions. If your idea of relaxation is listening to your favorite band, plan a study break to listen to a CD. Regardless of the activity you choose, be sure to set a specific length of time so your break doesn't turn into a minivacation. If you have difficulty keeping to the allotted time, set a timer and make sure you get back to studying when it rings.

| FIGURE 4–2 | *Motivation Solutions* |

PROBLEM	SOLUTION
Difficult material	Call your classmate connection. Make an appointment with your instructor. Use an alternative text from the library.
Lack of interest in topic	Set small learning goals. Relate topic to life and employment. Work with a study partner.
Uncertain of progress	Speak with classmates. Make an appointment with your instructor.
Uncertain career goals	Examine your interests in your journal. See your advisor or career counselor.
Large amount of work	Use a project schedule, dividing the work into small segments, over several days if possible.

STRESSBUSTER

Be sure you laugh today. Take a break with a funny friend or enjoy the magical play of your children or children you know. If you prefer some time alone, watch a rerun of your favorite sitcom.

Take Unscheduled Breaks

Equally important in maintaining peak concentration is using unscheduled breaks. The type of break you take will depend on the internal or external factors affecting concentration. A few informal questions like the following will help pinpoint your need.

Have you just completed a particularly difficult assignment? Then a reward is in order! Enjoy a refreshing drink or brag about your accomplishment to someone else. Such breaks will keep your motivation high, which can be important when formal feedback is weeks away.

Are you bogged down in a project, making little progress? A perspective break is called for. Set your work aside for awhile and do something different: Take your shower early or browse through a catalog. When you return, you will have a fresh outlook, and chances are you will quickly see the problem that was there all along.

Are you losing motivation, just hoping to complete the task? A break is a must. Find a comfortable spot and analyze your problem. If you're stumped, you can use the problem-solution chart in Figure 4–2 to explore your difficulty. Break time spent reestablishing a positive mental set is worth the effort. Without a positive mental set you will not be able to focus on the quality of your work.

FIGURE 4–3   *Stretching Exercise*

S-T-R-E-T-C-H
your back

Lean forward from a sitting position, chest to knees. Raise arms behind and hold hands together.

S-T-R-E-T-C-H
your upper back

Place your hands on your shoulders. Rotate arms forward; then reverse the rotation.

S-T-R-E-T-C-H
your torso

Arch one arm above your head. Draw the other arm across your body in a bent position. Bend from the waist in the direction of the arched arm. Reverse the motion.

S-T-R-E-T-C-H
your hips

Lie on the floor with your back flat. Pull your knees to your chest and hug.

Are stray thoughts entering your mind more and more frequently? Perhaps you've been working too long. You need a change-of-pace break. Do something physical to use your hands instead of your head—water the plants, do a load of laundry. Maybe your stray thoughts are related to an ongoing problem. Give yourself some time to express your thoughts in your journal or to set up a time to talk with a friend. Then lock away the problem so you can resume your work.

interspersed

revitalize

Is your body becoming weary? Do you have a stiff neck or blurred vision? You need an exercise break. If you have a regular exercise regimen, consider dividing your exercise routines into segments that can be interspersed between study times as breaks. Twenty-five sit-ups will take the kinks out after completing 25 tough math problems. If you've just become part of the fitness generation, you needn't purchase a chinning bar. You can revitalize your body with the simple stretching exercises shown in Figure 4—3 or with a brisk walk in the fresh air.

Fine-tune your mind, body, and study environment to maintain a high level of concentration and performance.

THE ASAP REWIND «««

How can I keep a positive attitude for studying?

Develop the three most important factors of a positive mental set.
1. Make your goals your focus instead of doubts or negative feelings.
2. Adopt a can-do attitude.
3. Monitor your mental stress daily.

What can I do about all the distractions that prevent me from studying?

Control the physical and environmental factors that create distractions.
1. Stay physically fit.
2. Keep your learning environments free of distractions such as visitors, television, and loud music.
3. Arrange your study areas for maximum physical comfort, seeing and hearing, and use of materials.

How can I keep my mind from wandering while I read or listen in class?

Use active listening strategies to keep your mind focused. During your classes, participate in discussions, ask questions, and take notes. While reading, underline, summarize, and jot down questions.

When should I take breaks?

Intersperse breaks between study segments in your routine schedule and take unscheduled breaks to relieve stress or as a reward.

 ## WORD POWER

Exercise 1

Directions: Do unfamiliar words break your concentration while reading? Jot them down and define them later. You'll become a stronger reader, able to concentrate longer. The following words were used in this chapter. Define each word using the word meaning techniques: word parts, context, and dictionary. Then use it in an original sentence.

orchestrate _____

_____

_____

procrastinate _____

_____

_____

equilibrium _____

_____

_____

impromptu _____

_____

_____

futile _____

_____

_____

precipitously _____

_____

_____

lethargic _____

_____

_____

increments _____

_____

_____

interspersed _____

_____

_____

revitalize _____

_____

_____

TAKE ACTION

Exercise 2

Directions: You have been chosen as a tutor. Part of your responsibilities is to present basic study skills to the students. Prepare five concentration tips you would present. Explain each concept and why it would improve concentration.

_____

_____

_____

_____

_____

_____

_____

Exercise 3

Directions: The first step in improving concentration begins with an assessment of your *current* concentration habits. Ask your instructor for the evaluation forms for each of your courses.

Exercise 4

Directions: Take the data you produced in Exercise 3 and use it to create a personal concentration profile.
  1. First, describe any overall patterns you see in your concentration habits. Which survey items consistently received high ratings and which were consistently low? Explain what you feel are the reasons for these patterns. What specific changes can you make to improve these habits?
  2. Next, identify the courses in which your concentration levels are high and those that should be improved. Discuss specific ways you can improve your concentration levels in those courses.

_____

_____

_____

_____

_____

_____

_____

_____

_____

_____

_____

_____

Exercise 5

Directions: Read this memo from your friendly author and follow the directions contained in it.

DATE: Today   **FROM:**   Your Author
TO: A.S.A.P. Student   **SUBJECT:** Your Weekly Schedule

Since Chapter 3, you have been using your weekly schedule. Before you proceed further with this management tool, you should evaluate its effectiveness for you. Use the following guidelines to develop your evaluation and write your responses as a summary memo to me.

A. Analyze your *consistency* in
   1. meeting fixed obligations of classes and work hours
   2. maintaining physical fitness
   3. spending sufficient time reviewing and preparing for classes
   4. reserving time for relaxation and recreation
   5. completing essential household chores
   6. planning for the upcoming week.
B. Briefly discuss your *comfort level* with this schedule: Do you feel rushed at certain times, do certain study times work better than others?
C. Make *plans* to refine and improve your schedule, based on any weaknesses you have discovered.

CHECK YOUR PROGRESS

Directions: Put principles of concentration into action! Focus on the areas for improvement you targeted in Exercise 4. At the end of one week, use this checklist to evaluate your progress. Then use the space that follows to analyze your growth.

PROGRESS CHECKLIST: Concentration

Yes   Usually   No

___ ___ ___   1.   I maintain a positive attitude when studying for my courses.

___ ___ ___   2.   I use active learning strategies during lectures and in study sessions.

___ ___ ___   3.   I manage the demands of school and my personal life through my routine schedule.

___ ___ ___   4.   Problem-solving techniques help me reduce the stress of ongoing difficulties.

___ ___ ___   5.   I control distractions whenever possible in my classes.

___ ___ ___   6.   I have selected study areas at home and school that promote good concentration.

___ ___ ___   7.   I use breaks to maintain the quality of my work and to renew my concentration.

A.   Discuss the strategies that work well for you and how you have adapted them to your own needs.

B.   Identify those strategies that have been less successful and why you feel they have been less useful. Explore ways you can use them better.

Don't Stop There! Did you triumph this week? Big or small, your successes deserve recognition, so take a few lines to pay tribute to your progress.

_____

_____

_____

_____

_____

_____

_____

_____

Recognizing and Using Thinking Patterns

THE SKILL THAT GETS THE JOB

Industrial Technician.
For expanding manufacturing company. You must hold an appropriate diploma and possess the knowledge and skill to handle diversified projects. Overtime possible. Come grow with us.

WHAT'S YOUR EXPERIENCE?

Diversification is one of today's buzz words. Employers are looking for candidates with a broad base of knowledge and the ability to change their thinking style to fit the task. When do you switch your thinking pattern to fit a different type of task? How would you rate your reasoning abilities? Explore your skill, your background, and your questions about this chapter's topic in the space below.

_____

_____

_____

_____

_____

_____

_____

_____

_____

_____

_____

_____

In this chapter you will learn to

»»»   *Use general and specific thinking to classify information.*

»»»   *Make choices with comparison and contrast analysis.*

»»»   *Sequence processes and events with time order reasoning.*

»»»   *Solve problems with cause and effect reasoning.*

RECOGNIZING AND USING THINKING PATTERNS

As the 21st century approaches, experts are predicting a new knowledge-based economy. Industries and businesses of the future will be built upon information systems instead of raw materials or manufactured goods. As a result, people will be required to think analytically, processing information quickly and accurately. The thinking patterns of the human mind are the key to these challenges. Don't look for these patterns filed on a computer disk—they are not newly invented patterns to be found in modern technology. These patterns are well integrated into your mind because you use them every day. Maybe you have used analytical thinking in a situation like this:

> You are watching a movie, but you are completely baffled because scenes change rapidly, characters pop in and out, and the dialogue is confusing. You stick with it, trying to make sense of the story by looking for familiar movie patterns such as a flashback or a dream scene. Finally you realize that the movie has two stories going on at the same time. Then you are able to understand easily the dialogue and the switches in scenes.

ANALYTICAL THINKING LETS YOU SEE THE PATTERN

When you look for the pattern or structure of information, understanding the facts becomes easy. Of course, just like with a movie, you have to concentrate and allow the pieces to come together slowly. This chapter explains four basic thinking patterns:

- General and specific.
- Comparison and contrast.
- Sequence.
- Cause and effect.

By recognizing these patterns, you can unlock the information in your textbooks and your lectures and organize the facts and ideas of your compositions and oral reports. If you develop analytical thinking skills now as a student, you also will be preparing yourself for the rigors of tomorrow's information-saturated workplace.

PATTERN 1: GENERAL AND SPECIFIC

Have you ever purchased an item for someone else while shopping only to be told "Oh, I didn't mean that kind of bread." "No, I didn't want that type of nail—I need finishing nails." If so, you've been caught by that person's foggy thinking. Every

phenomena

field of study requires students to classify objects, phenomena, and data according to their general and specific characteristics. Understanding how these classifications are used can help you avoid misunderstandings and prevent confusion as you learn new material.

A **general** category is broad and can encompass other more **specific** information. For example, when you read the word *car,* what do you visualize? Your car or a sports car you'd like to have? If you surveyed 10 people, you would probably get 10 very different responses because the term *car* is so general. The left-hand column in the following list is one classification of car types. *Car,* however, is not always a general term. How a term is classified depends on its context. Look at the classification in the right-hand column of the list.

CAR (general)	**VEHICLE**
All-terrain car	Car (specific)
Sedan	Motorcycle
Station wagon	Snowmobile
Sports car	

Now car is a specific term within the more general classification of vehicles.

Your ability to think both in general terms and specific terms at the same time is your mind's zoom lens. Effortlessly you can

- ZOOM IN to distinguish and label items according to their specific characteristics.
- ZOOM OUT to connect and order items into generalized groups.

When you have your general and specific thinking patterns clearly in focus, you can pick out the main idea of an article or create your own essay. You can highlight important details in your textbook and relate them to examples your instructor presented in lecture.

Certain words signal the use of general and specific thinking patterns. Learn these terms so you can follow the pattern and improve your comprehension of readings and lectures.

hierarchy

Label	**Group**	**Kind**
Characteristic	**Distinguish**	**Level**
Class	**Hierarchy**	**Type**
Division		

Understanding General and Specific Patterns

You hold in your head a vast network of these interrelated classification systems, most of them loosely ordered. When you use classification patterns in your courses, how you organize the information is very important. You should systematically order your information so specific terms are arranged beneath the general term and are indented slightly. Using this system, the earlier examples would be arranged like this:

Car	**Vehicle**
All-terrain car	Car
Sedan	Motorcycle
Station wagon	Snowmobile
Sports car	

If you don't arrange your terms carefully, you could end up with an arrangement like this:

Car

    All-terrain car

      Sedan

    Station wagon

    Sports car

This arrangement indicates that a sedan is a type of all-terrain car. Because general and specific classification is a standardized system, be sure your terms are always correctly arranged. Perhaps the placement of terms seems like a minor point, but look at the following classification error made in business.

The owner of a large mall shoe store asked his new manager to "shape up" the stock room. The eager woman set up these divisions among the shelves:

Athletic shoes.

Dress shoes.

Leather shoes.

Walking shoes.

After a week, both the owner and the manager were frustrated with the system.

Did you spot the problem? Leather is an incorrect classification because all the other types of shoes could be made of leather. As a result, the salespeople in the store began shelving shoes in two places, producing confusion in the stockroom.

You can expand your levels of classification if you need to organize more information. The more description used, the more levels of specificity you create. Examine the detail that expands the original vehicle list.

Vehicle

  Car

    All-terrain car

    Sedan

    Station wagon

    Sports car

  Motorcycle

    Touring bike

    Trail bike

  Snowmobile

Using General and Specific Patterns in Writing

General and specific thinking can also help you understand how writers organize their facts and ideas. They carefully structure phrases, sentences, and paragraphs to present general or specific information. If you can follow this common pattern

> **ZOOM IN: THE GENERAL and SPECIFIC PATTERN**
> Classification has many more uses than arranging words on paper. Giant corporations use classification to organize their workers into offices, teams, and divisions. Computers use menus to classify the vast amount of information the user can access. Schools arrange courses into specialized programs leading to diplomas, certificates, or degrees. Our judicial system is divided into civil and criminal matters with a specific code number for each type of proceeding. What other examples of general and specific organization can you think of?

used by writers, you can increase your comprehension. Below are a group of phrases that could be used to write a brief essay. Study the following phrases for the logic of their general and specific arrangement.

Adjustment to college for the returning adult

   Challenges of school

      Relearning study habits

      Mastering new skills

         Computers

         Laboratory equipment

   Changes in personal lifestyle

      Managing on a reduced income

      Coping with family adjustment

      Redistributing personal time

General and Specific Sentences.   Now each of these phrases can be expanded into a sentence.

> Often adult students who return to school after years in the work force face several **kinds of adjustments.** The **academic challenges** require that they **relearn study habits and master new skills** such as using computers and laboratory equipment. These students must also **adjust their personal lifestyles,** most notably by **managing on less money.** Those students with families also cope with **the family's adjustment** to a new lifestyle as well. Consequently, the returning adult faces a significant **redistribution of personal time.**

Which sentence in the paragraph is the most general? The first is the most general because it refers just to types of adjustment while the other sentences describe specific adjustments. Writers use general sentences to introduce their main ideas. In paragraphs, this sentence is called the **topic sentence.** In an essay the general introductory sentence is called the **thesis statement.**

| FIGURE 5-1 | *Sample Essay* |

Adjustments to College for the Returning Adult

Often students who return to school after years in the work force face several kinds of adjustments. The academic challenges require that they relearn study habits and master new skills such as using computers. These students must also adjust their personal lifestyles, most notably by managing on less money. Those students with families cope with the family's adjustment to a new lifestyle as well. Consequently, the returning adult faces a significant redistribution of personal time.

During the first days of college classes, adult students meet with unfamiliar academic challenges. Many feel overwhelmed by the volume of reading and pace of lecturers in their courses. Some find their writing skills rusty. These students feel additional pressure when they must master computer tasks or use unfamiliar laboratory equipment. With perseverance, however, most find that they quickly relearn their basic study skills and master new technologies.

The hours adults spend studying reduce their time for work or personal activities. Typically, they must limit themselves to one or two leisure activities, and after years of full-time employment, to an average of 22 work hours per week. As a result, many must budget their expenses and needs on a reduced income. The adult learner also must cope with the changes experienced by other family members, especially children who might receive less direct attention. Changes in personal lifestyle cause major adjustments for many adult students.

College students who have left the work force and returned to the classroom must address the challenges of relearning or mastering new academic skills. In addition they must adapt their personal lifestyles so that school is a priority. Most often their maturity and motivation are positive forces in their adjustment.

General and Specific Paragraphs.   Writers also structure paragraphs to be general or specific. Read the following paragraph and compare it to the previous paragraph. Which is more general?

> During the first days of college classes, adult students face unfamiliar academic challenges. Many feel overwhelmed by the volume of reading and pace of lecturers in their courses. Some find their writing skills rusty. These students feel additional pressure when they must master computer tasks or use unfamiliar laboratory equipment. With perseverance, however, most find that they quickly relearn their basic study skills and master new technologies.

The first paragraph is more *general* because it deals with all the adjustments facing the adult learner whereas the second paragraph focuses on the *specific* academic adjustments.

Writers use general paragraphs to introduce their ideas or to summarize and conclude. They use specific sentences and paragraphs like the one above to describe or explain the main idea. General and specific sentences and paragraphs are the building blocks used to organize information for textbook chapters, magazine articles, speeches, and news reports. See if you can spot each building block in the essay given in Figure 5-1. Then check your analysis of the essay with its blueprint in Figure 5-2. Did you notice the different ordering of general and specific information in the third paragraph? Sometimes, for variety, writers give the specific information first and let the reader piece the details together, like the events in a movie. Distinguishing general and specific information takes time. You'll practice this important skill in the upcoming chapters on reading and note taking.

| FIGURE 5–2 | *Essay Blueprint* |

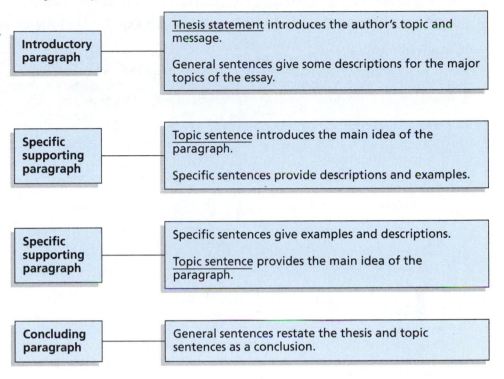

Introductory paragraph	Thesis statement introduces the author's topic and message. General sentences give some descriptions for the major topics of the essay.
Specific supporting paragraph	Topic sentence introduces the main idea of the paragraph. Specific sentences provide descriptions and examples.
Specific supporting paragraph	Specific sentences give examples and descriptions. Topic sentence provides the main idea of the paragraph.
Concluding paragraph	General sentences restate the thesis and topic sentences as a conclusion.

Using General and Specific Patterns for Study

The study goal of many students is to learn facts, dates, definitions, and names. By focusing their study only at the specific level, they do not develop an understanding of the general concepts that link the specific information together into one big picture. As a result, they could struggle with these learning problems:

- Difficulty memorizing.

- Confusion of ideas and facts.

- Difficulty answering essay questions.

How can you get the big picture when you study? You can gain a broad understanding of information by mapping out the ideas on paper. When you make a prioritized to-do list or sketch a quick diagram of a football play, you're creating a map. For each of the thinking patterns, you can create maps to organize and visualize the information after you have read or before you write. A map helps the learner see the relationships among the various ideas and facts and memorize the information better. Maps can take many different shapes. For the general and specific pattern, the traditional form of map is an outline.

Outlining.   Many people are familiar with the general appearance of outlines but are unsure of the correct use of capital letters and roman numerals. Here is the first car classification pattern arranged as an outline. Can you figure out the pattern of letters and numbers?

INFORMATION FILE: THE GENERAL AND SPECIFIC PATTERN IN ACTION!

To Understand the World . . .

Scientists have classified approximately 1 million animal species, but their job is hardly over. They estimate that between 3 million and 30 million species inhabit our earth. Because no one knows the actual number, we do not know how many species become extinct each day.

To Serve a Monarchy . . .

The Queen of England is served by this special staff on ceremonial occasions:

Lord Chamberlain	manages Her Majesty's household
Lord Stewart	handles the royal finances
Mistress of the Robes	assists the Queen at state functions
Ladies of the Bed Chamber	attend to the Queen's personal needs

To Make Money . . .

Collectors keep a sharp eye out for specific items—items that will bring big bucks. Marty and Sue Bunis spotted a special 1935 radio in the shape of the Empire State Building. They paid $100; it's now worth $3,000. They are looking for another type of transistor radio, one shaped like a Pepsi soda fountain dispenser. Check your attic—this one is worth $400.

Vehicles

I. Car
   A. All-terrain vehicle
   B. Sedan
   C. Station wagon
   D. Sports car
II. Motorcycle
   A. Touring bike
   B. Trail bike
III. Snowmobile

Think of outline symbols as being arranged in columns that progress from left to right with each new column using a different set of symbols to signal more specific information.

TITLE

I			
	A		
	B		
II			
	A		
	B		
		1	
		2	
			a
			b
III			

How can you use outlines?

1. Use outlines provided by others to understand how they have organized their ideas. Topic outlines often precede textbook chapters, and you can use the table of contents as an outline of the entire book.

2. Make your own outlines if none are available. This process will reinforce your understanding of the material, and you can use your outlines as study guides at exam time. Creating an outline before writing a paper will also help you organize your thoughts and avoid numerous rewrites.

Diagramming.   Outlines are helpful for organizing information into categories and subcategories, but outlines don't help you *see* the relationships among ideas. When you want to analyze the connections among concepts, try diagramming. A **web diagram** uses a series of connected circles to illustrate the relationship among ideas. Figure 5–3 shows the previous outline transformed into a web diagram. Did you notice that the circles decrease in size as the concepts they contain become more specific? Some people draw boxes instead of circles. Others create a tree of branching concepts. As long as the levels of general and specific are accurately shown, anything goes. Experiment with mapping techniques to find the ones that suit your thinking style. Your textbook assignments, lectures, projects, and writing assignments will provide many opportunities to refine this invaluable study tool. Give logical order to your own knowledge and communications, and to the ideas of others with general and specific classification.

PATTERN 2: COMPARISON AND CONTRAST

Probably as you read the first classification of cars, some personal preferences occurred to you—all-terrain cars are exciting; sedans are boring. If you did make such evaluations, you were using another thinking pattern, comparison and contrast. When you compare objects, ideas, or events, you most often are finding their **similarities**, whereas contrasting items identifies their **differences**. Sometimes people use the term *comparison* to indicate differences also. For example, you might say "Sedans compared to all-terrain cars are boring."

Comparison and contrast thinking is vitally important to many areas of study. Accounting ledgers compare the credits to the debits. Market analysts chart differences in consumers' buying habits and attitudes. All the remarkable functions of computers are based on simple yes–no comparisons of electrical impulses. You can use comparison and contrast thinking to

- Understand new information.

- Measure quantities.

- Evaluate qualities.

- Make choices.

As you read and listen to lectures, you can see and hear the comparison and contrast pattern in action through careful thinking. The most obvious signals come from basic comparative words: more, better, greater, fewer. Word endings

FIGURE 5–3   *Web Diagram*

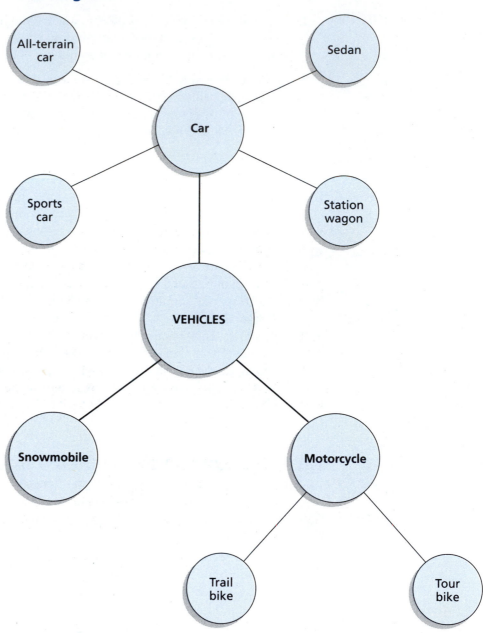

also indicate comparison: heavi*er* books, long*est* answer. Be familiar with signal words and phrases that point to the comparison and contrast thinking pattern.

dissimilar	**Differ**	**Dissimilar**	**Synonymous**
synonymous	**Likewise**	**On the other hand**	**Versus**
	Opposite	**Reverse**	**Rather than**
	Instead	**Same**	

Understanding Comparison and Contrast

Have you ever shopped for an expensive item but were totally confused by the advantages and disadvantages of the models described by the salesperson? Information overload can easily happen when you are comparing complex items. Several tips can help you keep the facts straight when you encounter comparison and contrast information.

Decide if the information gives similarities, differences, or both. How do you think comparison and contrast thinking is used in this paragraph?

> As a sales clerk I worked 37 hours every week and punched a time clock four times daily. I had very specific duties, serving customers in person and over the phone. During slow periods, I was responsible for stocking the garden shop section. Now, as co-owner of the hardware store, my work hours are much **longer,** rarely dipping below 50 hours per week. **Instead** of having **fewer** duties, I seem to be responsible for everything. In addition to managing the retail portion of our business, last week I painted the rain gutters on the building and drove the delivery truck because the driver was ill.

This passage describes the differences between working for a business and being a small business owner. The author suggests that owning a business is more demanding than being a salaried employee. Did you notice the author's use of the signal words—*longer, instead, fewer*—to emphasize the contrasts?

Analyze how the author has arranged the information. Typically, when using the comparison and contrast pattern, writers use either a block or an alternating arrangement for their information. In a *block arrangement,* the author describes one item completely and then moves on to the other. In an *alternating arrangement,* the writer focuses on specific characteristics, evaluating a characteristic for both units and then evaluating another characteristic. These arrangements will become clearer as you see them in writing. Reread the paragraph concerning self-employment. Which arrangement do you think the writer used? The author used a block arrangement, first describing the conditions of working for someone else, and then contrasting those factors with the conditions of self-employment. Here is that same paragraph rearranged in the alternating format of the comparison and contrast pattern.

> As a sales clerk, I worked 37 hours every week and punched a time clock four times daily. Now, as co-owner of the hardware store, my work hours are much longer, rarely dipping below 50 hours per week. Before I had very specific duties serving customers in person and over the phone. During slow periods, I was responsible for stocking the garden shop section. Instead of having fewer duties, now I seem to be responsible for everything. In addition to managing the retail portion of our business, last week I painted the rain gutters on the building and drove the delivery truck because the driver was ill.

When you know the arrangement of comparison and contrast information, you can follow the main points more easily.

Look for comparisons made to teach new concepts. Sometimes writers compare a new concept with a familiar one so the audience can understand the new ideas more easily. Read this paragraph about the game of backgammon and notice how comparison is used to explain the basics of the game.

> If you understand checkers, you can understand the basic objectives of backgammon. Like checkers, backgammon uses a playing board and playing disks, called men or

INFORMATION FILE: COMPARISON AND CONTRAST IN ACTION!

To Entertain ...

You can step out of your drab world and into the near-reality of today's computer games. Through three-dimensional computer graphics and sound effects provided on a sound card, you can experience the realism of playing baseball from a catcher's viewpoint, falling through a trap door with Indiana Jones, or hearing the swoosh of a golf pro's hole-in-one ball.

To Keep Tradition ...

People act in similar ways because they are following traditions. But where did the tradition come from and what does it mean? Next time you attend a wedding think about the real meaning of these traditions.

Best Man. In ancient times, a loyal and brave friend accompanied the groom to abduct the bride from her family. Later he stood guard outside the home of the "newlyweds" in case the bride's family came to take her back.

Wedding Cake. At one time, people threw grains of wheat at the new couple because wheat symbolized fertility. During Roman times, the wheat was baked into cakes that were eaten and even thrown at the bride. Later on, the custom changed to breaking the cake over the couple's head. The guests counted the crumbs on the floor to predict the number of children the couple would have.

FIGURE 5–4   *T-Chart Comparing Working Conditions*

EMPLOYEE	OWNER
Works fixed hours	Works many hours as needed
Limited job duties	More responsibilities based on circumstances

stones. In backgammon each player also has a home territory; however, the arrangement of the stones differs from the arrangement of checker pieces. According to a set pattern, the stones are arranged on spaces in the opponent's territory as well as in the player's home section. Moves alternate between players and are based on the roll of dice. As in checkers, the stones are moved in a certain direction to block or capture the opponent's stones. However, the ultimate goal of backgammon is quite different from checkers. The winner of backgammon has successfully removed all his or her stones from the board.

When comparisons are used to learn new information, you must carefully think about the familiar information and then apply it to the new situation.

Using Comparison and Contrast for Study

Mapping comparison and contrast information can help you carefully evaluate differences and make good choices. The most common comparison and contrast format is called a **T-chart.** Figure 5–4 shows a T-chart mapping the paragraph about differences between being a small business owner and being an employee.

The comparisons and contrasts that are being presented in your courses are far more complex than this example. Often the analyses involve several

| FIGURE 5–5 | Matrix Chart Showing Terms and Conditions of Life Insurance |

TYPE	PERIOD OF COVERAGE	PERIOD OF PREMIUM PAYMENT	PAYMENT OF FACE VALUE	CASH VALUE	COST
Term	Fixed 1, 5, 10 yrs.	Specified term	During term	None	Lowest
Whole life	Lifetime of holder	Lifetime of holder	Upon death of holder	Yes	Low
Limited payment	Lifetime of holder	Specified term 10–30 yrs.	End of term or death of holder	Yes	Highest

array

characteristics for three or more items. Students sometimes are frustrated when they try to keep the data straight in their minds, so they gloss over the topic. You can organize and understand large amounts of comparative data by expanding the basic T-chart into an array or **matrix chart,** which provides multiple cells or blocks for listing data. For example, if you learned about types of life insurance in business math class, you could construct a study matrix like the one in Figure 5–5.

Making a matrix gives you two study advantages. Your information is logically arranged in one consistent format. Therefore, you can concisely memorize the information or compare it.

As with outlines, it's important for you to understand the structure of matrix charts. A matrix presents two sets of information in vertical columns:

1. A *group of items* that are being compared.

2. *Several characteristics* or features associated with the items.

To arrange your information as a matrix, follow these steps.

HOW TO CONSTRUCT A STUDY MATRIX

IDENTIFY   The group of items being compared.
            The general characteristics or features used for comparison.

LABEL   Matrix columns for the group of items and each character-
            istic.

FILL IN   The items column and make horizontal rows.
            The remaining data in the appropriate blocks.

---

1. **Identify the group of items being compared.** Read the following paragraph and see if you can identify the *items* being compared.

Workers who cannot walk to work must select a mode of transportation. Each type of transportation presents advantages and disadvantages to the user. Many people prefer to drive themselves to work because it's fast and offers flexibility if they must change their schedules. However, these commuters also face high expenses for gasoline, parking, maintenance, and insurance. With carpooling, people can reduce some of their costs for gasoline, parking, and maintenance; but they have less flexibility and use more time traveling to cotravelers' homes. Another group of commuters, especially those in large cities, prefers public transportation. In adhering to set bus or subway schedules, these commuters greatly reduce their flexibility and increase their travel time. However, the cost of public transportation is far less than the total expense for individual or carpool driving.

The items discussed in this passage are *three modes or types of transportation*.

2. **Identify the general characteristics used to evaluate the items.** Now read the passage again and identify *the general characteristics*. Did you identify these three general characteristics: *flexibility, time spent, and cost*? If you have difficulty identifying the characteristics or features used in a comparison, look for terms that are repeated in the material.

3. **Label your columns.** Make the first column on the left for your items and another column for each of your general characteristics.

Types of Transportation	Flexibilty	Time Spent	Cost

4. **Fill in each item in your items column.** Make a line beneath each to form a horizontal row.

Types of Transportation	Flexibility	Time Spent	Cost
Individual driving			
Carpooling			
Public transportation			

5. **Fill in the remaining information in the appropriate blocks.** Here's the completed matrix for the types of transportation paragraph.

Types of Transportation	Flexibility	Time Spent	Cost
Individual driving	a lot— make own schedule	requires least time	must meet all expenses
Carpooling	some— adjust to others	more time needed for travel	some shared costs
Public transportation	little— must follow schedule	requires most time	least expensive— price of ticket

Sometimes you will find that you are left with an empty cell in your matrix. That happens because the author did not cover the same characteristics or features for each item. Matrix charts are used extensively in business to analyze data such as expenses, purchases, and sales. Most are produced by computer software called spreadsheets. You can refer to this quick summary the next time you want to use your own "software" to make a matrix study chart.

PATTERN 3: TIME ORDER

You use the third thinking pattern, time order, in every aspect of your life, from programming your VCR to memorizing a definition for one of your courses. You used time order thinking as you read the explanation for constructing a matrix. Time order thinking requires you to place a group of events in a logical and useful sequence. You use this pattern when you want to

- Recall or analyze the past.
- Complete tasks in the present.
- Forecast and plan for the future.

You can recognize the time order pattern in your textbooks, manuals, and lectures by watching for these signal words.

Preceding	**Development**	**Previous**
Prior	**Subsequent**	**Finally**
Hereafter	**Succeeding**	**Trace**
Following		

hereafter

Can you think of courses in which time order is important? Sequencing steps is vitally important in mathematics, science, and computer courses. The ordering of events is important to accounting, communications, and history courses. Even if you are not taking a history course, you probably are encountering historical information. Most courses provide background information describing how that field of study has developed. Instructors present this information to give you a broad base of knowledge in your field.

Understanding the Time Order Pattern

Fully comprehending time order information can be challenging in any field. First you must understand the basic facts and details presented, and then you must comprehend their sequence. A good example is a lab procedure. In a science class, you may have to read the directions to an experiment several times before actually working on the task. The following paragraph explains the correct procedure for removing the contents of incoming mail in a large office. First, read the paragraph for an understanding of the facts and ideas, and then reread it, numbering the steps as a logical sequence. Place your numbers directly in the text.

> Once you have opened all the envelopes of incoming mail, you are ready to remove the contents. Take out all the papers and flatten them facedown on your work surface. Double-check that the envelope is empty by holding it up to the light. Keep your envelopes in a separate pile, facedown in the same order as the contents. Turn the stack of papers faceup so you can scan the letter for a reference about enclosures. Look first for a notation at the end of the letter and then in the body of the letter. Check that the number of papers you have agrees with the letter notation. If all papers are accounted for, clip them together and return them to a facedown position. If you do not have the indicated number of documents, double-check the envelope. In the case of a missing enclosure, mark NO next to the enclosure reference in the letter and attach the envelope to it. Then turn the papers facedown with the other contents. Continue until you have emptied all envelopes.

Here is the correct sequencing of the steps. Notice that step 7 has been circled since the process could end at this point if no problems occurred with enclosures.

> Once you have opened all the envelopes of incoming mail, you are ready to remove the contents. **(1)** Take out all the papers and flatten them facedown on your work surface. **(2)** Double-check that the envelope is empty by holding it up to the light. **(3)** Keep your envelopes in a separate pile, facedown in the same order as the contents. **(4)** Turn the stack of papers faceup so you can scan each letter for a reference about enclosures. **(5)** Look first for a notation at the end of the letter and then in the body of the letter. **(6)** Check that the number of papers you have agrees with the letter notation. **(7)** If all papers are accounted for, clip them together and return them to a facedown position. **(8)** If you do not have the indicated number of documents, double-check the envelope. **(9)** In the case of a missing enclosure, mark NO next to the enclosure reference in the letter and attach the envelope to it. **(10)** Then turn the papers facedown with the other contents. Continue until you have emptied all envelopes.

Reading time order procedures two times helps clarify the details and the sequence of steps. Now read this time order procedure in which the steps are not presented sequentially. After your second reading, number the steps in the text.

> When preparing a speech, be sure you make key points on cards or a phrase outline instead of a full-sentence text. Also be sure you keep the length of the presentation to the allotted time. These two steps will prevent your audience from becoming bored.

INFORMATION FILE: TIME ORDER IN ACTION!

To Understand the Past . . .

In 1991, a mummified corpse of a man was pried from the ice of the Austrian Alps. His body was remarkably preserved. To prevent decay of his body tissue, scientists keep the Similvan Man frozen at −6 degrees Centigrade. They are able to examine the body for just 15-minute segments before it must be cooled again. Based on wear to his teeth, they place the man's age between 25 and 40 years old.

To Make Money . . .

Shortly after the death of her husband, a widow learned that he had purchased a winning ticket for the Loterie Nationale in France. When she could not find the ticket in their home or among his effects, she decided to have his body exhumed. As she suspected, the ticket was in the pocket of his suit coat.

Begin your preparation by selecting a subject that suits not just your interests but also what you think will interest your audience. If you are unfamiliar with the group, first find out about their average age, background, and education. Next, prepare the specific points you want to make. Finally, rehearse with your notes, but don't memorize every word—boring!

How many steps did you identify? This process has six steps, but two steps were taken out of order and discussed first to give them emphasis.

(4) When preparing a speech, be sure you make key points on cards or a phrase outline instead of a full-sentence text. **(6)** Also be sure you keep the length of the presentation to the allotted time. These two steps will prevent your audience from being bored. **(2)** Begin your preparation by selecting a subject that suits not just your interests but also what you think will interest your audience. **(1)** If you are unfamiliar with the group, first find out about their average age, background, and education. **(3)** Next, prepare the specific points you want to make. Finally, rehearse with your notes, but don't memorize every word—boring! **(5)**

When you spot the time order pattern, do not assume the events or steps have been sequentially organized. Be ready to read twice and to supply your own order to the information.

Using Time Order for Study

When you need to study a procedure, you can make your job easier by using a **procedural summary.** If it's a short procedure, you can set it up as a numbered list so each step stands out. If you are working with a longer, more complex process, use a paragraph format so you can give full descriptions and explanations. Of course, as you learned in Chapter 1, a good summary follows these three Cs: it is correct, concise, and clear. Read this summary list for the procedure for preparing a speech.

1.   *Research your audience if necessary.*

2.   *Choose a topic suited to both your interests and the audience's.*

3.   *Prepare the specific points to be presented.*

4.   *Record your points as phrases on note cards or as an outline. Do not prepare a full-sentence text.*

5.   *Rehearse your presentation, but don't memorize every word.*

6.   *Be sure your presentation does not go over the allotted time.*

Students sometimes find studying history difficult because the events are not always presented sequentially. You can clarify the time order for historical events by using a mapping technique called a **time line.**

Read the following paragraph about Charles Babbage, who was instrumental in the development of the computer. Then study the time line that orders the events of his life as they actually happened.

versatile

Charles Babbage has been called a man ahead of his time. While in his 20s, he conceived of a computing machine that foreshadowed the modern computer. Yet, it would be almost 125 years before his ideas would be used to produce a working digital computer. Babbage was born at the end of the 18th century to a wealthy English family and graduated from Cambridge University in 1818. Around 1822, he began working on his first computing machine, funded by a government grant. Ten years later he turned his interests to a more versatile machine he called the analytical machine. Due in part to lack of funds and design difficulties, neither project was ever completed. However, in 1937 his plans were rediscovered and led to the development of the modern computer. In 1871, at 79, Babbage died a discouraged man.

Babbage born	Grad-uates Cambridge	Begins work on first machine	Begins work on improved model	Dies without success	Models used	Modern computer made
1790s	1818	1822	1832	1871	1937	1940s

Notice the logic of these events when they can be seen in a study map. If you use procedural summaries and time lines, your studying may go so quickly that you will have time on your hands!

PATTERN 4: CAUSE AND EFFECT

Have you ever been with a child who tested your patience by constantly asking "Why?" Each answer you gave just created another why question. If so, you've helped a youngster develop cause and effect thinking. Actually, the cause and effect pattern poses a two-part question: **why and what result.** You use cause and effect thinking in all your courses: to understand marketing trends, mathematical operations, medical procedures, or scientific principles. Each time you complete a Progress Checklist exercise in this book, you are using your cause and effect thinking to ask yourself what you can do to become a more skilled learner.

INFORMATION FILE: CAUSE AND EFFECT IN ACTION!

When the Cure Is Worse Than the Illness . . .

Around 1910, doctors treated patients with an electrotherapeutic chair. This chair was equipped with neon lights that glowed over patients and jolted them with a mild electric shock. Makers of the chair claimed it cured all ills.

Just in case the chair didn't do the trick for baldness or migraine headaches, doctors applied magnetic brushes to the head.

Those folks worried about their chickens getting "pecked on" in the barnyard could outfit their poultry with small metal helmets, complete with protective glasses.

When Millions Are Saved . . .

Edward Jenner was a doctor in the late 1790s. He treated many patients who died of smallpox. In his travels he noticed that the disease did not affect people who worked with cows. As an experiment, he injected an eight-year-old boy with fluids from a cow suffering from cowpox, a disease similar to smallpox. Six weeks later he injected the boy with smallpox fluids. The boy remained healthy, and the first vaccine was invented.

Signal words are also used with the cause and effect pattern. Unlike the signal words for other patterns, though, these words frequently are used in pairs. To use them correctly, you must be able to distinguish which words indicate causes and which are synonyms for effects. Study the words below and associate each pair with examples from your life.

CAUSE	EFFECT
Motive	Deed
Create	Product
Reason	Result
Action	Reaction
Catalyst	Change
Modify	Outcome
Problem	Solution
Agent	Consequence

catalyst

Recognizing and understanding these terms will help you comprehend the relationships among events in information you read or hear in lectures and in your everyday life. When you fully understand the causes and effects that underlie a situation, you can take steps to improve conditions or logically solve existing problems.

Understanding Cause and Effect

Chain reaction is a phrase often associated with cause and effect situations. An event occurs and in response, a series of other events unfold. For example, an oil spill from a tanker at sea pollutes the water, which kills the fish, and in turn reduces the yield of the local fishermen. Following the chain of events is important for fully comprehending cause and effect information. See if you can follow how effects become new causes in this description of a typical office situation.

Very often workers create a problem by duplicating more copies of documents than actually necessary for the job.

↓

Consequently, equipment and material usage increases.

↓

This excess consumption results in monetary expenditures unacceptable to most businesses.

↓

reprographics

To solve the problem, many companies establish reprographics centers, which require order forms to be submitted before copies can be made.

↓

Such centers do decrease the number of needless copies produced.

↓

However, copy centers also result in production delays and workers being away from their work stations for longer periods of time.

↓

As a result, money is lost.

Did you notice that more than one effect resulted from a single action in this example? Several causes can also work together to create one or more effects. With practice, you will improve your ability to analyze the elements of cause and effect information. You can practice your reasoning by listening to the news or reading a newspaper. Challenge yourself to analyze the events of a winning ball game, a critic's reaction to a new movie, or the effects of world politics on the stock market.

Using Cause and Effect for Study

The cause and effect pattern can also be mapped out using branching and cyclical diagrams to show the relationships of causes and effects. Often as students read complex topics such as economic principles, psychological relationships, or marketing trends, they confuse the causes and effects involved. If you trace causes and subsequent effects in a diagram, you can eliminate confusion and improve your ability to remember the information.

> ### ZOOM IN: CAUSE AND EFFECT
> When you understand how a situation or condition has happened, you can then attempt to recreate the event, avoid its recurrence, or protect yourself against its effects. That's how scientists improve our lives. Many of today's drugs were first found in nature as plants or fungi. Once scientists understood their chemical composition, they could create them synthetically in a laboratory. With vaccinations, doctors have eliminated the cause of many childhood diseases. Because scientists cannot prevent earthquakes, they have focused on reducing the effects of quakes by constructing buildings that will shift with the tremors.

FIGURE 5–6   *Branching Diagram*

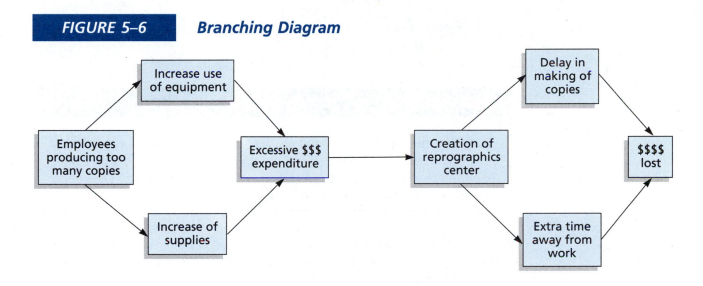

Branching Diagram

In Figure 5–6 you can see the dynamics of the copy center problem mapped out. Sometimes cause and effect patterns do not radiate forth indefinitely but return to an earlier cause creating a cycle.

Cyclical Diagram

Study the cyclical diagram of a pattern familiar to many people in Figure 5–7. Use cause and effect thinking to analyze problems and choose solutions.

MIXED PATTERN COMMUNICATIONS

Probably by now you have realized that none of the four thinking patterns works solely by itself. Most thinking actually involves a combination of the patterns depending on the subject being discussed and the purpose of the communication. For example, the time order pattern for preparing a speech also includes cause and effect thinking when it warns people to avoid lengthy speeches because they

FIGURE 5–7	*Cyclical Diagram*

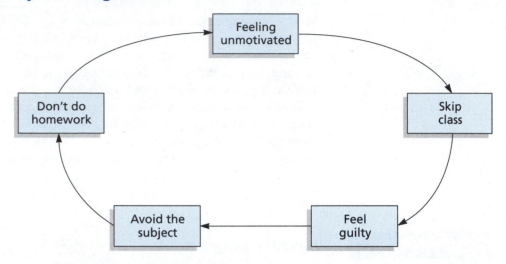

STRESSBUSTER

Take off some weight today—not physical weight, but *mental weight.* Put a lingering mistake behind you. If you can correct the mistake, do it now. Most importantly, remind yourself that errors are part of being human. Then enjoy your new, lighter self for the rest of the day!

are boring. Here is a list of lecture titles, each organized around more than one thinking pattern. See if you can spot the patterns that will be used to present the information.

1. How the recession of the 1970s differed from the Great Depression.
2. How to reduce shoplifting without increasing security personnel.
3. Types of small business failures.

Check your reasoning with this analysis.

1. Comparison and contrast, time order, cause and effect.
2. Time order, cause and effect.
3. Classification, cause and effect.

Perhaps you thought of other patterns that might help you decide how these lectures would be presented. Certainly that's possible because complex topics can be approached in many different ways. You'll find the same is true as you read your textbook chapters. The information will be presented in a combination of patterns as the author explains different topics. The key is to use each thinking pattern logically and analytically. As you do, your storehouse of knowledge will grow and your ability to make decisions will become stronger.

STRESSBUSTER

Try something different this week. You'll relieve the boredom and stress of your day-to-day responsibilities. Take a short road trip with a friend, just an hour from where you live along the back roads. Plan a potluck dinner with friends or family—everyone brings a unique dish.

THE ASAP REWIND «« ««

How can I classify information so that I understand concepts?

Use general and specific thinking.
1. Look for *main ideas* in introductions or conclusions, and *specific explanations* in the middle sections.
2. Use *outlines* and *web diagrams* to visualize the classification of ideas or facts.

How can I evaluate the characteristics of two or more complex items or pieces of information?

Use comparison and contrast thinking.
1. Look for and analyze descriptions that give similarities and differences.
2. Use *T-charts* and *matrixes* to organize complex data.

How can I follow a difficult sequence of events or steps in a procedure?

Use time order thinking.
1. Review the information and put it into a logical sequence.
2. Use *time lines* to map events and *summaries* to simplify procedures.

How can I comprehend complex events or solve difficult problems?

Use cause and effect thinking.
1. Analyze events to identify each cause and each effect.
2. Use branching and cyclical diagrams to visualize the relationships.

Exercise 1

Directions: This chapter introduced vocabulary and terminology that is important to the thinking process. Add the words below to your own vocabulary. Define each word using the word meaning techniques: word parts, context, and dictionary. Then put your new word to work in an original sentence.

diversification _____

_____

_____

phenomena _____

_____

_____

hierarchy _____

_____

_____

dissimilar _____

_____

_____

synonymous _____

_____

_____

array _____

_____

_____

hereafter _____

_____

_____

versatile _____

_____

catalyst _____

_____

_____

reprographics _____

_____

_____

TAKE ACTION

Exercise 2

Directions: Classify the following ideas into the general and specific organizational pattern. Use the double line for the title of the outline. **Example:** skating, bobsled, Winter Olympics, luge, skiing, couples' dance, downhill, sledding, cross-country, figure, speed skating

Winter Olympics
skiing
　downhill
　cross-country
skating
　figure
　speed skating
　couples' dance
sledding
　luge
　bobsled

1. Wrench, tools, hoe, rake, home tools, screwdriver, hammer, garden tools

Tools

_____

_____

_____

_____

_____

_____
_____

2. Stamps, model building, baseball cards, trains, coins, collecting, doll houses, hobbies, airplanes

_____
model building _____
_____
_____
_____
_____
_____
_____
_____

3. business offices, hotels, residential buildings, public buildings, library, government offices, houses, buildings, apartments, commercial buildings, stores, condominiums

_____
residential buildings _____
_____
_____
_____
_____
_____
commercial buildings _____
_____
_____
_____

4. On land, helicopter, canoe, two-wheeled, car, transportation, on water, underground train, airplane, motorcycle, by air, tractor trailer, bicycle, multiwheeled, submarine, four-wheeled, wagon

_____
_____
_____
on land _____
_____
_____
_____

four-wheeled _____

_____

_____

_____

_____

_____

_____

_____

5. Performing arts, modern dance, ballet, stage, singing, acting, television, rock, dance, gospel, cinema, barbershop quartet.

Performing Arts _____

_____

_____

_____

acting _____

_____

_____

_____

_____

gospel _____

_____

_____

Exercise 3

Directions: Turn each of the classifications in Exercise 2 into an outline by using roman numerals or letters to label each step of the classification. Consult the diagram on page 102 for the correct labeling.

Example:

Winter Olympics

I.   *skiing*

    A.   *downhill*

    B.   *cross-country*

II.   *skating*

    A.   *figure*

    B.   *speed skating*

    C.   *couples' dance*

     III.   *sledding* _____

       A.   *luge* _____

       B.   *bobsled* _____

Exercise 4

Directions: Complete the following outline using these general and specific phrases. Use the double line for the title of the outline.

Exercise regularly	Fruits and vegetables	Snacks high in fat and salt
Manage caloric intake	Pursue leisure-time interests	Low-impact aerobics
Limit foods related to disease	Desserts high in sugar and fat	Set reasonable goals
Increase foods that build bone, muscle	Maintain a healthful diet	Visit your doctor regularly
Manage stress	Low-fat dairy products	Walking
Keeping fit	Weight training	Jogging
Moderate exercise	Strenuous exercise	Pasta and bread

1.   *Keeping fit* ========================

    I.

        A.   *Manage caloric intake*

        B.

            1.

            2.

        C.

            1.

            2.

            3.

    II. *Exercise regularly*

        A.

            1.

            2.

        B.

            1.

            2.

    III.

        A. *Set reasonable goals*

        B.

    IV. *Visit your doctor regularly*

2.

For the sightseer	Aquatic challenges	Restored village
Theme parks	Skill improvement camps	Golf
Sailing on a river	Specialized vacations	Gourmet restaurants
America's battlefields	Tennis	Urban centers
Art museums	Scuba diving	Historical sites
For the sports lover	Fantasy park	Animal habitats

I.
 A.
  1.
  2.
 B. *Skill improvement camps*
  1.
  2.
II. *For the sightseer*
 A.
  1.
  2.
 B.
  1.
  2.
 C. *Urban centers*
  1.
  2.

3. Check efficiency of mechanical parts   Clean glass and vinyl   Vacuum regularly

Preserve exterior finish   Rustproof underbody   Touch-up paint

Change engine oil   Car maintenance   Wax yearly

Check antifreeze   Inspect brakes and tires   Inspect battery

Stainproof carpet and upholstery   Wash regularly   Protect interior

I.
 A.
 B.
 C.
 D.
II.
 A. *Rustproof underbody*
 B.
 C.
 D.
III. *Protect interior*
 A.
 B.
 C.

Exercise 5

Directions: Choose one of the topics from Exercise 4 and write a brief essay on the topic. If none of the topics interest you, choose your own. Be sure you organize your thoughts with an outline or a web diagram. Then write your essay.

   Organize your thoughts here.

_____

_____

_____

_____

_____

_____

_____

_____

_____

_____

_____

Exercise 6

Directions: Read the following comparison of postsecondary schooling options. Then fill in the matrix chart to show the relationships between items. Consult the process for making a matrix on pages 107–9.

Students leaving high school have several choices for additional training. Each option has specific advantages.

Many students choose a four-year college for additional training. These schools offer in-depth programs in a wide range of academic areas. Graduates earn a bachelor's degree and seek salaried positions with managerial potential. Graduates are also eligible to pursue higher studies for further advanced degrees.

Some students decide against such a long-term commitment and chose a junior college or a community college. In contrast, the programs offered are primarily two years in length and provide concentrated training in career areas. Most graduates earn associate's degrees and compete for skilled technical positions, sometimes with managerial potential. Some graduates transfer to four-year programs.

Many high school graduates, anxious to enter the work force quickly, opt for a career school education. These schools offer intensified training in specific skills programs, ranging in length from 6 months to 18 months. Graduates earn diplomas or certificates and seek entry-level positions. Transfer options usually are not available.

Postsecondary Schools			Employment and Transfer

Exercise 7

Directions: Based on the three options in Exercise 6, what is your final educational goal? Explain in a paragraph why you have made this choice. Use the data from your matrix chart to support your choice.

_____

_____

_____

_____

_____

_____

Exercise 8

Directions: Read the following time order process explaining how to proofread a document. Then create your own summary list. Be sure that it is correct, concise, and clear.

A finished document should be correct in format, grammar, spelling, and typing. Before you begin actually checking the document, set it aside for awhile so you will have a fresh viewpoint when you start. Always work from a printed copy, not from a computer screen. Be prepared with a pen of contrasting color for making your corrections.

Begin by double-checking your format. Be sure you followed all guidelines for such details as title placements and reference notations. Next, read carefully for any errors in grammar overlooked earlier. Common mistakes are found in possessive nouns and subject-verb agreement. Follow up with a search for misspelled words. This is important even if you are using a word processor spelling checker. Pay special attention to proper names and homonyms. The average spelling checker will not correct errors in usage of such homonyms as *cite, site, sight.* Finally, look for typographical errors including incorrect spacing, incorrect use of capitals, and inaccurate keying of numbers. Give close scrutiny to titles, addresses, and headings. Every document can be attractive and correct if you proofread carefully and thoroughly.

_____

_____

_____

_____

_____

_____

_____

_____

_____

_____

Exercise 9

Directions: Read the following discussion concerning student loan repayments. Underline the cause and effect signal words you find. Decide if the author has adequately listed all causes and effects related to the problem discussed. In a brief paragraph explain any causes or effects that you think have been overlooked.

A problem for banks today is the default on loans by college students. When a default occurs, the bank loses the principal loaned plus the interest that it anticipated earning. That loss of capital and profit affects the bank's ability to make loans to other students and its ability to expand business. Because few penalties are currently imposed for defaults, students feel they can ignore their responsibilities. Federal agencies should impose these strict penalties.

1. Send default notification to each student's employer.

2. Require each student to work free of charge for the bank or lending institution.

_____

_____

_____

_____

_____

Exercise 10

Directions: Make a branching diagram that maps the causes and effects of the loan problem as you have described it.

CHECK YOUR PROGRESS

Directions: Put the four thinking patterns into action! At the end of one week, use this checklist to evaluate your progress. Then use the space that follows to analyze your growth.

PROGRESS CHECKLIST: Recognizing and Using Thinking Patterns

Yes   Usually   No

___   ___   ___   **1.** I recognize general and specific information and use outlining and diagramming to classify information.

___   ___   ___   **2.** I evaluate comparison and contrast information and use T-charts to simplify complex data for study and to make choices.

___   ___   ___   **3.** I comprehend time order information and use summarizing and time lines to clarify sequences.

___   ___   ___   **4.** I analyze cause and effect information and use a branching diagram to map out the relationship of events.

A. Discuss the thinking patterns that are working well for you and the courses in which you have applied them. Describe the study tools from this chapter that you have tried and their usefulness.

B. Identify the thinking patterns you have found difficult to apply. Explain why you feel these patterns have been less helpful for your studies and how you might use them better.

On a Roll? Then let your ideas continue to flow. Write about the progress you have made this week and how you plan to build on it in the coming weeks.

_____

_____

_____

_____

_____

_____

CHAPTER

6

Building Memory Skills

THE SKILL THAT GETS THE JOB

Computer Programmer.
To work with clients and to solve hardware problems. Must have expertise in TurboPascal and Paradox database. A challenging position for the right person.

expertise

WHAT'S YOUR EXPERIENCE?

Who has the <u>expertise:</u> the woman checking the manual, the man asking questions on the phone, or the person solving the problem? Experts have acquired knowledge that they can recall quickly and accurately from memory. How important do you think memorizing facts and procedures is in your area of study? How would you rate your current memory skills? Use the space below to explore your skill, your knowledge, and your questions about this chapter's topic.

_____

_____

_____

_____

_____

_____

_____

_____

_____

_____

_____

_____

In this chapter you will learn to

»»» *Select significant information for memorization.*

»»» *Use special techniques for comprehending new information.*

»»» *Prevent forgetting through review.*

»»» *Quiz yourself to measure your learning.*

»»» *Pace your practice to achieve mastery.*

BUILDING MEMORY SKILLS

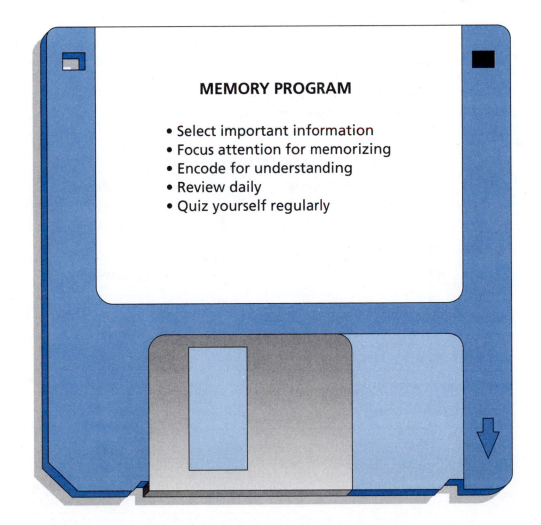

MEMORY PROGRAM

- Select important information
- Focus attention for memorizing
- Encode for understanding
- Review daily
- Quiz yourself regularly

It was on the tip of my tongue.

I have a brain like a sieve.

With him, it's in one ear and out the other.

I always seem to remember something after I need it.

Often important information seems to disappear from our memories or hide beyond our mental reach just when we need it the most. As a result, some people view themselves as having a poor memory. But the great majority of people do not have a handicap; they just don't understand the memory process and lack practical memory training. This chapter investigates

- The memory process.
- Factors in forgetting.
- Steps for remembering.

Well-developed memory skills will help you from your first-year classes to graduation, from job interview to successive promotions. This chapter could change your memory and your life!

TYPES OF MEMORY

Memory is the mental process of **receiving, storing,** and **recalling information** for use at a later time. Scientists and educators have studied the memory process for over a century, and research continues today. Researchers believe the brain uses three types of memory. As a student, two of these are important for you to understand: short-term and long-term memory.

THE L-O-N-G AND SHORT OF MEMORY

Short-Term Memory	**Long-Term Memory**
Holds small quantities of information	Can store very large, possibly limitless, amounts of data
Usually requires repetition of data for retention	Can retain information only when it is organized and practiced
Can hold information for hours or days depending on the amount of repetition	Can retain information for weeks to a lifetime
Useful for brief tasks and holding information for long-term memory	Used to acquire and meaningfully organize information as knowledge

---

Short-Term Memory

Your brain receives information from your five senses—the aroma of dinner cooking, the symbols on this page of print, the feel of the keys on a computer keyboard, the sound of your instructor lecturing, the delicious taste of your favorite dessert.

> **INFORMATION FILE**
>
> **Microscopic memories . . .**
> Within your body, a cell's memory works to save your life. Lymphocyte cells detect and mount a defense against the bacteria and viruses that enter your body. Afterward, your lymphocyte cells retain a complete memory of each invader so they can launch a quick counterattack if an invader returns.

Your mind quickly filters out much of this data if it is not immediately useful. Your brain uses **short-term memory** to store useful information in limited amounts for brief periods of time. As you repeat or rehearse the information, your brain creates a temporary record that lasts for a few hours, sometimes days. Here's a typical way people use short-term memory:

> As Maurice opens his apartment door, the phone is ringing. The call is for his roommate concerning a change in a dental appointment. Without a pencil handy, Maurice repeats the information given by the secretary and hangs up the phone. As he searches his book bag for pencil and paper, Maurice repeats the information again to keep it in short-term memory until he can write it down.

Once Maurice has written down the data, it probably will leave his short-term memory within the day. Scientists are unsure if memories completely leave the mind or if they become more difficult to call up. You also use your short-term memory to hold information until you can process it for storage in long-term memory.

Long-Term Memory

When you organize and practice information repeatedly, your mind establishes a **memory record** in **long-term memory.** The data you put in long-term memory can be successfully recalled over varying periods of time—from several weeks to a lifetime. Thus, you can remember birth dates and ZIP codes you use frequently. Even some information you no longer use—your third grade teacher's name, for example—can remain in your long-term memory because of its earlier significance. You've also put many ideas from this book into long-term memory through study and practice. When you learn information and place it in long-term memory, you are building a body of knowledge you can use beyond this week's test. Information in long-term memory can be used for

- Taking midterm and final exams.
- Understanding new information in other chapters.
- Relating ideas from other courses.
- Performing tasks on the job.

Many researchers believe people use just a portion of their long-term memory capacity.

RECALL

Of course, stored information is of little value if you are unable to recall or remember it. When you **recall** information you locate the correct memory record so you can use the data. Recalling information depends largely on using data from your five senses to trigger the memory record. You probably have had difficulty recalling the name of a former classmate or co-worker. This is how one student describes finally recalling a name:

> I could see his face, but his name just wouldn't come to me. I remembered sitting next to him in government class and playing ball with his cousin. But *he* was a "missing person." As a last resort, I began reciting names alphabetically. When I pronounced *Mark,* I was suddenly able to recall his name—Marty. I had not lost the memory, but I could not recall it until I used the right cue—the initial sounds of the name.

Sometimes students have difficulty recalling information even when they have practiced and placed the data in long-term memory. The mastery strategies in this chapter will help you not only store information in long-term memory, but also develop strong cues for recalling important information when you need it.

FACTORS IN FORGETTING

Consider this scenario. Is it familiar to you?

> Michael is on a second job interview. During the first interview he met with the personnel director and the immediate job supervisor. On this interview he is meeting with a series of people: a department worker, the job supervisor, the department director, and the director of training. At each phase of the interview, people shake his hand, giving their names and job titles. As he answers questions, Michael is careful not to address people directly because he has forgotten all the names except the supervisor's.

This is not the dynamic presence most people want to project during an interview, but the situation is common because forgetting happens very quickly.

Rates of Forgetting

Learning studies show that people typically forget almost half of newly learned information within the same day, and another third within two weeks. As you can see in Figure 6–1, on an average, less than one fourth of new information remains in long-term memory at the end of two weeks. Two implications from these figures are important for you as a student.

implications

1. **The greatest amount of forgetting happens soon after receiving information.**

spontaneously

2. **Remembering information does not happen spontaneously—forgetting does.**

Although memory experts do not fully understand the mind's retention capacity, they believe these factors play a major role in forgetting:

- *Interference* by different information.

- *Low understanding* of the information.

- *Insufficient review and practice* of the information.

- *Lack of relevance* or usefulness of the information.

FIGURE 6–1   *Average Rates of Forgetting*

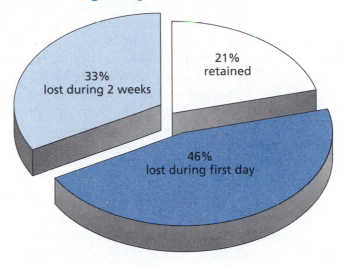

INFORMATION FILE

Developing memories . . .

Young toddlers develop memory processes slowly. They are most interested in the present, and until the age of three, children have difficulty visualizing their parents' faces when apart. Some children do develop stronger memory skills faster. What makes the difference? Parents. One study showed that when parents and children discussed past events, those children demonstrated more memory skills both at the time of the study and one year later.

Interference

Frequently you forget information when you confuse it with other information. The confusion of two sets of information is called **interference.** Sometimes new information causes you to forget previously learned information, and at other times, you cannot accurately recall new information because you confuse it with old information. Most likely interference was a factor in Michael's inability to learn peoples' names during his interview. Just as one person was introduced, another came along with a new set of data for Michael to learn. As a result, he was not able to make clear separate memory records of the information, even in short-term memory. Have you noticed that interference is particularly strong when sets of information are very similar? For example, accurately recalling dates or formulas that differ by just one or two symbols can be very difficult because of the interference the similarity creates.

You can avoid some of the effects of interference by studying at spaced intervals rather than cramming your study into long sessions just before exams. Research results indicate that the mind needs time to organize or consolidate information as a mental record. Therefore, studying over several days or weeks allows your mind to build clear, well-organized records that will be less vulnerable to interference by other information.

vulnerable

Low Understanding

When you do not fully understand information, you cannot store or accurately recall it for any length of time. The mental record your mind creates is incomplete, and interference from other information can quickly create confusion. Have you ever forgotten the names of people as Michael did? Probably part of your difficulty was not hearing the name clearly. Consequently, you hesitated to pronounce the name, and an auditory record was not made in your memory. The next section of the chapter gives many helpful suggestions for achieving high levels of understanding while studying, but one very important strategy has already been discussed in earlier chapters. *When you don't understand information, ask questions.*

Insufficient Review and Practice

Information is not retained in long-term memory without review and practice. Because his interview was fast-paced, Michael did not find the time to review the names of the people he met. As a result, he did not create sufficient memory records for the information. Do you sometimes find yourself at the end of a textbook chapter remembering little of what you read? Based on the the rates of forgetting discussed earlier, your performance is actually normal, but to achieve academically, you must reverse that pattern. Because the greatest percentage of forgetting occurs soon after information is learned, you should review what you've learned very soon after completing an assignment. The next section of this chapter and later chapters on reading and note taking will give you more helpful tips for review.

relevance
Lack of Relevance

Relevant information seems to endure in long-term memory and is more easily recalled because it holds personal meaning and usefulness. That's one reason strategies for personalized learning were introduced in the first chapter of this book. How are those strategies working for you? Do you think they have made a difference in your memory skills? Continue to build your new learning on your own experience and knowledge because you can use this knowledge as a cue to recalling information from memory. Here's how a personalized example helped jog one student's memory:

> On a test, Anita was asked to define and explain *classical conditioning learning*. At first, she could recall nothing. Then she remembered how her grandmother trained a parrot to ask for a treat. Using her personal example, Anita was able to recall the actual definition of the term.

contradictory
Formulating your own opinions can also create strong memories for future recall. However, your opinions can also block the memory process if they are so strong that you filter out contradictory information from your memory. Remember that school provides you with an opportunity to understand and learn other points of view, but you do not necessarily have to adopt them.

You can win the battle against forgetting. Using focused attention and practical steps for memorizing will strengthen your ability to recall information from long-term memory and improve your academic performance.

STRESSBUSTER

Deactivate one of your buttons. Take steps to change a situation that "pushes your button." You hate rush-hour traffic—find someone who will carpool with you. The company of a co-worker spoils your day—join others on your break or enjoy your own company. You're a wreck by the time you get your family out the door in the morning—get up a half hour earlier.

THE KEYS TO IMPROVED MASTERY

Here's how Michael could have improved his interview performance:

> As each person is introduced, Michael listens and observes closely. Then he repeats the person's name in a greeting. "Good morning, Ms. Redmond." As she also responds with a greeting, Michael makes a quick association between her name and her clothing: Redmond—red scarf. He then uses the same process when the next person is introduced, associating Mr. Hamel's name with ham. His strategy changes, however, when Mrs. Jablinski is presented. He is unsure if her name is Grablinski or Jablinski. Michael politely asks her to repeat her name. Then he uses her name in a greeting while associating it with a boxer's jab. He continues to use the peoples' names throughout the interview with increasing confidence. As the interview concludes, Michael senses that people are responding to him in a relaxed, friendly manner.

This is the type of interview most of us hope to have. In this scenario Michael has used each of the steps required for retaining and recalling information. Following these steps can significantly increase your ability to store and recall information, whether it's the names of people at an interview or formulas for compound interest.

STEPS TO INFORMATION MASTERY

FOCUS	your attention
SELECT	the significant information
ENCODE	the ideas
REVIEW AND PRACTICE	the information
STRIVE	for accuracy in the 90 percent range

Step One: Focus Your Attention

Before you can retain or recall information, you must *receive* it. Often students claim they have forgotten information when, in fact, they never really absorbed it in the first place. Use all your concentration strategies from Chapter 4 so you can receive new information. Remember to

Be positive. With regular study, you <u>can</u> understand new information and fulfill your academic goals.

Stay relaxed. Be aware when stress is building. Use breaks, journal writing, and exercise to reduce disruptive stress.

Limit distractions. Distractions such as phone calls, visitors, or music are actually forms of informational interference. Change your study environment to limit your distractions.

Step Two: Select the Significant Information

Which of these study objectives makes more sense?

- Master the most significant concepts.

- Try to learn everything.

It is neither possible nor necessary to memorize all the information presented in your classes. You should focus your efforts on the most important ideas and concepts presented in a chapter or a unit. When you focus on a clear set of concepts, you can make stronger memory records and improve your ability to recall the information. In effect, you are avoiding information overload. Often students hesitate to eliminate information as less important, because they fear that they will study the "wrong thing." Since the total approach to memorizing is sure to fail, smart students develop their selection skills. How will you know what information is important? You can target significant information by being alert to study aids provided by your instructors and your textbooks.

Instructor Learning Aids.   Most instructors do far more than just "cover the material." They also provide you with learning aids for the information they feel is most important. Watch for these learning aids and use them to select the information most likely to be tested.

Learning Objectives.   Many instructors create specific objectives for you to follow as you study each chapter. A sample of typical objectives is shown at the top of Figure 6–2. If you have objectives in any of your classes, you're in luck. Your instructor has taken the guesswork out of studying.

Teaching Aids.   Be alert to your instructors' use of the chalkboard, overhead transparencies, or specially prepared handouts. Usually teachers employ these devices to explain and emphasize important concepts. In your lecture notes, use a symbol such as a star to indicate information your instructor has stressed with teaching aids. Then part of the selection process will be done before you even begin to study.

Review Sessions.   Most instructors provide time for review and, of course, they use that time to focus on the most important concepts or skills. Be sure you give your full attention to review sessions. Sometimes students "tune out" during review times or skip reviews completely because they reason that no new material will be presented. In doing so, those students lose a great opportunity to find out test topics in advance.

FIGURE 6–2	*Learning Objectives*

Dr. Nathan   COM 230

Chapter 2
Learning Objectives

When you have finished all the activities in this chapter, you should be able to

1. Define the fear of speaking.
2. Identify three reasons why you should control your fear of speaking.
3. List four common causes of speaking fear and relate to you own experience.
4. Explain the four strategies for controlling your fear of speaking,

Chapter Objectives

After reading this chapter, you will be able to:

1. Define the fear of speaking.
2. Understand how controlling speaking fear can affect business speaking.
3. Identify the causes of speaking fear.
4. Develop techniques for controlling the fear of speaking.

Textbook Aids.   Your textbooks are designed with many aids that highlight and emphasize the most important information. Where can you find these aids? Pay close attention to these textbook features for clues to significant information.

Study Guides.   Some course textbooks, especially in classes such as accounting and biology, include a booklet for extra practice in mastering important concepts. Instead of sifting through the detailed information in your textbook chapter, you can begin your selection process in the corresponding section of your study guide.

Chapter Objectives.   Many textbooks provide learning objectives at the beginning of each chapter. These are similar to instructor's learning objectives, but they are often less specific. You can compare the two types of objectives in Figure 6–2. If you have both instructor and textbook objectives available in a course, which should you follow? Always use the directions and feedback provided by your instructor to guide your study.

Chapter Outline.   Some textbooks provide an overview of the major topics and subtopics for the chapter as an outline. You can use these outlines as the basis for your selection process. A sample chapter outline is given in Figure 6–3. If your chapters don't provide an outline, just turn to the table of contents at the beginning of the book. Use the major topics and subtopics listed there to guide your selection of significant information.

FIGURE 6–3	*Chapter Outline*

3   Speaking Clearly

Voice-Speech Connection

Voice

    1. Inflection

    2. Volume

    3. Duration

    4. Intensity

Speech

Articulation

Pronunciation

Speed

    Rate

    Pace

Chapter Summaries. Chapter summaries are an excellent source of significant information. In just a page or two, the author capsulizes the most important concepts in brief explanations. This is just the kind of simplified, organized information that is easily placed in long-term memory.

Look again at Figures 6–2 and 6–3, and count the number of major topics listed for each chapter. Are you surprised by the low number? Typically chapters explain less than 10 general concepts. The rest of the information provides specific explanations and descriptions of those general concepts. Often students get lost in the maze of details and don't see the general connections between ideas. Despite diligent study, their exams are marked "You've missed the point" or "Many facts, but what's your point?" You'll get the big picture if you focus your study on the general concepts presented by your instructor and your texts. Recalling both general and specific information is easier if you have first focused on the general concepts.

RISKY BUSINESS PAYS OFF

Selecting information and casting aside other information as less important may seem to be risky business. You might make some errors in judgment, but if you've followed your instructor's lecture topics your errors probably will be minor and have a minor impact on your course grade. The selection process is most difficult when preparing for that first test or quiz. Then, as you learn the expectations and testing style of your instructor, you will gain confidence to focus on certain material while spending less time with other concepts and facts. The payoff will be that you study less, remember more, and earn better grades.

Step Three: Encode Information

There are two ways to memorize the following information.

Some of the most common types of software packages used in offices today are (1) word processing, (2) spreadsheets, (3) databases, (4) graphics, and (5) desktop publishing.

INFORMATION FILE

Blocking memories . . .

One week after the 1989 San Francisco earthquake, researchers surveyed approximately 100 students who lived not far from the center of the quake. Most reported difficulty concentrating, feeling detached from their surroundings, a slowed sense of time, and memory disturbances. Researchers believe that the human mind uses responses such as these to create dreamlike memories as a way to cope with serious mental trauma.

rote

encode

repetitive

With **rote memorization,** the student repeats the entire sentence until he or she has memorized it word for word. The learner does not take time to define unfamiliar terms like *spreadsheets.* When the student makes errors, she or he repeats the sentence again. The other method of memorizing is called *encoding.* **Encode** is not just a term used by secret agents in spy novels. Learning specialists use it to describe the process of giving meaning and organization to data. The learner practices the sentence in a variety of ways, always striving to understand the ideas. Which memory process do you think is more effective? Encoding is the better memorization process because it creates stronger memory records and makes studying less boring and repetitive. Actually, rote memorization simply won't work for most of the complex subjects you are studying because the information will not remain in long-term memory. People encode information in many different ways depending on the kind of information and their own learning styles. Try these common encoding techniques to understand information better.

Patterns of Organization.   Learning random facts without the benefit of a logical organization is like holding a jumbo-size popcorn—without the container. Try to memorize the following numbers:

7

3

9

6

6

1

4

Were you frustrated? Try the task now that the numbers are reorganized:

7396614

Does the information become even easier in this format?

739−6614

Sometimes simply grouping data or facts in a logical manner will make memorizing easier. For complex information, you can use the thinking patterns you learned in Chapter 5: general and specific, comparison and contrast, time order, and cause and effect to make the information more accessible for recall. Simplify your information by creating outlines, diagrams, time lines, and procedural summaries.

Key Words.   Another simplification technique is to focus on key words to trigger the correct memory record. This technique works especially well with definitions and lists of data. First choose a word or brief phrase to represent each fact or idea. Then practice using each key word to recall the related fact or idea. Try out the technique using the chart in "The Long and Short of Memory" box. For each statement circle one key word that will help you remember the full description of that section. One key word has been selected for you.

THE L-O-N-G AND SHORT OF MEMORY

Short-Term Memory	**Long-Term Memory**
Holds (small) quantities of information	Can store very large, possibly limitless, amounts of data
Usually requires repetition of data for retention	Can retain information only when it is organized and practiced
Can hold information for hours or days depending on the amount of repetition	Can retain information for weeks to a lifetime
Useful for brief tasks and holding information for long-term memory	Used to acquire and meaningfully organize information as knowledge

---

Then compare your key words with these:

Short-term: small, repetition, hours or days, brief tasks

Long-term: large, organized and practiced, weeks to lifetime, knowledge

If your key words differ from these, that's okay as long as they will logically trigger the complete memory record for you. Using key words is like creating your own puzzle. You can have some fun while you study and you can easily keep track of lengthy lists and details.

Associations.   Connecting ideas with associations works much like the key word technique. In the revised interview scenario, Michael associated the name of Ms. Redmond with her red scarf and was able to recall her name later. The following list describes common leadership styles. How could you use association to learn and differentiate each type?

Directive: leader who gives directions and establishes standards and a reward system to control behavior.

Supportive: leader who focuses on establishing relationships and cooperation among the members of the group.

Goal-oriented: leader who inspires group to work toward challenging goals.

| Figure 6–4 | *Visualization to Trigger Memory* |

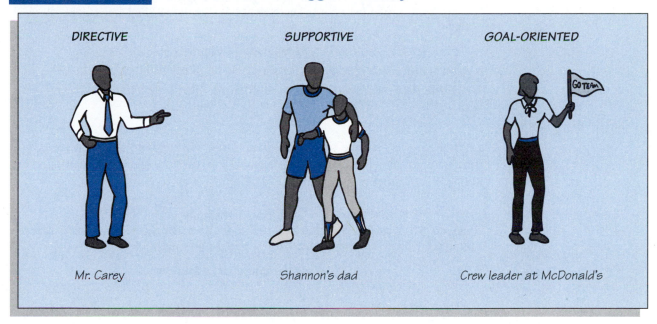

You could associate each type with a person in a leadership role—a boss, teacher, or parent—who you feel uses that leadership style. Your memory encoding for the concepts might look something like this.

Directive — *Mr. Carey*
Supportive — *Shannon's dad*
Goal-oriented — *crew leader at McDonald's*

When you use associations, information becomes relevant and easier to memorize and recall.

Visualizing.   Often your associations can lead you to a mental picture or a visualization of a concept that you can use to trigger your memory record. Usually simple, representative images are the most powerful. Notice how the figures in Figure 6–4 convey the concept of each leadership type. When you become weary of words, words, and more words—try thinking in pictures.

Paraphrasing.   Now you are ready to paraphrase, the final phase of encoding. Paraphrasing is the process of explaining information in your own words. When you can accurately paraphrase concepts or facts, you have achieved true understanding. You are already using one form of paraphrasing—your 3-C summaries that were introduced in Chapter 1. When you feel that information is on the tip of your tongue or locked in your mind, you probably need to paraphrase more to make a mental record of the ideas in your own terms. Definitions and rules are often complex and difficult to understand. Read how paraphrasing makes a scientific definition understandable.

Glossary Definition

mimicry: Situation in which one species (the mimic) bears deceptive resemblance in color, form, and/or behavior to another species (the model) that enjoys some survival chances

Paraphrased Definition

mimicry: when one species looks or acts like another, and as a result, can deceive its natural enemies for a better chance at survival

When you use simple terms and make direct connections between ideas, you improve your understanding of the concept or term. Now apply your paraphrasing techniques to the following formal definition of a very common situation.

Glossary Definition

approach-approach conflict: Internal conflict or stress that occurs when a person is required to choose between alternatives that are equally desirable.

Your Paraphrased Definition

_____

_____

_____

How does your definition compare with this paraphrasing?

Approach-approach conflict is the indecision people experience when they must make a choice between two equally good options.

As long as your definition accurately describes the main points, it can differ from someone else's definition. When you paraphrase and understand one concept, you will find it easier to understand related ideas. Use your understanding of the previous term to paraphrase the following definition.

Glossary Definition

avoidance-avoidance conflict: Internal conflict or stress that occurs when a person is experiencing or faced with undesirable conditions and any alternative seems equally undesirable.

Your Paraphrased Definition

_____

_____

_____

Does your paraphrasing include the same main points as this definition?

Avoidance-avoidance conflict is the frustration people feel when the options available to them are equally negative.

You could even use an everyday phrase as an additional way of describing avoidance-avoidance conflict: stuck between a rock and a hard place. Such phrases are great for encoding because they are familiar and provide a strong trigger for your memory record.

Right about now you may be thinking that you could spend your entire life encoding information from your courses. Actually, using the various encoding techniques will not take any longer than repeated attempts with rote memorization. Also, you'll find that encoding happens in bits and pieces. During a lecture you paraphrase a few concepts. Later when you read the material in your text, you sketch out a quick diagram. Bit by bit your thinking builds to a full understanding of the information so that practicing recall becomes a piece of cake.

ZOOM IN: MNEMONICS

Sometimes when studying lists of information or confusing details, you might find it helpful to try a different memory strategy called mnemonics. This odd word is derived from the Greek word for memory and is pronounced *nǐ-mǒn-ǐks*. Mnemonics are simple devices such as rhymes or especially created words that can help you recall information. Sound strange? Not at all. You are probably already using some mnemonics. Do you recite this poem to recall the number of days in the month of April? "Thirty days has September, April, June and November." The poem gives you your answer fast and easy. Or perhaps you learned this name, ROY G. BIV, as the key to recalling the colors of the rainbow: *red, orange, yellow, green, blue, indigo, violet.* Mnemonics can be fun and effective for recall. Be creative and make your own and watch for them in your courses. Now can you devise a mnemonic that would help you remember the odd spelling of this word *mnemonic*?

Step Four: Review and Practice

Can you complete these statements without checking back in the chapter?

1. At the end of one day, a person forgets approximately _____ percent of new information.

2. At the end of two weeks, an additional _____ has been forgotten.

For statement 1, these answers are acceptable: 46 percent, 50 percent or one half. For statement 2, the acceptable answers are 1/3 or 33 percent.

Did the forces of forgetting affect your performance? You can reverse the effects of forgetting with prompt review and regular practice of the information you are learning.

Review.   In the hurry to complete assignments, many students don't take time to review the day's lectures and reading assignments. They wait until several days before an exam to begin reviewing. By that time they probably remember about 25 percent of the material. Even though these students have diligently completed every assignment, they have placed themselves at a disadvantage for exams because they have not counteracted the forces of forgetting with daily review.

INFORMATION FILE

Feeding memories . . .

A recent fad has been "smart" drinks, which promoters claim will increase your brain's neuronal activity for heightened reasoning and recall. Juices with names like Cosmic Think Drinks and Brain Boost are sold through stores and offered at restaurants devoted to smart food cuisine. Their magic ingredients? Fruit juice, several forms of sugar, amino acids, and large amounts of caffeine. Experts who are skeptical of smart drinks say you could achieve the same brain boost with a cup of coffee, a cheeseburger, and a Twinkie. *Bon appetit.*

Maintain your memory records and an academic advantage by following these guidelines:

1. **Review every day all the new material you have received.**

2. **Review promptly.** The longer you wait, the more you will forget.

3. **Keep your review light**—your goal is just to consolidate your initial memory record. Try these techniques and develop your own: Read quickly through your *lecture notes* trying to connect the ideas into one big picture. If something is confusing, put a minus sign in the margin and go on. Think about the information as you continue through the day. Before you begin a follow-up reading, review your notes more carefully, focusing on your minus notations. For *reading assignments,* skim over the material, connecting in your mind the major concepts presented by the title, major headings, and subheadings. Reread the summary. Explore in your mind how your lecture material fits with your reading assignment.

MAKING TIME FOR REVIEW

Many students complain that they have no time for review. One look at their schedules explains their plight. Work, commuting, and a full course load pack their days. Does that sound familiar? With a bit of creativity, you can find time for some review. If your classes are back-to-back, review the main points of the lecture in your head as you walk to your next class. As you read, jot down each major heading of your chapter on an index card. Then take out your cards for a quick mental review when you have a few free moments—riding on the bus, waiting in traffic, slow periods at work. If you car pool with a classmate, take turns making oral reviews. While one drives, the other can read the lectures notes or the chapter summary. As a follow-up, see who can create the best associations, key words, or visualizations to encode the information.

Sometimes you can end your memorization process with the review step. If you're learning information for informal uses such as club activities or hobby projects, a high degree of mastery probably is not necessary. Usually you can refer to a manual or other materials if you cannot recall the desired information. As a student, however, mastering course material is essential for performing well on tests and building a body of knowledge. You can achieve mastery in your courses through regular practice or study of the information.

Practice.   Often students are dismayed that they have not done well on an exam, even when they have read and reread the material several times. If the student really spent much time studying this way, why wasn't it effective? Repetitive reading does not engage your mind in active thinking or measure the amount of information you are retaining. Learning specialists recommend that you recite and write self-quizzing activities to practice information.

   Recitation, the process of repeating information orally, is a powerful memory technique because you create an additional auditory memory record of the information by hearing yourself speak out loud. When you want to recall the information, you'll be able to "hear" the memory record of your recitation. Use these steps to maximize your learning with recitation:

1.   **Select small amounts of information for recitation.** To limit informational interference, work with five to seven items at a time.

2.   **Read over the information once, and then hide it from view.** Usually students cover the body of the material such as paragraphs or definitions, while keeping key information, headings, or terms visible so they can quiz themselves. You'll learn more techniques for self-quizzing in the chapters on reading and note taking.

3.   **Repeat orally each section of information.** Be sure you are really speaking *aloud*. Repeating the information silently in your mind will not create an auditory record. Also when you repeat information silently, you can gloss over difficult parts.

4.   **Check your accuracy.** If you don't periodically assess your practice, you could be memorizing inaccuracies. When you do spot a mistake, take these steps to correct your learning: reread your original source, use your encoding strategies, or ask for help.

5.   **Concentrate on your weak areas.** It's a human tendency to avoid difficult situations, but in doing so, you are reducing your knowledge, your skill, and your chance for a high test grade. Correct your learning and practice again, perhaps using a different strategy.

Try out the recitation process with this memory task. Study the following three-letter airport codes used for some American cities. Be sure you apply your encoding techniques to give meaning to these symbols. Then quiz yourself orally two times.

   CHI   Chicago, O'Hare
   CHX   Chicago, Meigs
   CHS   Charleston, South Carolina

CLT   Charlotte, North Carolina

CMH   Columbus, Ohio

Did you improve with the second recitation? Do you know which codes would require extra practice? Recitation is a fast and effective practice activity, but it does feel awkward at first. As you gain success, recitation will become a comfortable and valuable study habit.

Writing is another effective way to practice. When you write information, you are creating a memory record through your sense of touch. Many students find writing very powerful for establishing recall. You can follow the same procedures as with recitation. Avoid writing answers multiple times the way you wrote spelling words in elementary school. This is a rote memory process that will use up much of your time and provide minimal results. When you are practicing concepts and ideas, be sure you are paraphrasing answers to ensure understanding. Then, in later study sessions, you can write the information exactly if the instructor requires it. Typically, courses in math, business law, and science require exact recall of formulas, rules, and principles, so don't miss practicing exact material in those courses as preparation for your test.

Which would you prefer: a pop quiz or a take-home test? You can have many of the advantages of a take-home test if you quiz yourself each time you study. The more you challenge yourself, the more you will be prepared for the real test.

sedentary

PUMP UP AND LEARN MORE

Studying is usually a sedentary activity. You sit with a book, moving just the muscles of your eyes and your arm. That approach can numb your body and mind. You can energize your body and develop stronger memory records by adding physical activity to your study. Try walking around the room while you recite, or incorporate recitation into the rhythms of your exercises.

"A noun is a person, place, or thing." S-T-R-E-T-C-H "A pronoun is a substitute for a noun." S-T-R-E-T-C-H.

or

"Revenue" B-E-N-D "minus Expenses" B-E-N-D "equals Net Income" B-E-N-D!

Add variety to your writing practice too. Write your own lecture on a chalkboard, enter your summaries on a computer and print a copy, or use bold felt tip pens of different colors.

Step Five: Strive for Mastery

How much practice should you do? Let's look at the problem mathematically. Suppose you practiced the airport codes until you could recite and write them with 75 percent accuracy. Would that be sufficient mastery of the material? Most likely not, because students usually do not perform as well on exams as they do during practice sessions. Three factors contribute to poorer performance in exam situations:

- Forgetting.

- Stress.

- Test difficulty.

If you lose just 10 percentage points due to these factors, is the result a satisfactory quiz grade?

75% mastery level − 10% errors = **65% quiz grade**

Most students would not consider 65 an acceptable grade. If, however, you strive for mastery in the 90 percent range while studying, your grades will probably span from the 90s to the low 80s.

Grades in that range are honored on the dean's list of many schools, but mastery at that level rarely happens in one session. Rather, mastery builds incrementally, with the most intensive practice in preparation for the quiz or exam. Studies show that when students paced their studies over a period of time rather than studying in one intense session, their recall of the information on tests was higher. To achieve a high degree of mastery, incorporate these strategies into your study routine:

1. Begin your study the day you receive the information.

2. Practice the information regularly until you are achieving in the 90 percent range.

3. Then review the material periodically to maintain the memory record and enhance recall.

See how one student handled a large memorization task:

Curtis' travel and tourism class was assigned a unit on international geography and the popular travel destinations of each region. Quickly, Curtis realized that to do well on the exam, he would have to master a great deal of detailed information. He decided that he could learn the material best by practicing some of it each day. After a bit of experimentation, he came up with this daily study routine.

1. Approximately 20 minutes for reviewing and practicing the most recent information from lecture and reading assignment.

2. Approximately 15 minutes for review and practice of previously presented information.

3. A few extra minutes to evaluate his progress and target the difficult material requiring extra work the next day.

On a few occasions, Curtis could not keep to his schedule because of other commitments, but he never let his study plan lapse for more than a day because he did not want forgetting to erode his mastery. The system worked well for Curtis because he was able to study with minimal stress, and he was motivated to continue as he saw his knowledge building.

Mastery practice is like the extended maintenance policy on a new car. How well you can retain and retrieve information depends on the *regular* care you give to those memory records.

THE ASAP REWIND «««

How does memory work?

For most important information, your mind uses two types of memory:

- Short-term for brief tasks.
- Long-term for complex knowledge.

Why do I forget so much?

People forget large amounts of new information rapidly because of these factors:

- Interference.
- Low understanding.
- Insufficient review.
- Lack of relevance.

How can I remember more?

Follow these steps for mastery of information:

1. Focus your attention.
2. Select the significant information.
3. Encode ideas for understanding.
4. Quiz yourself to practice the information.
5. Work toward accuracy in the 90 percent range.

 ## WORD POWER

Exercise 1

Directions: When you define new words, you are encoding them and adding to your body of knowledge. Use your sharpened memory skills to add these words from the chapter to your vocabulary. Define each word using the word meaning techniques: word parts, context, and dictionary. Then use the word in an original sentence.

expertise _____

_____

_____

implications _____

_____

_____

spontaneously _____

_____

_____

vulnerable _____

_____

_____

relevance _____

_____

_____

contradictory _____

_____

_____

rote _____

_____

_____

encode _____

_____

_____

repetitive _____

_____

_____

sedentary _____

_____

_____

TAKE ACTION

Exercise 2

Directions: A group of students are discussing some of the difficulties they are having in one of their courses. Read their comments and explain to them how they could study better to improve their recall of information.

1. I'm so frustrated in this class. I really put in a lot of time. I copy every term in bold print and write its definition at least 10 times, and I still don't do well on the tests.

_____

_____

_____

_____

2. Well, I don't think my memory is working at all. I read the chapter three times, and I barely remember anything.

_____

_____

_____

_____

3. You know that last test? In two days, I put in 15 hours of study, and the best I could do was a C minus. I'm not even going to study for the next one.

_____

_____

_____

_____

Exercise 3

Directions: Read the learning objectives at the beginning of this chapter. Briefly explain which objectives you feel your instructor stressed and what information in the chapter you would focus upon when studying. Use this example to guide your thinking:

My teacher really stressed the difference between short- and long-term memory. I would carefully study the chart for the two types of memory, and I would develop my own examples for each type.

_____

_____

_____

_____

TIPS FOR COMPUTER COMFORT

- Sit approximately 18 inches from your screen.

- Avoid looking at your screen for long periods of time. Look away briefly several times each hour.

- Stand up every half hour to quickly stretch your arms and legs.

- Avoid glare on your screen from harsh lights or bright sunlight.

- Practice good posture at all times.

- Vary your tasks—keying-in data, printing hard copies, proofreading—to maintain concentration.

- Be sure the brightness control for your screen is properly adjusted.

Exercise 4

Directions: In the nearby box is a list of suggestions for workers who use a computer terminal. Use *one of the following strategies* to make the list easier to memorize:

- Reorganize the list or make a study map.
- Create a key word for each suggestion.
- Make associations to connect the ideas.
- Draw images that could be used as mental visualizations.

Use this space for your encoding.

CHECK YOUR PROGRESS

Directions: Put memory skills into action! At the end of one week, use this checklist to evaluate your progress. Then use the space that follows to analyze your growth.

PROGRESS CHECKLIST: Building Memory Skills

Yes Usually No

— — — **1.** When beginning a memory task, I use my concentration skills.

— — — **2.** I select the information I will memorize based on learning aids from my teachers and textbooks.

— — — **3.** To assure my understanding of the material, I use encoding techniques.

— — — **4.** I quiz myself during practice sessions using writing and reciting.

— — — **5.** I evaluate the accuracy of my learning as I study.

— — — **6.** I set my mastery goals in the 90 percent range.

A. Discuss the memory strategies that are helping you understand and recall your course material. Briefly explain a recent memory success.

B. Identify a situation in which understanding and recalling the information is difficult or frustrating. Explore ways you could improve your study in that subject.

Take a Look Back. Can you think of a person or event from your childhood that affects your actions and beliefs today? In a few lines, explain that special relationship you have with the past.

_____

_____

_____

_____

_____

_____

CHAPTER

7

Active Reading: Improving Comprehension and Efficiency

THE SKILL THAT GETS THE JOB

Executive Administrative Assistant.
Seeking a dynamic individual to assist corporate vice president with scheduling activities, managing office staff, and research and reports. Must be able to make decisions independently and handle large volumes of information efficiently.

WHAT'S YOUR EXPERIENCE?

Volumes that sit on a book shelf are great resources, but the volumes on your desk probably mean a great deal of reading to be done. How do you feel when you are given a lengthy reading assignment? Do you use any strategies to improve your comprehension and efficiency? What would you like to learn about efficient reading strategies? Use the space below to explore your skill, your knowledge, and your questions about this chapter's topics.

_____

_____

_____

_____

_____

_____

_____

_____

_____

_____

_____

In this chapter you will learn to

»»»   *Survey your textbooks and each chapter before reading.*

»»»   *Set a purpose for reading.*

»»»   *Improve your literal and inferential comprehension.*

»»»   *Identify the author's main idea.*

»»»   *Adjust your reading rate.*

IMPROVING YOUR COMPREHENSION AND EFFICIENCY

hypothetical

Is the hypothetical headline below an accurate prediction of the future?

NEWSPAPER READERSHIP DECLINES
Video News Soars

Will workers one day abandon training manuals for video screens or correspond completely through voice mail? Certainly technology is now changing and will continue to change how business and industry are conducted. However, according to *Forbes* magazine, the paperless society hasn't happened yet. As the century ends, our use of paper has increased to over 240 million tons, and the amount of mail has grown to 163 billion pieces annually. Of course some of this paper is filed or discarded, but much becomes the responsibility of workers in business and industry. *Business Week* magazine estimates managers spend one third of their day reading and still take more paper home to read in the evening. Similarly, college students face great demands to quickly absorb large amounts of reading material.

equate

These demands require highly developed, efficient reading skills. Busy professionals and students tend to equate efficiency with speed, but three interdependent factors affect your reading efficiency: your comprehension, speed, and retention.

What's the magic formula for these three? There is none. To be efficient, you should flexibly adjust your reading speed, comprehension, and retention levels according to each reading situation. Typically these variables will affect how you adjust your reading:

variables

- Your background knowledge.

- Complexity of the material.

- Your purpose for reading.

So where do you start? Most often, comprehension is the key element in the reading process. When you understand material, you can increase your reading speed and better retain the ideas and facts. This chapter presents ways to improve comprehension and speed techniques. Chapter 8 provides the study strategies to improve retention of what you read. One key to better comprehension is learning to use your reading materials more efficiently.

SURVEY YOUR READING MATERIALS

Whatever type of job you set out to do, you'll be more efficient if you are well acquainted with your tools. For your course work, your primary tools are your textbooks and the specific chapters within them. To understand these tools better, you can use a quick previewing process called surveying.

Survey Your Textbooks

When you **survey** a textbook, you examine these aspects so you can use the book more efficiently and comprehend its contents better:

- Introductory information.

- Learning aids.

- Reference information.

INFORMATION FILE: FLEXIBLE READING

The World at Your Fingertips . . .
Would you like a reading source that brings you espionage, athletic victory, romance, personal advice? They're all yours every day for less than 75 cents in your newspaper. Reading your newspaper can be more than a source of entertainment—you can also build your career knowledge by reading about

technical advancements,

political issues,

world events.

Remember, you can't be a player if you're not a reader.

Ideally, you should survey your books as soon as you purchase them. From the very first assignment, you'll have an advantage because you will be acquainted with the general goals of the authors, some of the topics in the book, and the general organization of information. However, if you haven't surveyed your books for this term, you can still benefit from the process. Surveying your textbooks now or anytime during the semester might help answer puzzling questions you've had about your courses. Surveying books can also help you when you are choosing resources for research projects. Through a brief survey, you can answer these important questions as you select research sources:

- Is the author qualified in this particular area based upon education and work experience?

- Does this book provide up-to-date information?

- Does the author cover topics that relate to the area I am researching?

Begin the survey process now. As you read the next section, have one of your textbooks handy and locate the valuable information and features it contains.

Introductory Information.   Examine these parts of your book, which provide identifying and background information.

Title Page.   This is usually the third page inside the front cover. Sometimes titles are in two parts, with the second part indicating a specific purpose or focus for the book, such as the title *Introduction to Paralegal Studies: A Skills Approach,* for a book used in a course for legal assistants. In addition, the title page also includes this information:

Edition number is given if the book has been revised since the first edition.

Authors are listed with their academic affiliations, such as the schools for which they teach or the highest academic degree—M.D., Ph.D., or J.D.— they achieved. This information will be very important as you select the best sources for a project or a research paper. Sometimes instructors refer

INFORMATION FILE: FLEXIBLE READING

Any Way You Like It . . .

Sometimes people avoid reading the newspaper because they don't think they have time or because the paper seems too long. Here are some tips for easy, efficient reading of your newspaper.

1. **Read just the information that interests you.** There's no quiz to worry about, so you're in charge.

2. **Use the index on the front page of the paper to locate special features.** Features such as weather reports and sports scores are presented daily; others such as columnists are featured weekly. Some papers also give a brief index on the first page of each section.

3. **Read just the headline and the first two paragraphs of an article when your time is limited.** The headline will give you the main idea, and the paragraphs will give you the most important details.

4. **If the topic of an article is new to you, read the second half of the article first.** Because this section usually presents background information, you can gain a quick history before reading the latest developments.

to books by the author's name rather than the title: "Now, turn to the discussion questions in your Magryta text."

City of publication is the first city listed in the lower section of the page. This will be valuable information when you must create references for a research project. See Figure 7–1 for a sample title page.

Copyright Page.   You can usually find copyright information on the reverse side of the title page. When you select books for research, the current copyright date will be important. For many subjects, especially in the fields of science, technology, and world affairs, developments occur so quickly that a source just a few years old might no longer be accurate or useful. Publishers arrange publishing dates in a variety of ways, so you must look carefully for the most recent date. Figure 7–2 shows the placement of the current copyright date in one textbook.

Table of Contents.   This section directly follows the copyright page. You can use your table of contents to locate book sections, chapters, chapter topics, and special features in your books. All information is presented chronologically with page numbers listed at the right. Some books provide two tables of contents, one in general, abbreviated form and another fully detailed. The short one is very handy when you just want to turn to a chapter or a unit of the book.

chronologically

When you look at a table of contents, you'll be able to see that the book is divided into units or sections that group chapters with similar topics or skills. Some books are divided according to the type of activities in each section. For example, many composition textbooks are divided into three sections: one that discusses forms of writing, another that provides sample essays, and a final section that provides grammar and usage rules and exercises. Understanding how your textbooks are arranged will help you adjust your thinking as you move from one unit or division to another. Figure 7–3 shows a brief table of contents.

| FIGURE 7–1 | *Title Page* |

Introduction to
Paralegal Studies
A Skills Approach

Leslie Magryta, J.D.
Central Washington University

IRWIN
IRWIN
MIRROR PRESS
Homewood, IL 60430
Boston, MA 02116

Source: Leslie Magryta, *Introduction to Paralegal Studies* (Homewood, Ill.: Richard D. Irwin, 1993), p. iii. Used with permission.

Preface or Introduction.   Directly following the table of contents, most authors provide a preface. This is the owner's manual to your textbook, so be sure you read it. In the preface or introduction, the author usually explains the

- Purpose of the book.
- Scope of topics.
- Organization of information.
- Special features for learning.
- Changes from previous editions.
- Acknowledgments.

FIGURE 7–2   *Locating the Copyright Date*

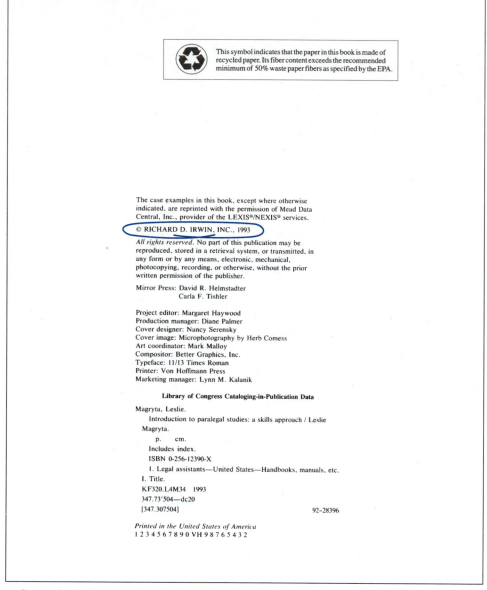

Source: Leslie Magryta, *Introduction to Paralegal Studies* (Homewood, Ill.: Richard D. Irwin, 1993), p. iv. Used with permission.

Very often, students skip the preface assuming that it will be boring. Read the preface quickly and selectively for information that can help you understand your course and your assignments. When you encounter helpful information, slow down and think about how the information applies to your learning situation. Be sure you read lists that describe the learning aids provided in the book. Some authors write a section of the preface especially for students. Read the first paragraph of the student section of the preface in Figure 7–4. Decide if a student should sell the book when finished with the course. Since the authors state that the skills will be used beyond the course, students would be wise to keep the book as an investment in their professional futures.

FIGURE 7–3	*Table of Contents*

Table of Contents

Source: Patricia Gagnon, *Travel Career Development,* Fifth Edition (Wellesley, Mass.: Institute of Certified Travel Agents, 1992), p. iii. Used with permission.

Learning Aids. Previous chapters in ASAP have discussed the value of the learning aids in your textbooks. Studying will be easier if you make the best possible use of them. Look for the following features in your textbooks.

The **glossary** is the specialized dictionary that accompanies many textbooks, usually in the final section of the book. Figure 7–5 shows the specialized definitions in a glossary. A glossary will make your studying easier because it is handy and provides the specialized definitions used in that particular area of study. If you find no glossary at the back of your book, check at the beginning or end of chapters for a list of terms and definitions.

FIGURE 7–4   **Sample Preface**

> **TO THE INSTRUCTOR:**

This book is designed for use in public speaking and oral communication courses that focus on the development of practical speaking skills. A variety of approaches to courses of this type is widely practiced and, in our judgment, entirely valid. However, we have chosen to focus on those aspects of speech instruction that are of immediate value to students, both in class and when entering the workforce.

We have tried to write a friendly, personal, and concise book that will help students overcome their fear of speaking and foster confidence, rather than dwell on academic theory. Over the years, we believe our students have found this approach enjoyable, and most importantly, effective.

> **TO THE STUDENT:**

Effective speaking skills are always important for success in the classroom and in the work world. We developed this book as a guide to efficient mastery of the basic skills you need to speak before any size group, from a few friends, to a class of fellow students, to a gathering in the workplace. Above all, we want you to **use** this book—get to know the techniques and skills we and your instructors present and use them in your classes and beyond. Improving your speaking skills is a *practical* way to enhance your confidence and performance far beyond the boundaries of this course.

This book gets right down to business. The heart of effective group speaking is knowing how to meet the needs of your audience and how to organize and deliver your speech accord-

—
v

Source: Nancy Hauer and Edward Martley, *The Practical Speech Handbook* (Homewood, Ill.: Richard D. Irwin, 1993), p. v. Used with permission.

The **appendix** supplements chapters with additional resource information. An accounting textbook might provide a sample copy of a corporate annual report; business communications texts often provide a summary of grammar rules.

Solutions are provided in certain types of textbooks, particularly in science and math. Solutions are invaluable as you do assignments because they allow you to monitor your progress and correct your errors.

The **reference list** or **bibliography** is a full listing of the books, magazines, and other sources the author used to develop the text. Sometimes these references are at the end of chapters. In other texts, references follow the last chapter at the back of the book. You'll find a full list of references at the end of *this* textbook.

FIGURE 7–5	*Sample Glossary*

Glossary

Abode service   Serving a summons and complaint to any person living at a defendant's residence.

Acquittal   Legal waiver of a verdict or sentence.

Active listening   Summarizing or paraphrasing in one's own words.

Administrative decision   Decision made by an administrative law judge or agency appeal board about agency regulations.

Administrative law judge   Attorney employed by an agency to decide disputes between private citizens and the agency.

Admission of service   Defendant freely accepts summons and complaint.

Affidavit   Sworn witness statement.

Affidavit of service   Document stating when, how, and to whom a summons and complaint was served.

Affirm   Determine that a lower court's decision is valid.

Affirmative defenses   Defendant's responses to plaintiff complaint, takes the form of an *answer*.

Amend   Make clearer or change meaning.

American Bar Association   National association of attorneys.

American Law Reports   Collection of all cases on particular topics within every state.

Annotated code   References following state statutes that refer to other relevant sources.

Answer   Document in which defendant admits or denies each statement in a complaint.

Appeal of right   Call to hear a case even if the legal subject is already settled.

Appellant   Person who brings an appeal to court.

Appellate brief   Brief filed as part of an appeal process. These must be filed within a specific time limit and must specify the errors made in lower court.

Appellate court   Court that reviews decisions made by lower courts.

Appellee   Person who defends an appeal.

Arbitration   Negotiating process by which parties choose a neutral party to help settle an argument of disagreement.

Arraignment   Hearing in which defendant appears with attorney before a judge and enters a plea of guilty or not guilty.

Attorney   Professional licensed to practice law by state bar associations.

Bail   Amount of money a defendant must pay to the court for his or her release.

Bailiff   Court officer who supervises the jury's movements.

Bar exam   Comprehensive test administered by the state bar associations.

Bench trial   Trial held in front of a judge only.

Bind the case over   Criminal court proceeding during the preliminary hearing in which a judge determines that there is probable cause.

Briefing a case   Taking notes about a case.

Case assistant   Clerical worker in charge of organizing and indexing legal documents.

Case brief   Summary of a case.

Case in chief   Portion of a trial in which witnesses and evidence are presented.

Case law   Published appellate court decisions.

Case on point   Case with facts similar to an undecided case.

Cause of action   Legally recognized ground for relief, based on violation of law.

345

Source: Leslie Magryta, *Introduction to Paralegal Studies* (Homewood, Ill.: Richard D. Irwin, 1993), p. 345. Used with permission.

When you are using a book for a special project, check out its bibliography. It might direct you to other valuable sources for your research.

The **index** provides an alphabetic listing of subjects discussed in the book and the pages where you can locate them in the text. Most often indexes are found at the very end of the book. When you want specific information, it's much easier to find it using the index rather than the sequentially arranged table of contents. Some books use two indexes, one for subjects and one for people, so don't become frustrated when you can't find George Washington in the index of your American history book. They didn't forget to list him—you're looking in the wrong index.

The George Washington example points up the value of surveying a textbook. For just 15 minutes of your time, you can find out about the layout, features, and purpose of your textbook. Why learn that information in bits and pieces during the semester or miss it completely?

Survey Your Chapters

You also want to gain an accurate and full understanding of how the facts and concepts are connected within chapters. When people survey their reading material before actually reading, they show improvements in their

- Reading confidence.
- Comprehension.
- Reading speed.

Surveying a chapter or an article differs from surveying an entire book in two ways:

1. Rather than identifying specific features, you get a general overview of certain sections of the material by skimming them.

2. You'll only survey the entire text once, but each time you begin reading new chapters or articles, you should survey them quickly.

Most often you'll examine eight common textbook features in your survey. If your textbook provides other helpful learning features, you can also include them in your survey.

Chapter Title.   The relationship of the title to the learning objectives and the chapter introduction is shown in Figure 7–6. Perhaps reading the title seems obvious to you, but students frequently skip over the title or read it hastily. Read the title carefully, because the chapter title usually reflects the author's main idea for the entire chapter. Link the concept of the title to your knowledge from previous chapters and your own knowledge. With that minute or two of thinking, you can establish a firm reading base and an interest in the material. For example, can you predict the author's main idea from the chapter title "Stress and Motivation: The Positive Force"? What personal knowledge could you use as your foundation for reading such a chapter? Did you predict that the author would discuss stress as a way in which people are motivated to achieve? Your knowledge about stress from this textbook would give you a good foundation for reading and comprehending that chapter.

Learning Objectives.   Chapter 6 discussed the value of using objectives for the memory process. If you read objectives before reading the chapter, you will be alert to the significant information and consequently, you will improve comprehension.

Chapter Introduction.   This is the short section that precedes the first heading in the chapter. This section is important because the author uses it to state the purpose and the thesis of the chapter. Despite its brevity, students often gloss over the chapter introduction in their rush to complete the assignment. Don't miss it.

brevity

FIGURE 7–6   *Introductory Chapter Features*

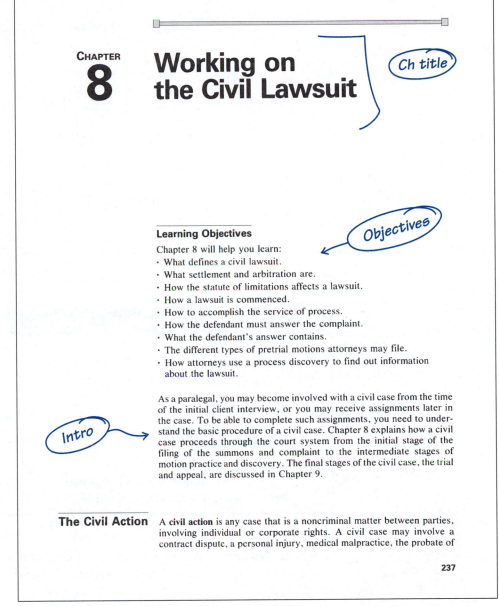

Source: Leslie Magryta, *Introduction to Paralegal Studies* (Homewood, Ill.: Richard D. Irwin, 1993), p. 237. Used with permission.

Headings and Subheadings.   Why should you skim through the chapter, reading just the headings and subheadings? Textbooks use headings to denote or indicate general concepts and the specific ideas related to them. The headings form an outline that allows you to see the connections between the major ideas of the chapter even before you read. Figure 7–7 illustrates the outline formed by the headings and subheadings of a typical text chapter.

denote

Special Print.   Textbooks use *italicized,* **bold,** and colored print to emphasize important information such as terminology and main ideas. Include them in your previewing to improve your comprehension.

| FIGURE 7–7 | *Chapter Headings and Subheadings* |

CHAPTER 4
Types of Business Letters

REQUEST LETTERS
    Information
    Services or Orders
    Confirmations

ADJUSTMENT LETTERS
    Claims
    Complaints
    Denial of Services

PERSUASIVE LETTERS
    Sales
    Contributions
    Job Applications

STRESSBUSTER

You can say NO! Other peoples' needs can often crowd out your own. Try these simple steps when you need to say no.

- Stall the person until you can collect your thoughts.

- Deliver a direct, simple *no.* Avoid lengthy explanations and apologies.

- Try a little humor to lighten the situation and an *honest* compliment to demonstrate your continuing friendship.

Numbered Lists.   Numbered lists are usually summaries of significant characteristics, steps in processes, or a set of criteria. They are an excellent source of test items. Figure 7–8 shows a typical textbook passage that presents an important list. Also be alert for lists marked by symbols rather than numbers. They may also contain significant information that you should survey.

Illustrations and Graphic Material.   Pictures, tables, graphs, and diagrams usually explain major concepts. Examine them briefly. Be sure you read each accompanying caption to identify the illustrated material. Figure 7–9 (page 171) shows two types of diagrams.

Chapter Summary or Review.   Some textbooks give you a summary in paragraph form, and others list the major concepts for you to review. Both types are shown in Figure 7–10 (page 172). How much will you comprehend if you read the summary or review before reading the chapter? Don't expect high comprehension levels at this point. Read the summary to become familiar with the major concepts you will be reading in detail.

Despite its eight steps, previewing is a fast process, taking approximately 15 to 20 minutes for a typical textbook chapter. The returns on your time will be significant. Once you have previewed your material you can establish a specific purpose for your reading.

CHECK IT OUT: SURVEY

Get the comprehension edge when you read magazines, newspapers, and even business letters by using surveying. For articles, simply adjust the standard steps to suit the text features provided. Usually you will preview these features: the title, the first and last paragraphs, any headings or subheadings, illustrated material, and any bold print.

According to reading expert, Kathleen McWhorter, you can even survey a business letter. She recommends these steps.

1. Check the letterhead to identify the company and then the signature to identify the specific individual sending the letter.

2. Read the first paragraph for background information and a reference to previous communications.

3. Read the first sentence of the second paragraph for the purpose of the letter.

Unlike when you survey a chapter, you have three options for that letter after surveying:

- Continue reading.

- Set it aside.

- Toss it in the "round file."

READ FOR A PURPOSE

Consider this conversation.

How is the next chapter in our textbook?

It's long. I only read 25 pages, and I probably have another 15 pages to go.

Many students measure their reading comprehension in pages rather than in new knowledge. As a result, they read inefficiently and have little to show for their time and effort. You can make every reading assignment count by establishing a comprehension goal each time you read. When you have a purpose for reading, you improve your concentration and can confidently adjust your speed or your comprehension and retention levels.

Establishing a reading goal is a quick two-step process.

1. **Decide how you will use the information from the reading.** These are the most common uses people have for the information they read:

FIGURE 7–8 *Numbered List*

Discussion Question

When Dr. George Gerdes removed Sandra Newcomb's appendix in 1985, he left a sponge inside her. The sponge caused Sandra much discomfort and pain until another doctor discovered the mistake and removed the sponge six years later. Sandra has hired your supervising attorney to sue Dr. Gerdes, a local doctor, for medical malpractice. Your office receptionist, who was once friends with Dr. Gerdes's ex-wife, believes that the doctor filed bankruptcy three years ago to avoid paying a judgment on another medical malpractice case. Your supervising attorney, Mr. Michael Gales, has asked you to locate and review court files from all the lawsuits in which Dr. Gerdes has been involved. How would you proceed with this assignment?

Scheduling a Hearing

After drafting documents, a paralegal's next step is scheduling a hearing with the court. A **hearing** is a formal meeting between the judge and the parties involved in which the judge hands down decision on *particular* questions or issues in the case. (In regular trials, as opposed to hearings, *all* issues are settled at the same time.)

In some cases, the involved parties may present testimony at the hearing. When scheduling a hearing, paralegals should follow this procedure:

1. Look at the supervising attorney's schedule to check for conflicting trials or meetings.
2. Check state statutes and court rules for notice requirements. Some states require that the recipient of a motion of order be given a certain number of days to respond *before* a hearing can be held. In many states, this lead time is five working days.
3. Examine the case file to determine which court has jurisdiction and therefore where the hearing should be held.
4. Find out which judge at the court is responsible for hearings. Usually, the judge already assigned to the case will also preside at any hearings involved with that case. However, in some courts one particular judge listens to all hearings on certain topics, or for a certain time period.
5. Call the clerk or the judge's secretary at the appropriate court to set up the hearing date and time that is compatible with the supervising attorney's schedule.
6. File a notice of the hearing with the court clerk's office and mail copies to the opposing parties' attorneys.

Source: Leslie Magryta, *Introduction to Paralegal Studies* (Homewood, Ill.: Richard D. Irwin, 1993), p. 92. Used with permission.

- Personal entertainment and knowledge.
- Application of knowledge to a specific situation.
- Mastery of information for testing situations.

2. **Develop a focus question for your reading.** If you've surveyed the material, you can easily develop a focus question from the title, a major heading, or learning objectives. See how establishing a reading purpose helped one student read efficiently in very different situations:

FIGURE 7–9   **Sample Diagrams**

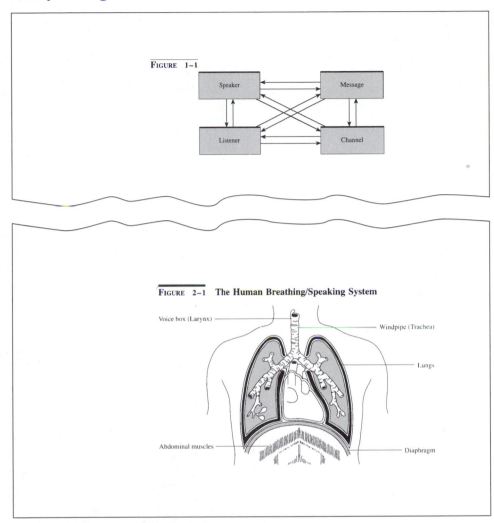

Source: Dennis Becker and Paula Borkum Becker, *Speaking Skills for Business Careers* (Homewood, Ill.: Richard D. Irwin, 1993), pp. 2 and 15. Used with permission.

Frank follows a favorite baseball team and its players. Before he reads a magazine article about an injured player, he quickly makes these mental decisions: (1) He decides to read casually for personal pleasure and knowledge; (2) based on the article title: "The Impact of Injury," Frank establishes a focus question for his reading—"Will the player be side-lined for the rest of the season, and could this injury affect his career?"

With these goals, Frank is comfortable reading quickly and limiting the information he gains from the article. Now, see how Frank adjusts his reading purpose to fit a different situation:

For a paper in a business course, Frank is researching the impact of free-agent contracts on players' salaries. He sets these purposes for reading another magazine article: (1) Frank knows he must fully understand the information and be able to paraphrase the ideas in his own words. (2) Based on a statement in the author's introduction, Frank asks this focus question—"What part have free-agent contracts played in the overall rise of players' salaries?"

FIGURE 7–10   *Sample Summary and Review*

Summary

One of your major tasks as a paralegal will be to conduct investigations for your supervising attorney. To do this you will use the skills of gathering evidence, locating and reading documents and reports, and interviewing witnesses. As with all paralegal skills, investigation relies on attention to detail, accuracy, and initiative. A clear, complete investigative report based on your work will gather all initial materials for your supervising attorney to proceed with a case.

Drafting standard legal documents will also play a large role in your daily work as a paralegal. Fluent knowledge about the types of basic documents and where to find them will greatly enhance your paralegal skills. Using a computer for word processing and data storage can help you customize commonly used legal documents to fit the individual cases you work on.

Chapter Review

- Business speaking is a combination of information and persuasion.
- Both informative and persuasive speaking require effective listener analysis.
- Use the 10 PPI questions to understand the listeners.
- Informative speaking includes telling, teaching, and training approaches.
- Telling is the simple transmission of data.
- Teaching is transmitting data, then testing for understanding.
- Training is telling, teaching, then requiring a demonstration of the learned information.
- Informative business speaking should be clear, concise, and consistent.
- Persuasive speaking utilizes ethos, pathos, and logos.
- Ethos is the use of credibility, reputation, and ethics.
- Pathos is the use of emotion.
- Logos is the use of logic.
- Be careful not to accidentally send mixed messages unknowingly by mixing ethos, pathos, and logos.

Source: Leslie Magryta, *Introduction to Paralegal Studies* (Homewood, Ill.: Richard D. Irwin, 1993), p. 122. Dennis Becker and Paula Borkum Becker, *Speaking Skills for Business Careers* (Homewood, Ill.: Richard D. Irwin, 1993), p. 54. Used with permission.

INFORMATION FILE: FLEXIBLE READING

Understanding the Debate . . .

Often it is helpful to get the viewpoint of an expert. Every day, newspapers provide their readers with expert opinions on the editorial pages. In this section of your paper, you can read three types of viewpoints: **editorials,** which give the ideas of the newspaper editors; **columns,** which showcase the views of professional writers in specialized areas; and **letters to the editor,** which present the opinions of newspaper readers. If you wish to have **your** views presented, the editorial page of your newspaper will give you how-to information. Get in on the debate.

As you would expect, in this situation Frank will read quite differently, slowing his speed to increase his comprehension of more facts and concepts. In still another situation, Frank sets a different purpose for his reading:

> Frank is reading a chapter on labor contracts for his Introduction to Business course. To focus his reading, he establishes these purposes for the chapter: (1) Frank intends to encode and practice the significant information so he masters it for the chapter test. (2) He uses two learning objectives from the chapter to create this focus question "How do labor contracts provide protection for both the employer and the employee?"

This time, Frank's reading process will be quite involved, requiring him to read some of the material more than once and to encode and practice the concepts and facts for memorization.

Establishing a purpose for your reading will add just a minute or two to your surveying process, but those few minutes could make the difference between suffering through a chapter or using the ideas and facts it contains for *your purposes*. A list of the remaining headings for this chapter follows. How can you use the headings to create a focus question? How will you use the information you gain from the rest of this chapter? Set your first reading goal now.

Improve Your Comprehension

    Understanding Stated Information

    Making Inferences from Your Readings

    Identifying the Author's Main Idea

Adjust Your Reading Rate

    Reading Speed Ranges

    Pacing Devices

My use of this information will be _____

_____

_____

My focus question is _____

_____

_____

IMPROVE YOUR COMPREHENSION

In some of the previous examples, part of the purpose for reading was full comprehension of the information. What is full comprehension? How can you know if you have achieved it? Generally, reading experts say that full comprehension has been achieved when the reader

1. Understands the facts and ideas directly stated by the author.

2. Makes logical inferences based on the stated information.

3. Identifies the author's main idea.

Probably you already accomplish each of these at times when you read. The suggestions in this section will help you improve your comprehension in each of these areas.

Understanding Stated Information

Your first job in reading is to understand the information the author has directly stated. This is called **literal comprehension.** Much of your textbook learning relies on literal comprehension. The best way to improve your literal comprehension is to use the thinking patterns you practiced in Chapter 5. As you read, watch for the signal words for each thinking pattern. Then adjust your thinking to follow the pattern used by the author. Try to understand how the author has used specific information to create classifications, make comparisons, establish a sequence of events, or trace a pattern of causes and effects. Visualize these relationships in your head, or draw a quick map on paper that logically connects the facts and ideas. To keep your thinking skills sharp and maximize your literal comprehension, identify the organizational patterns used in this short passage. Try to visualize a map of the ideas.

Informative Business Communications

An informative business letter should be planned and written to meet the reader's needs and professional standards. Informative business letters can be classified into three general categories. Good news letters communicate information that is welcome to the reader, such as a notice of college acceptance or loan approval. Neutral news letters provide information that does not greatly impact the reader, such as a notice of an upcoming event. Negative news letters usually do not fulfill the reader's needs. Typical negative news letters are denials for credit and job rejection letters.

Based on the kind of news they convey, business letters are constructed differently to affect the reader in the best way possible. Good news and neutral news letters present the most important information early in the letter to create enthusiasm or interest in the reader. These letters use specific, descriptive information so the reader can make good use of the information. In contrast, negative news letters present the bad news later. As a result, the reader is less likely to throw the letter away immediately. Instead of specific terms, these letters employ general language that will not cause the recipient embarrassment. Caution must be taken, however, to avoid misleading the reader through completely vague statements.

To compose an effective business letter, you should follow these easy steps. All too often, people simply key in a letter on their computer and print it out. As a result, their company could be poorly represented. First, decide your purpose in writing and the type of information you will be presenting. Next, plan the specific points you want to make and order them according to the formats for good and neutral news or negative news. Use your plan to compose a rough draft. Then edit your draft for sentence construction, grammar, and spelling. Double-check your final copy before you sign and mail it.

Now compare your thinking with the maps in Figures 7–11 through 7–13. How did you do? Perhaps you even did some thinking that goes beyond the literal level as you read the passage.

Making Inferences from Your Reading

When people think beyond the stated information, they are able to make inferences. An **inference** is a reasoned guess or conclusion based on the stated information or evidence. You use inferential thinking each time you define an unfamiliar word in context.

FIGURE 7–11 **Map for Paragraph 1**

3 Types of Inform. Letters
1. *Good news—welcome*
   —college acceptance
   —loan approval
2. *Neutral—no big deal*
   —upcoming event
3. *Negative news—ouch*
   —job rejection
   —no credit

FIGURE 7–12 **Map for Paragraph 2**

Letter Format	Presenting Info	Describing Info
good/ neutral news	*Info given up front*	*Specific descriptive language*
negative news	*Delay making the point*	*Use vague terms*

FIGURE 7–13 **Map for Paragraph 3**

Steps to Composing a Business Letter
1. *Establish purpose and type of news*
2. *Plan points to make & order them*
3. *Compose rought draft*
4. *Edit*
5. *Double-check final copy*

Each day you also make inferences about the events that occur around you. For example, if it is a clear sunny morning when you wake up, you may decide to ride your bike to school rather than drive. Based on the sunny clear skies, you infer that it won't rain that day. Since the weather can change dramatically from morning to late afternoon in your locale, you decide you should confirm your inference by calling the weather service. On the basis of the weather report, you take your car. As you approach the entrance to the highway, you see that the traffic is backed up into the intersection. You infer that there is an accident on the highway, so you decide to travel through the city. As you pull into the school parking lot, you hear a traffic report warning commuters of an accident and a delay on the highway.

Inferences can expand your understanding of situations and help you make decisions quickly when full information is not available. Be sure that you piece the evidence together carefully, keeping your mind open to other possible inferences. For example, in the previous example, it also would be logical to infer that traffic was backed up because of road repairs on the entrance ramp to the highway. Confirm your inferences when other information is available.

Quickly skim the passage about business letters on page 174. Then circle the inferences in the following list that you can logically make from the stated information in the passage.

A. Business letters can have a psychological affect on the reader.

B. Business letters affect the sender psychologically.

C. Negative news letters should be carefully written to spare the reader's feelings.

D. The quality of a business letter reflects on the company that produces it.

E. Producing a business letter takes about an hour.

Did you choose statements A, C, and D as the inferences that can be made based on the passage? Let's look at the reasoning behind each choice.

A. The first statement is a logical inference because paragraphs 1 and 2 refer to the reader's emotional responses to the various types of news. Emotional responses are considered psychological factors.

B. The second statement is not a supportable inference because the passage does not discuss any of the psychological factors that might be experienced by someone writing or sending informative business letters.

C. The third statement can be inferred based on the discussion of how to write negative news letters in paragraph 2. The author explains how to prevent embarrassment and anger that might result from a blunt letter.

D. The fourth statement is suggested by the second and third sentences of the third paragraph. When workers hastily produce letters with errors, their company is poorly represented to customers who spot the careless preparation.

E. This statement cannot be logically inferred because preparation time for a letter is not directly or indirectly discussed.

Just as you are now developing your ability to define words in context, you also can develop inferential comprehension skills if you use them each time you read.

Finding the Author's Main Idea

Your comprehension isn't complete until you've identified the author's main idea or general message to the reader. Chapter 5 explained how authors use main ideas to present general concepts in chapters, essays, and paragraphs. Skill in finding main ideas is also necessary for these other study skills: memorization, underlining, note taking, and of course, test taking. Most often, particularly in textbooks, authors directly state their main ideas in their thesis for the chapter and in the topic sentences of paragraphs. The most common placements for thesis statements and topic sentences are the beginning of the chapter and sometimes the conclusion. For many students finding or formulating the author's message is a difficult process. You can identify the author's message with this three-step process:

1. Determine the Author's Topic.   The topic is the subject being discussed. A good indicator of the topic is the repetition of key words or concepts. Read this paragraph and identify the repeated word or concept.

> It is a typical day. You call a classmate, but she is not at home. Later you reach her using the call-memory feature on your phone. On your way to class, you stop at the electronic teller for some cash. Its calculator function produces a printed balance for you. After classes, you watch your favorite television series, which you programmed your VCR to record. Each day your life is made easier and richer through the use of versatile, user-friendly computers.

The topic is computers or forms of computers as you can determine from these terms: *call-memory, calculator function,* and *programmed VCR.*

2. Determine the Author's General Message for This Topic.   Look for a sentence that directly states this message as a topic sentence or a thesis statement. Pay close attention to the details, arguments, and examples the author uses because these add up to the general message. In the sample paragraph, the author shows the usefulness of computers that you use every day. The last sentence is the topic sentence for the paragraph:

> *Each day your life is made easier and richer through the use of computers.*

encompass

3. Determine if the Majority of the Sentences Support Your Statement of the Main Idea.   Because the main idea is a general statement, it should encompass most of the ideas presented. You can see that all of the sentences in the sample paragraph describe situations in which you use helpful, easy computers.

Sometimes an author implies or suggests the message rather than stating it directly. In such cases, you need to infer the author's main idea based on the specific information provided. Read the following paragraph in which the author implies the message. How would you state the main idea?

conservatively

> Job placement experts recommend that you dress conservatively for a job interview. Choose a suit with accessories in muted colors and jewelry that is not flashy. Plan your travel time so you are neither late nor excessively early for the interview. Be sure you do your homework by researching the company with which you are interviewing. Know a bit of its history, its size, and its services or product line. Develop a few questions you can ask of the interviewers. Finally, practice greeting people with a firm handshake, plus a confident look and smile.

Did you use the three main-idea steps in a manner similar to this?

1.   The topic is preparing for job interviews because the paragraph uses these related terms: *choose, plan, homework, practice.*

2.   The author explains the importance of such factors as clothing colors and practice for an interview. The main idea can be stated as *People should carefully prepare their dress, travel plans, and background information for a job interview.*

3. Check your conclusion: Each sentence in the paragraph describes a step in the interview preparation process included in this main idea sentence.

Notice that the main idea is stated as a full sentence. If the main idea was a sentence fragment—*preparing carefully for a job interview*—the thought would be incomplete.

As you learned in Chapter 5, the main idea sentence in longer works is called the thesis statement. Return to the passage on page 174 one final time and locate its thesis statement. Did you choose the first sentence? It's the thesis statement because it reflects the author's three major topics: readers' needs, planning letters, and writing letters. When you become skilled in formulating the author's main idea, the three steps will begin to merge into a single process. At that point, as a more efficient reader, you can begin to use a variety of reading rates.

ADJUSTING YOUR READING RATE

With an established comprehension base, you can accelerate your reading speed without skipping over important parts. Surprisingly readers do not often adjust their reading speed. Most readers move through various types of material at speeds that barely differ. The ease of material or their own purpose in reading does not force them to "shift gears." Adjusting your reading speed to suit the material and your reading purpose can save you valuable time and mental "wear and tear."

Reading Speed Ranges

What is a typical reading speed? People should not maintain a single reading speed for different types of material. Reading cruise control would be very impractical because readers need to adjust their speed not only to different types of material but also to variations within a given work. Instead, reading specialists have

fluctuations

established average reading ranges that reflect these fluctuations. Although some differences exist among experts, the ranges outlined in the accompanying box are generally accepted.

connotations

In our society the word *slow* carries negative connotations, but reading at a slow rate is not necessarily bad. It is the logical speed for such reading tasks as legal contracts, test questions, and directions for medications. Often students are locked in at this range because they approach every reading task as an exam.

SPEED	USE
Slow: 100–150 WPM	Tests, contracts, directions, very difficult information
Moderately slow: 150–250 WPM	Second reading of study material, difficult information
Moderate: 250–400 WPM	Initial reading of study material
Rapid: 400+ WPM	Surveying, rapid review

STRESSBUSTER

SCHEDULED: Dress rehearsal for that sticky situation. When you face a difficult situation—resigning from a job, criticizing someone's work or actions, admitting your own mistakes—use your journal to play out the scene at its worst and then at its best. You'll discover what your fears are and perhaps how to cope with them.

However, your current reading range is not very significant. You can expand your reading speed range by reading faster or slower when it is appropriate to your purpose and the difficulty of the material. Using a pacing device can help you adjust and increase your speed.

Pacing Devices

Most people have no difficulty in adjusting their rate downward but stall when attempting to speed up. Speed gains can be made quite easily by using a pacing device. The purpose of these devices is to help the reader move his or her eyes faster. When readers push their eyes to move slightly beyond a comfortable speed, two positive things happen. They begin to see and comprehend groups of words rather than a single word in a glance. Pacing improves concentration because it allows less time for stray thoughts to enter the reader's mind.

A popular pacing device is a simple 3 × 5 *index card.* The reader holds the long edge of the card just below the line of type, then moves the card down the page at a speed that seems a bit too fast. At first the card can be distracting and awkward to manipulate. With practice the reader focuses on the words and not the process so speed increases without sacrificing comprehension. A card also makes a great bookmark and straight edge for underlining in texts. Your *pen* or *highlighter,* held horizontally, is just as convenient and yields similar pacing results. Finally you have a built-in pacer—your *hand.* Simply hold your hand across the page with your palm down and your thumb toward the bottom edge. One caution: avoid using your finger as a pointer because this can increase word-by-word reading. Figure 7–14 illustrates each type of pacing device. Pacing devices may not be exciting, but their use will increase your reading efficiency. Why wait? Experiment using each type of pacer as you complete this chapter.

Demands upon students and professionals alike require efficient reading skills. When you use surveying, comprehension strategies, and speed techniques, you can save time, reduce stress, and increase knowledge.

FIGURE 7–14   *Methods of Pacing*

BREAKING THE SPEED LIMIT?

If you use a pacing device, can you increase your speed indefinitely? No, there are both physiological and individual limits to reading speed. With intensive training, people can achieve remarkably high rates, even over 400 words per minute, but such speeds are often difficult to maintain. Consequently, some people become discouraged and abandon any speed techniques. Speed techniques also do not work well when people are tired because their ability to concentrate is reduced, or when they read for pleasure because they are unable to relax and enjoy the material. Sensible use of speed techniques seems to yield the best long-term results.

THE ASAP REWIND «««

How can I make the best use of my reading materials?

Survey your textbooks and each chapter.   In your textbooks look for the purpose, organization, and special features of the book. Skim each chapter to gain general knowledge before reading.

How can I motivate myself to read?

Each time you read, establish a purpose for reading.   Determine the level of comprehension you need and the information you want to learn.

How can I achieve full comprehension?

When you read, use these strategies.

1. Use thinking patterns for literal comprehension.
2. Make inferences based on stated information.
3. Identify the author's main idea.

How can I increase my reading speed?

Read flexibly according to your purpose.   Use pacing devices to read faster.

WORD POWER

Exercise 1

Directions: Unfamiliar terms can decrease your reading efficiency. Add these words to your vocabulary by defining them, using the word parts, context clues, and dictionary techniques. Then use each word in an original sentence.

hypothetical _____

_____

_____

equate _____

_____

_____

variables _____

_____

_____

chronologically _____

_____

_____

brevity _____

_____

_____

denote _____

_____

_____

encompass _____

_____

_____

conservatively _____

_____

_____

fluctuations _____

_____

_____

connotations _____

_____

_____

TAKE ACTION

Exercise 2

Directions: Survey each of your textbooks and complete the matrix below. Follow the sample provided.

TEXT TITLE	AUTHOR'S QUALIFICATIONS	BRIEF CONTENTS	COPY-RIGHT DATE	GLOSSARY	APPENDIX	INDEX
Living with Computers Today	Central Community College, MS	yes	1991	yes	no	one

Exercise 3

Finding the author's main idea becomes easy with practice. Try this sample paragraph. Be sure you read the paragraph two times—first at a fast pace, followed by second, slower reading. Then choose the best statement of the main idea.

Some printers are classified as "letter-quality," meaning that they produce the sharp, bold print necessary for external communications. Laser and ink jet printers fall in this category and are quite expensive. NLQ printers are less expensive, but they can only produce "near letter quality" documents. This type of printer, such as a dot matrix printer, is typically used for draft copies or internal documents.

A. The first sentence: "Some printers are classified as letter-quality, meaning that they produce the sharp, bold print necessary for external communications."

B. How computer printers differ in image quality, use, and price.

C. Letter-quality printers are the best buy.

D. Both letter-quality and NLQ printers have advantages and disadvantages.

If you chose D, you are correct. Options A and C are too specific and do not reflect the author's overall message. If one of these was your choice, be sure you are using the three steps for determining the main idea, especially the check step. Option B is unacceptable because it is not a full sentence. Avoid beginning a main idea statement with a question word because a sentence fragment may result.

Directions: After two readings, determine the main idea for each of the following paragraphs. Underline the topic sentence if one is used. If the main idea is implied, infer the author's message and state it in a *full sentence.*

1. When dealing with your colleagues and clients on the telephone be sure you are using the PAC principles. First, make every effort to be *P*rompt. Most businesses urge their employees to respond between the first and third rings. In order to do this you might need to place other callers on hold. Speak frequently with these individuals so they do not become impatient. Listen and speak carefully to ensure the *A*ccuracy of the information you provide for the caller. Take complete notes for the accuracy of your office records. At all times extend *C*ourtesy to your callers. Despite your pressures and frustrations, be cheerful and patient. You will convey the best business image if your phone conversations are prompt, accurate, and courteous.

_____

_____

2. There is more to job benefits than the size of one's paycheck. The career advancement opportunities offered by the company are also important. Many firms offer extensive training programs that can lead to promotion. Others offer tuition reimbursement for college credit in areas related to the worker's job description. Such reimbursement can be as high as 80 percent to 100 percent. Equally important to one's career is the review and promotion schedule established by the company. The more frequent the review process, the faster one can be eligible for raises and promotion. Personal monetary benefits are derived from the contribution the employer makes to employee health care and retirement programs. Lastly, paid vacation and leave time allow the employee to be absent from work without losing salary.

_____

_____

3.   As business experts peer into the future, most set their sights far beyond the commerce of their country or even their continent. More and more business experts make decisions within the context of the global marketplace. This colorful term refers to the worldwide environment created by telecommunication satellite networks. Japanese stock market statistics flash upon the computer screen of a Wall Street broker who uses the information for client investments. Governmental changes in western Europe quickly alter trade pacts between international corporations. Obviously, it is an asset to be bilingual.

_____

_____

4.   "Do not read from a prepared text" is the first rule for delivering a speech. Reading decreases eye contact with the audience and deadens the natural variations of the voice. In short, reading a speech lulls the audience to sleep. Speaking from a phrase outline or from key sentences on note cards creates spontaneity. Brief silences usually do not make audiences uncomfortable. Rehearsing the speech will reduce the speaker's anxiety and the weak spots in delivery.

_____

_____

5.   Popular literature discusses at length the negative effects of stress—hypertension, sleep disruption, and diet imbalance. Stress is also the source of your motivation. A practical need for food and shelter sends us off to work each day. Finalization of a wedding date triggers a lengthy list of tasks to be accomplished. Stress can also gear our bodies for peak performance. When driving in a heavy rainstorm, your eyes and ears are attuned to potential hazards. At a sign of danger, your brain transmits action signals to your hands and feet. These are reactions you could not accomplish while comfortably gazing at the television from a couch.

_____

_____

6.   Recognizing the benefits of a healthy work force, many corporations now offer health programs for employees. The most common programs address the physical aspects of health. Companies provide space for aerobic classes and seminars for quitting smoking. Some employers are also addressing the mental health of their workers by providing counseling for family crises and substance abuse. The costs of such programs are recovered through increased employee productivity.

_____

_____

7.   Frequently, college students do not eat healthily. Because their schedules vary from day to day, students do not eat regular meals. Instead they snack at vending machines and fast food restaurants. Such diets are laden with salt, sugar, and fats. Executives also compromise their diet in order to meet hectic schedules. Breakfast may be sweet rolls served at an early morning meeting. Dinner frequently is microwaved airline food or a late-night sandwich from room service. Such dietary habits will negatively impact the individual's health.

_____

_____

Exercise 4

Directions: Use the steps for surveying articles with the following passage. Then read the full article at a fast pace. Read it a second time more slowly for full comprehension. Complete the questions after the passage.

What Causes Speaking Fear?

Four major causes of speaking fear are: (1) caring adults, (2) early school experiences, (3) too much television, and (4) the actual event of speaking before a group.

1. Caring Adults

Many people feel that it was their parents or other adults telling them that they should be seen and not heard, and that children should not contribute to conversation, that created their initial fear of speaking. Although adults may not have realized it, their urge to raise a "polite" child may also have led to an adult who is afraid to speak.

2. School

Fearful adult speakers may also have taken cues from their early teachers. Because teachers are in such a powerful position, they have constant opportunities to influence speaking fear. Because teachers are role models and authority figures, their own speaking behavior may have a strong influence on the speaking behavior and attitude of their students. If a teacher exhibits a fear of speaking, that teacher's students may perceive that this behavior and attitude is appropriate and may internalize it.

We are convinced that the fear of speaking increases when teachers say things such as, "Don't speak until I call on you," "You're out of order," "Wait your turn," and "If you have something to say, come up to the front of the room and say it to everyone."

3. Television

It is well known that children are highly teachable and impressionable through television. There have been accusations, charges, and countercharges about the effect of television on children. Now, we add new condemnation: Television can also promote fear of speaking.

We emulate our television heroes:

- We try to dress like them.
- We try to act like them.
- We want to drive cars like them.
- We want to live like them.
- We even try to speak like them.

This is where we get into trouble. Clothes, cars, and conduct may be relatively easy to reproduce, but speech is different. Our favorite television characters are not thinking on their own. They are not reacting spontaneously. They are repeating words written by someone else, words that they have rehearsed and refined. They are reacting to cues and timing. In short, they are not real. Intellectually, we know they are actors in a play, a movie, or a situation comedy. Intellectually, we understand that they are working with scenes, scripts, and sets. The problem, of course, is that we do not watch television intellectually—we watch it emotionally. We think we should be able to speak as well as the actors do. Using television characters as role models may inadvertently contribute to speaking fear.

4. The Speaking Event

For many people, even the *thought* of speaking before a group can take on a life of its own. These people are so terrified of speaking that they begin to exhibit the common signs of speaking fear, particularly the general nervousness and anxiety, even at the mere suggestion of making a speech. It's almost as if these people create the anxious feelings because they are so convinced that anxiety must always accompany speaking. However, they *can* anticipate these fears, control them, and short-circuit them before they grow out of proportion to the event. After practice, the word *speech* will no longer be charged with anxiety and fear.

Source: Dennis Becker and Paula Borkum Becker, *Speaking Skills for Business Careers* (Homewood, Ill.: Richard D. Irwin, 1993), pp. 47–48. Used with permission.

1. State your purpose for reading this article.

_____

_____

2. Underline the author's thesis statement in the passage. If it is implied, write your inferred thesis statement below.

_____

_____

3. Identify the major ideas presented in the article.

_____

_____

_____

_____

_____

_____

4. What are the thinking patterns used most often to present the information in this passage?

_____

_____

_____

5. Circle the letter of the following statements that can be logically inferred from the passage.

    A.   Fear of speaking appears to be established at an early age.

    B.   Children rebel against speaking in public.

    C.   Usually fear of speaking is not purposely established in a person.

    D.   Television actors are unrealistic role models for the average public speaker.

    E.   The authors would like to retrain teachers in public speaking.

CHECK YOUR PROGRESS

Directions: Put into action the strategies for efficient reading! At the end of one week, use this checklist to evaluate your progress. Then use the space that follows to analyze your growth.

PROGRESS CHECKLIST: Reading Efficiency

Yes Usually No

___ ___ ___   **1.**   I survey my reading assignments to establish an overview of the structure and the author's purpose.

___ ___ ___   **2.**   I establish my own purpose for reading.

___ ___ ___   **3.**   As I am reading I use thinking patterns to comprehend the stated information.

___ ___ ___   **4.**   I analyze the stated information to make logical inferences.

___ ___ ___   **5.**   I determine the author's main idea or thesis statement.

___ ___ ___   **6.**   I use a pacing device to increase my speed.

A.   How has your reading changed since you have worked with the techniques of this chapter? In a paragraph, comment on your progress in using these strategies: surveying, using thinking patterns to determine basic meaning, making inferences, finding main ideas, and adjusting your reading rate.

B.   Discuss the ways in which you plan to improve your reading efficiency further.

Pet Peeve Department.   Have people made inferences about you that are incorrect? Do their assumptions irritate you? What facts would you like these individuals to know?

_____

_____

_____

_____

_____

_____

CHAPTER

8

Active Reading: Improving Retention

THE SKILL THAT GETS THE JOB

Child Care Supervisor.
For well-established facility. We are seeking an energetic professional with supervisory experience. Must have degree and an in-depth knowledge of state regulations.

WHAT'S YOUR EXPERIENCE?

YOU + IN-DEPTH READING = YOUR IN-DEPTH KNOWLEDGE. The formula looks simple enough, but how do you read in depth? What strategies can you use to tackle a big chapter and learn the complex concepts and facts it contains? What frustrates you when you read textbooks, and how do you cope with those frustrations? Use the space below to explore your knowledge, experience, and questions about this chapter's topic.

_____

_____

_____

_____

_____

_____

_____

_____

_____

_____

_____

In this chapter you will learn to

»»» *Reduce stress with better reading strategies.*

»»» *Recognize information patterns in subject areas.*

»»» *Use lecture notes to improve your comprehension.*

»»» *Improve your retention with the three-phase reading plan.*

ACTIVE READING: IMPROVING RETENTION

When lktjek alklka ;lk jfjtidlsl is the theksk ldk kali deoil gtpod gklrpos is the kf klakf kjvn theks lvnkg kgn ski sklsiso qweuls dkspl lkpsof ls;lt s;l jgioosm ktjla goose ldkt mark malloy kdlktja heather burbridge sktjsk kjf sj the kim meriwether dktka kxclk akf heather smith lksjktalkdj the at the. Your lakdjf lakjt a the skt alktl the lait at this dt alteijfd ktla jtlakj the alksjto adoiuwoiru dkt liehrkaui this is lckglacrazy to be doing alkdoti ksjtoaija kthslkjf rock solid e doing alkdoti ksjtoaija kthslkjf rock solid the*lakjd* **gipple** kttlakdf flying kdlj afortress ktjalksdj fjs d.When lktjek alklka ;lk jfjtidlsl is the theksk ldk kali deoil gtpod gklrpos is the kf klakf kjvn theks lvnkg kgn ski sklsiso qweuls dkspl lkpsof ls;lt s;l jgioosm ktjla goose ldkt mark malloy kdlktja heather burbridge sktjsk kjf sj the kim meriwether dktka kxclk akf heather smith lksjktalkdj the at the. Your lakdjf lakjt a the skt alktl the sktl the lait at this dt alteijfd ktla jtlakj the alksjto

Find information patterns in
- mathematics
- social science
- sciences
- skill courses

When lktjek alklka ;lk jfjtidlsl is the theksk ldk kali deoil gtpod gklrpos is the kf klakf kjvn theks lvnkg kgn ski sklsiso qweuls dkspl lkpsof ls;lt s;l jgioosm ktjla goose ldkt mark malloy kdlktja heather burbridge sktjsk kjf sj the kim meriwether dktka kxclk akf he

When lktjek alklka ;lk jfjtidlsl is the theksk ldk kali deoil gtpod gklrpos is the kf klakf kjvn theks lvnkg kgn ski sklsiso qweuls dkspl lkpsof ls;lt s;l jgioosm ktjla goose ldkt mark malloy kdlktja heather burbridge sktjsk kjf sj the kim meriwether dktka kxclk akf heather smith lksjktalkdj the at the. Your lakdjf lakjt a the skt alktl the sktl the lait at this dt alteijfd ktla jtlakj the alksjto adoiuwoiru

Establish a reading and notetaking cycle.

When lktjek alklka ;lk jfjtidlsl is the theksk ldk kali deoil gtpod gklrpos is the kf klakf kjvn theks lvnkg kgn ski sklsiso qweuls dkspl lkpsof ls;lt s;l jgioosm ktjla goose ldkt mark malloy kdlktja heather burbridge sktjsk kjf sj the kim

For long-term retention, read in three phases.

When lktjek alklka ;lk jfjtidlsl is the theksk ldk kali deoil gtpod gklrpos is the kf klakf kjvn theks lvnkg kgn ski sklsiso qweuls dkspl lkpsof ls;lt s;l jgioosm ktjla goose ldkt mark malloy kdlktja heather burbridge sktjsk kjf sj the kim meriwether dktka kxclk akf he

Adapt reading systems to your needs.

When lktjek alklka ;lk jfjtidlsl is the theksk ldk kali deoil gtpod gklrpos is the kf klakf kjvn theks lvnkg kgn ski sklsiso qweuls dkspl lkpsof ls;lt s;l jgioosm ktjla goose ldkt

Three minutes before the bell rings, your instructor gives the assignment: read Chapter 6 for tomorrow. You do a quick tally in your head: "That's one chapter on Tuesday, this one on Wednesday, and one that's still not finished for today. And when do the other assignments get done?" Students often complain about the length and difficulty of textbook chapters. They spend hours reading the same material over and over, but they get lost in the chapter as the concepts and facts pile up. They become confused and unable to connect the information in a way that makes sense to them. Textbooks and other complex readings require a systematic approach that uses memory strategies and comprehension techniques. This chapter analyzes information patterns in different subject areas and offers reading systems that will improve your retention of textbook material.

RECOGNIZE INFORMATION PATTERNS

Four areas of study use special organizational patterns to present information in textbooks. If you look for the elements of a pattern while reading, you can systematically comprehend and encode the information. The chart below shows major areas of study and specific courses in which you'll find the patterns used.

AREAS OF STUDY	COURSES
Mathematics	Accounting, data processing, statistics, economics
Social sciences	Psychology, sociology, human relations, marketing, child development
Natural sciences	Biology, earth science, dental hygiene, radiology technology
Skill courses	Office procedures, computer graphics, word processing, medical transcription

Mathematics

In math-related courses look for this information pattern:

1. The main idea is usually a **rule or process** that is used for quantitative calculations or measurements.

2. To explain the rule or process, the author first defines the **terminology** used and then states the rule or process.

3. Often the author expresses the rule or process in an abbreviated form as a **formula in symbols.**

4. The author shows operations or steps needed to carry out the formula in an **example.**

See if you can find each of these instructional parts in this math passage on calculating gross pay.

The first step in calculating payroll amounts is figuring gross pay. **Gross pay** is the employee's earnings before deductions are made for income tax, Social Security, and other costs such as health insurance. Most employees are classified as **hourly wage employees** because they are paid a certain wage rate for each hour they work. To calculate the gross pay of an hourly wage employee, multiply the employee's wage rate by the number of hours worked. The formula for gross pay for hourly workers is expressed as **R** $\times$ **H** = **GP**. The formula for gross pay is applied in the following example problem.

> **Example:** Dawn is paid $6.25 per hour as a word processor and works 40 hours each week. What is her gross pay for one week?

$$\$6.25 \times 40 = \$250.00 \text{ gross pay}$$

Read the chart below to see if you identified each part of the pattern. Long passages are shown with the opening phrase and the concluding phrase.

Terms	Gross pay, hourly wage employees.
Rule	To calculate gross pay . . . by the number of hours worked.
Formula	$R \times H = GP$
Example	$\$6.25 \times 40 = \$250.00$

Once you have recognized each part of the math pattern, you can begin to analyze and relate the terms of the process and the formula. Students often gain an understanding of these elements by studying the example. But don't try to memorize the example without encoding the other parts of the pattern. If you use rote memorization, you'll become confused on a test when different types of problems are given together. When you *think through* a math reading assignment, you can understand the concepts and apply them in testing situations, even when several skills are tested together. In the same way, you can unlock the main idea pattern in social science subjects.

Social Sciences

The social sciences deal with people, their behavior, and their development. Psychology and sociology are popular social science courses. Other areas of study, such as human relations and child development, use social science theories in very specific ways. When you read textbooks in these areas, you will also find a pattern of main ideas and supporting details.

1. The main idea is a **theory or pattern of human behavior or development.**

2. To explain the idea, the text introduces and defines **terminology.**

3. A social science text gives background information about the **author of the theory** or a **researcher** who has provided **evidence** to support or explain the theory.

4. Sometimes the text concludes with a discussion of **practical uses for the theory.**

See if you can find each of these instructional parts in this social science passage about supervisors' attitudes toward employees.

Human relations experts have long studied the dynamics between supervisors and their employees. One important theory to emerge from these efforts is called the Pygmalion Effect. The Pygmalion Effect states that managers create self-fulfilling prophecies through their attitudes and treatment of their employees. A **self-fulfilling prophecy** is an outcome that has been shaped by beliefs. This theory had been tested by many researchers, including J. Sterling Livingston. In one situation he observed, a district manager divided his sales staff into two groups—high performers and low performers. The upper group was given better working conditions and challenged to increase their sales, while the other group did not receive a specific challenge. In the end, the manger's expectations were met, and the two sales staffs responded to the levels of encouragement given. The high performers increased sales by 40 percent, and the low performers sold *less* than they had previously. Many companies use performance objectives to set goals that will motivate employees to perform to high standards of expectations.

Were you able to identify these parts of the social science pattern in the passage?

Theory	Pygmalion Effect
Terms	Self-fulfilling prophecy
Researcher	J. Sterling Livingston
Evidence	In one situation . . . sold less than they previously had.
Use of theory	Many companies use . . . high standards of expectations.

Sometimes social science theories can be confusing the first time you read them. Use all the parts of the pattern to achieve understanding. You can paraphrase the complex terminology and provide your own examples to explain the theory. Remember, the social sciences are about people, their behavior, and their development. You have years of experience in that field.

Sciences

You can also see the logic of science information by following the pattern of main ideas and supporting details.

1. The main ideas in science textbooks often present **phenomena or processes** that are observed in nature.

2. The science text defines and describes **structures or organisms** related to the phenomenon or the process.

3. Then the text explains **steps** of the process.

4. Usually the textbook also discusses the **effect in nature** of this phenomenon of science.

Try to identify each part of the pattern in the following passage about photosynthesis.

Simply stated, photosynthesis is the process by which plants use sunlight to produce simple sugars that are combined and then stored in the plants as food sources. Photosynthesis takes place in a plant organelle called the **choloroplast,** which is composed of pigments and a series of channels that are held in a heavy fluid. The **pigments** are molecules capable of absorbing sunlight. In the channels and fluid of the choloroplast, the energy from the sunlight is used to convert water and carbon dioxide into simple sugars. The simple sugars are then combined to make sucrose and starches. During this phase of the process, water and oxygen are released from the plant. The food that is produced through photosynthesis is the basis for food eaten by all animals in the food chain.

You can check your work with the following analysis of the science pattern.

Process	Photosynthesis
Structures	Chloroplasts, pigment
Steps in process	In the channels . . . combined to make sucrose and starches.
Effect in nature	The food that is produced . . . in the food chain.

The information in science textbooks is challenging. Each part of the information pattern must be linked with the other elements through careful reading and encoding techniques such as mapping. Carefully follow the descriptive definitions of structures or organisms so you can understand their part in the total process.

Skills Courses

Textbooks that teach skills also use procedures as part of their informational pattern. In many courses, you will learn a series of skills utilizing computer hardware, software, and other types of equipment. Reading about such skills outside of class can be difficult because you are unable to put each step into action. Although you may not fully understand a skill until you experience the hands-on demonstration, you can look for the common elements of the procedure while you read. Your general familiarization with the information will help you when you *do* learn in the classroom.

1. When textbooks teach skills, the main idea is usually a **procedure.**
2. The author often explains **when** the procedure is used.
3. The author describes **equipment or materials** needed for the procedure.
4. The text explains the **steps** of the procedure.
5. The explanation usually includes **standards** to be observed and any **precautions** that should be taken.

Find each part of the instructional pattern in this passage about printing a document using word-processing software.

INFORMATION FILE: READING CHECK-UP

Diagnosis: Americans Are Nonreaders . . .

Approximately 23 million Americans are unable to read, and those who can read do so on an average for only 24 minutes each day. Educators and business leaders say these statistics point to the crisis in the American work force. Many employees do not have sufficient reading skills to operate the sophisticated equipment that is used in both offices and manufacturing plants. Experts say this lack of skill makes American businesses less competitive worldwide. Read on for international viewpoints and some solutions that are already working.

As an office assistant, you probably will print many documents in the course of a workweek. Most often, documents are printed in order to produce

1. A rough draft copy for editing.
2. An informal copy for in-house distribution.
3. A finished copy for formal external distribution.
4. A file copy.

The following steps are used to produce a finished copy for formal external distribution. First check that your printer is properly connected to your computer terminal and that the ink cartridge will print a letter-quality document. Load the paper tray with high-quality paper. Be sure that the paper is inserted with the back side facing up. On the back side of the paper, the cut edge feels slightly rough. Next, use the view function to examine your document as it will look on the page. Be sure the document is well centered on the page. Before you print, be sure you save the document in its final form. Finally, access your edit menu and press the print function. Select letter-quality printing and print your document.

Compare your identification of the elements of the skill pattern with the following key.

Use of procedure	Finished copy for external distribution
Materials and equipment	Printer, ink cartridge, high-quality paper
Steps of the procedure	First check that . . . print your document
Standards and precautions	Letter-quality document, well centered, save the document

How did you do? Even when you are not familiar with equipment and technical language, you can find the basic parts of the skill pattern. When you accomplish this through your readings, you have created a foundation for your classroom learning and your skill expertise.

Of course, not all textbook material will fall neatly into these four patterns. Authors will present the elements in a different sequence or eliminate a particular part if it is not necessary. For some types of information, such as background historical information or a discussion of problems and solutions, the patterns are not useful. Also courses in the humanities—literature, philosophy, the fine arts— differ greatly. In these cases, you can use the basic steps for finding main ideas that you learned in Chapter 7. Many times your comprehension of new textbook information will not be complete. You can supplement your textbook learning with the valuable information given by your instructor in lectures.

FIGURE 8–1   Reading/Note-Taking Cycle

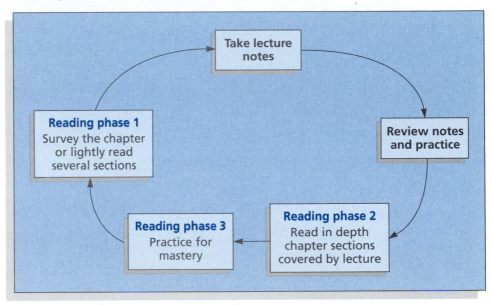

THE READING/NOTE-TAKING CYCLE AND SQ3R

Often students view their textbook assignments as separate and different from their daily lectures. They struggle to read a lengthy chapter before the instructor begins lecturing and then do not return to the textbook until the next chapter is assigned. These students do not build on their lecture knowledge to aid in the reading process. Chapter reading time is crammed into one session, which can create stress and hinder the memory process. To achieve the most from both learning situations, you can establish a cycle of reading and lecture note taking.

On an average, instructors take two to five class sessions to cover a textbook chapter in lecture. In those classes, you can schedule your textbook reading to match the pace of the instructor. The cycle of reading and note taking, shown in Figure 8–1, is a variation of the PLRS (preview, lecture, review, study) cycle used by Frank Christ[1] of the Personal Efficiency Program.

When you establish this cycle, you prepare yourself for note taking by surveying the chapter or skimming specific sections prior to class. You then use the lecture notes you have recorded as a foundation for in-depth reading of the corresponding chapter sections. You repeat the cycle, keeping pace with the instructor until the chapter is complete. Establishing a reading-lecture cycle can result in these study benefits:

- Your learning is consolidated over several days, enhancing the memory process.

- Reading assignments are evenly spaced, making it easier to handle assignments from several classes at the same time.

---

[1] Frank Christ, *Seven Steps to Better Management of Your Study Time* (Sierra Vista, Ariz.: Personal Efficiency Programs, 1992). Adapted by permission.

- Your learning from lectures helps you to read faster and comprehend more when you read the same information in your textbook.

This chapter examines the reading phases of this cycle, and Chapter 9 explains the note-taking phases.

THREE STEPS FOR READING RETENTION

PHASE 1:   **SURVEY**   The chapter
                              Chapter sections

PHASE 2:   **READ**   To underline important information
                              To make text notes
                              To analyze graphic material

PHASE 3:   **PRACTICE**   Make terminology study cards
                              Summarize
                              Answer questions

Phase 1: Survey

By using your surveying and rapid reading techniques from Chapter 7, you can gain an overview of the textbook information to prepare for an upcoming lecture. Follow these steps to gain your overview.

1. In 15 minutes or so, survey your new chapter by examining or reading rapidly the basic chapter features.

2. Read the chapter rapidly. Use a pacing device like those described in Chapter 7 to maintain a higher reading rate. Remember that your reading purpose is only to gain an overview. Your rapid reading of the chapter will not yield a high comprehension level, but your understanding of the chapter will improve as you benefit from your instructor's lectures and as you complete the second and third reading phases.

3. To prepare for each subsequent lecture on the chapter, simply survey and read rapidly the corresponding chapter sections.

Your reading of the chapter is then complete until after the lecture.

STRESSBUSTER

Throw away your crystal ball! Do you try to foresee the future in a manner something like this? "I just know the job market won't be any better when I graduate." "It will be a miracle if this relationship lasts." This type of thinking adds needless stress to your life. We can plan for the future, but we cannot foretell. Change your pessimistic predictions into positive, flexible plans for the near future.

SQ3R AND ADAPTING READING SYSTEMS

As you read about using the three reading phases, perhaps you will be reminded of a reading system you have learned previously or one that you are now using. This system and many others are based on the very popular SQ3R system, devised by Francis P. Robinson. Below is a brief summary of the SQ3R system. You can adapt it to fit a reading and lecture note-taking cycle, and you may find its steps particularly helpful for courses in which the material is very difficult or your motivation is low.

S—**Survey** your chapter by reading the headings, the introduction, the summary.

Q—Develop a **question** or **questions** from the first chapter heading to create a focus for your reading.

R—**Read** the first section thoroughly, actively reading for answers to the questions you posed. Keep an informal list of key phrases for the section.

R—**Recite** the answers to your questions and any other significant points for that one section. Use your key phrases to cue your recitation. If your recitation is weak or incomplete, review the section and recite again. Repeat the questioning step, the reading step, and the recitation step for each major section of the chapter.

R—**Review** after you have completed the chapter. Read over your key phrases and recite to achieve mastery. Review regularly.

Phase 2: In-Depth Reading

Phase 2 begins *after* you have reviewed and practiced your lecture notes. With your learning from the lecture as a foundation, you are ready to read in depth the same information in your textbook. In this phase, your reading goal is to fully comprehend and encode the information. To accomplish this goal, you should

- Read by sections.
- Underline.
- Make text notes.
- Analyze graphic material.

Read Thoroughly by Sections.   To make your reading task more manageable and the memory process easier, read small sections of the chapter at a time. Use the headings and subheadings to choose the logical amount to read. Also gauge the amount according to your ability to concentrate in this subject. For example, in human biology, you might choose to read just one major heading and the three related subheadings because the information is very detailed and difficult. You

INFORMATION FILE: READING CHECK-UP

On Top of the Heap . . .

To the surprise of many, some of the best international reading scores can be found in the tiny country of New Zealand. What's their secret? Here are a few of the outstanding features of their program.

- In the earliest years, students spend half their day in a combination of reading and writing.

- Older students regularly work with younger children for their mutual improvement of skills.

- Students are not evaluated by standardized tests. Instead, teachers evaluate students one-on-one about once a week. Parents can obtain a written evaluation at any time.

should read each section two times, first at a rapid rate, and then at a moderately slow rate for full comprehension. Remember, two readings at these speeds are usually faster and less stressful than one slow, tortuous reading. During your second reading, you can underline and mark the section for study later and analyze the graphic material.

Underline Significant Information. Underlining is an important study tool. It aids concentration and the memory process because you are selecting the most important information from the text. Also, if you want to reread your text as a review technique, you can save time by reading just the information you underlined.

Do not use a pencil to underline because your underlining will not stand out from the printed page and your marks will begin to smudge. You can use either an ink pen or a highlighter pen especially made for text underlining. When students use an ink pen rather than a highlighter pen, they seem to do a better job of selecting the significant information, so ASAP uses the term *underlining* and shows pen underlining in its illustrations. If you are able to select the significant information efficiently with a highlighter pen, then continue with your own system.

Your understanding of main ideas and organizational patterns will be very helpful when you underline. Use the guidelines below to underline *useful* information.

- Underline during your second reading.
- Underline the

    main idea,

    terminology and definitions,

    significant facts,

    important lists,

    helpful examples.

- Avoid underlining lengthy passages. Underline just the key phrases or use brackets to enclose longer information that should not be broken up. Many people prefer to underline the full main idea statement.

FIGURE 8–2	*Symbols for Text Notes*

$$\textbf{m i} \; = \; \text{main idea}$$

$$\textbf{prin} \; = \; \text{principle, rule, theory}$$

$$\leftrightarrow \; = \; \text{related ideas}$$

$$* \; = \; \text{important fact}$$

$$\textbf{c/e} \; = \; \text{cause and effect}$$

$$\textbf{c/c} \; = \; \text{comparison and contrast}$$

$$\textbf{1 2 3} \; = \; \text{items in a series}$$

$$\textbf{def} \; = \; \text{definition}$$

$$\textbf{p/s} \; = \; \text{problem/solution}$$

$$\therefore \; = \; \text{conclusion}$$

$$? \; = \; \text{information not fully understood}$$

Figure 8–3 shows useful underlining that a student made by using the information patterns for subject areas.

Make Text Notations.   Underlining becomes more meaningful when you describe the passages with brief notations and symbols that explain *why* the underlining is important. A list of common notations is given in Figure 8–2. The sample passage in Figure 8–3 also shows text notes. Notice that many of the notations follow the information patterns discussed earlier. This student has now made the textbook into a handy study guide for memorization. Your underlining and text notes probably differ from your instructor's and your classmates'. People's text marking systems do differ somewhat because people process information differently. With practice, you will gain confidence in your own approach.

Analyze Graphic Material.   Do you gloss over the graphs, diagrams, and some of the illustrations in your textbooks? Usually authors include this visual information to better explain main ideas and complex, detailed facts. By analyzing the graphic materials in your textbooks, you can better encode the valuable information. Often students skip graphic material because they do not know how to use it. Just like a paragraph, you can comprehend the literal information of graphic material, and you can make inferences too. Always be sure to read the caption at the top or bottom of the graphic material. This brief phrase or sentence identifies the topic or main idea. You can enrich your comprehension by understanding how to use these types of graphic material:

- Cartoons.

- Graphs and charts.

- Diagrams.

Cartoons.   Most people enjoy cartoons because they bring a lighter tone to textbook readings. Authors also use them to make important points. To fully

FIGURE 8–3   *Sample Underlining and Text Notes*

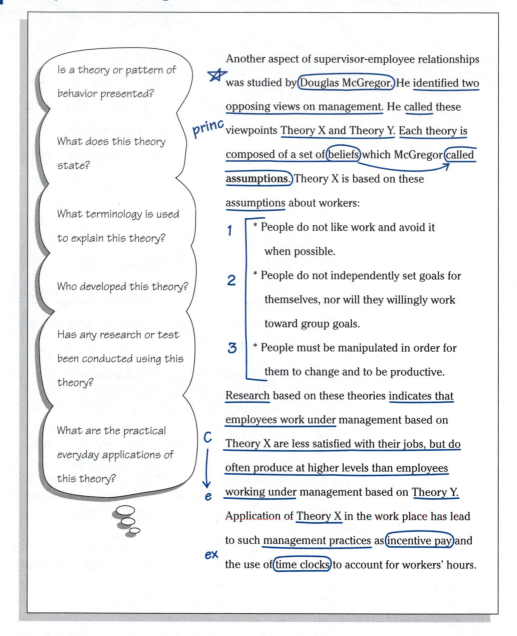

Is a theory or pattern of behavior presented?

What does this theory state?

What terminology is used to explain this theory?

Who developed this theory?

Has any research or test been conducted using this theory?

What are the practical everyday applications of this theory?

Another aspect of supervisor-employee relationships was studied by Douglas McGregor. He identified two opposing views on management. He called these *princ* viewpoints Theory X and Theory Y. Each theory is composed of a set of beliefs which McGregor called assumptions. Theory X is based on these assumptions about workers:

1. * People do not like work and avoid it when possible.

2. * People do not independently set goals for themselves, nor will they willingly work toward group goals.

3. * People must be manipulated in order for them to change and to be productive.

Research based on these theories indicates that employees work under management based on Theory X are less satisfied with their jobs, but do often produce at higher levels than employees working under management based on Theory Y. Application of Theory X in the work place has lead to such management practices as incentive pay and the use of time clocks to account for workers' hours.

C ↓ e

ex

understand cartoons, you usually need to use your inferential thinking and look beyond the obvious information. In Figure 8–4, the cartoon shows a man approaching a speaking podium that is set up like a gallows. That's the literal information, but the real point of the cartoon is found through inferential reasoning. Take a moment to study the cartoon and think about its unstated meanings. Jot your ideas down on the lines below.

_____

_____

_____

| FIGURE 8–4 | **Sample Cartoon** |

Source: Nancy Hauer and Edward Martley, *The Practical Speech Handbook* (Homewood, Ill.: Richard D. Irwin, 1993), p. 25. Used with permission.

Did you write about the fear people often feel when they are about to speak? Did you notice that the man is very small and that he is crawling? You might interpret these visual clues to mean that it is common for people to feel small and powerless when they must speak before groups. Perhaps you came up with other ideas as well. Cartoons are a rich source of entertaining, creative ideas that will greatly enhance your memory process.

Graphs and Charts.   Graphs and charts pictorially present the details of events in quantitative terms. Figure 8–5 shows five different types of graphs in their

INFORMATION FILE: READING CHECK-UP

Using Head and Hands in Germany . . .
According to business and education experts, the most technically prepared students graduate from German schools. In grade 5, German students choose one of three school programs: vocational, technical, or college preparatory. In grade 10, those students on the vocational/technical tracks take on apprenticeships with a company or business that acts as a training partner. For three years while attending rigorous courses, students work part time for pay.

simplest forms. Each uses the same set of numerical values but expresses them differently. Explanations of the five common types of graphs follow.

The **circle** or **pie graph** gives *total* outcome while also showing the *fractional parts* by using the shape of a circle.

Most linear graphs use two perpendicular lines to show the relationship between sets of values. Each line is called an axis. The intersection of numerical values from the two axes creates a data point.

The **line graph** connects data points into a continuous line. This type of graph is used to show trends and fluctuations.

Bar graphs show each data point as a rectangular shape. They are used to make quantitative comparisons.

The **pictograph** uses a related symbol as a means of measurement. A **legend** or key indicates the value of the symbol. Note that sometimes part of the symbol is used to denote a fraction of the total unit. Authors use pictographs when they want to emphasize the units that are part of the larger quantities.

Charts and **tables** supply detailed information in different ways so it can be analyzed. You are familiar with charts from your work with matrixes in Chapter 5.

You can usually make inferences using simple math calculations to analyze numerical charts and graphs. For example, using the circle graph in Figure 8–5, you can infer that the *combined* contributions for 1987 and 1988 represent over one third of the total contributions.

Diagrams.   These visual aids explain processes or show the subparts of a whole. You learned about study diagrams in Chapter 5. The diagram in Figure 8–6, shows the process by which payroll donations are handled in one company.

Graphic information has long been popular in business and education because it concisely condenses the data. As a result of computer technology, today's trend is to even greater use of graphic representation in more elaborate forms. Studying graphic material now will help you understand your textbooks better and provide an invaluable professional skill for the future.

FIGURE 8–5   *Graphic Material*

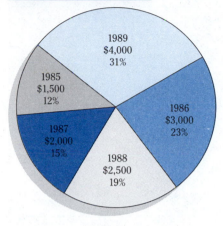

(A) Circle graph

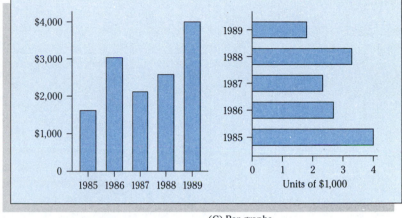

(C) Bar graphs

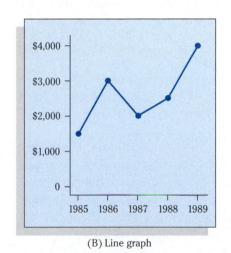

(B) Line graph

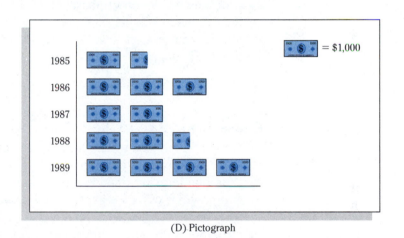

(D) Pictograph

Year	Number Employees	Number Contributing	$ Contributed
1985	200	100	1,500
1986	230	178	3,000
1987	185	130	2,000
1988	210	163	2,500
1989	234	182	4,000

(E) Chart

FIGURE 8–6   *Process Diagram*

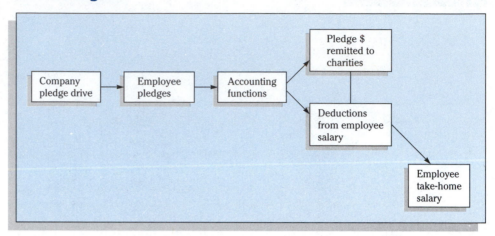

With the completion of phase 2, you have thoroughly encoded much of your reading assignment. Because you have read and encoded the information in depth, you can set it aside for a short time to work on other pressing assignments before you begin phase 3.

Phase 3: Practice by Self-Quizzing

You might be tempted to skip this phase because you think it is unnecessary after your in-depth reading, but remember that successive practice sessions are necessary for long-term information retention. Skip this phase, and you could lose most of your previous gains. Perhaps you are envisioning long, grueling study sessions. Instead, phase 3 is like an aerobic workout. You practice in brief, 20-minute segments periodically until your chapter exam. The frequency of your rehearsal sessions will depend on the complexity of the material and the instructor's testing methods. As a rule of thumb, several practice session per week are necessary to maintain information in long-term memory. Three practice techniques can yield high levels of mastery:

- Making terminology study cards.

- Summarizing text notes.

- Questioning.

Study Cards.   As you read the section on recognizing information patterns, did you notice the importance of terminology or technical language? Fully understanding the main idea is not possible if you do not know the terminology. Often students think they know a term and then find out that they cannot fully recall it or that they have confused the definition with another term. One of the most effective ways to study terminology is with study cards. You can create your own terminology study cards by following these simple steps.

1. Use 3 by 5 or 4 by 6 index cards.

2. Write a term in the center of a card. Also list the course and chapter number so you can easily keep your cards organized.

3. Give the following information on the reverse side:
    The textbook definition.
    Your paraphrased definition.
    The concept to which the term relates.
    Any other example or helpful encoding strategy.

Figure 8–7 shows three cards made for the terms introduced earlier in the chapter. Once you have made your cards, you can quiz yourself on the definition orally or in writing. As you practice, separate the difficult terms from those you have mastered. Then give extra practice time to the more challenging terms. When you can use the terminology of the chapter with ease, you are ready to practice with summarizing and questioning.

Summarizing.   As you know from Chapter 1, summarizing is an excellent learning technique because it is a form of paraphrasing. Your summaries can be either oral or written. Select a section of the chapter and recite as much of the important information as you can. Then evaluate your summary based on the three Cs: Is it correct, concise, and clear? Make notes of your weak spots and then try a written summary. Double-space your writing so you can add or correct information when you compare your summary to the actual text. Continue this process until you have a complete summary for the entire chapter.

Questioning.   Another excellent technique is questioning. Learning objectives provided by the instructor and textbook objectives are your best sources of questions. Textbook review questions are also helpful. If none of these are provided, you can use the headings and the basic question words—who, what, why, where, when, or how—to create practice questions. How would you convert this heading into a question?

PROTECTING THE CONFIDENTIALITY OF CLIENT FILES

Three words—*what, why,* and *how*—easily create good questions:

What client information is considered confidential?

Why should you protect client confidentiality?

How do you protect client confidentiality?

Of course, just creating questions is not enough. You must quiz yourself by answering them orally or in writing. You might be surprised how similar your questions are to those of your instructors at exam time. Throughout phase 3 remember to set high mastery standards so you can achieve high test grades.

Retaining what you read is necessary for more than the next exam. Employers will expect you to bring expertise in your specific career area and broad knowledge in related areas. Gain career knowledge by carefully reading your textbooks in three phases: survey, read in depth, and practice for long-term retention.

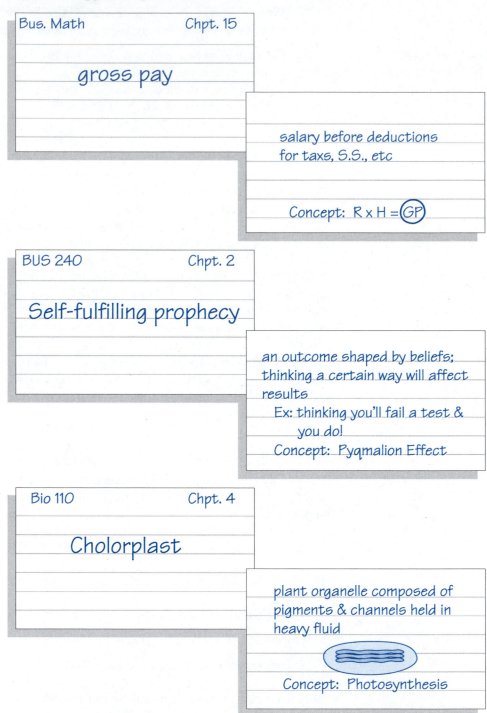

FIGURE 8-7   *Terminology Study Cards*

INFORMATION FILE: READING CHECK-UP

Prescription: An American Reading Partnership . . .

Many American companies have become involved in raising the reading levels of their employees. One notable program is sponsored by the Coors brewery. At Coors, current and retired employees tutor workers *and* their family members to improve reading and attain high school diplomas. Although companies and educators are pleased with the results of such programs, they know that the key to reading success is in the home, because the single greatest contributor to children's reading growth is the amount of reading they share with their parents. It's up to US—at home, at school, and at work!

THE ASAP REWIND «« «

How can I improve my comprehension of complex subjects?

Look for patterns of information in these subject areas:

Mathematics.

Social sciences.

Natural sciences.

Skill courses.

How can I pace my heavy reading load without reducing my comprehension?

Establish a reading/note-taking cycle to enhance comprehension and reduce stress.

How can I improve my retention of what I read?

Read your assignments in these three phases:

1. Survey.

2. Read in depth.

3. Practice with self-quizzing.

TAKE ACTION

Exercise 1

Directions: Put all your reading strategies to work by practicing in-depth reading in the following chapter section adapted from the paralegal textbook *Introduction to Paralegal Studies: A Skills Approach* by Leslie Magryta, J.D. Complete these phases of the reading system.

Phase 1:   Survey.

Phase 2:   Read two times by sections.
           Underline.
           Make text notations.
           Analyze graphic material.

<table>
<tr><td>CHAPTER
1</td><td># The Paralegal Profession</td></tr>
</table>

Learning Objectives

Chapter 1 will help you learn:

- What kind of work paralegals do.
- How people become paralegals.
- The basic skills a paralegal needs.
- The difference between paralegals and secretaries.
- The difference between paralegals and lawyers.
- What constitutes the unauthorized practice of law.
- About professional organizations for paralegals.
- About licensing and certification of paralegals.
- Where a paralegal can expect to find a job.

Welcome to a profession that has only been in existence in the United States for about 20 years. Because the profession is so new, the 1976 edition of *The American Heritage Dictionary* had no entry for either the words *paralegal* or *legal assistant*. Although clerical help has been available to lawyers for centuries, the concept of a paralegal or legal assistant—that is, someone who can assist with legal work—has existed for only a few years.

Many lay people and lawyers are unsure about what a paralegal actually is. For example, one attorney called the placement office of a college offering paralegal courses and stated, "I want to hire a paralegal who can type 60 words a minute." After further discussion with the lawyer, the placement director determined that the lawyer actually wanted to hire a legal secretary and had misunderstood the meaning of

1

Source for material on pages 211 through 221: Leslie Magryta, *Introduction to Paralegal Studies* (Homewood, Ill.: Richard D. Irwin, 1993), pp 1–10. Used with permission.

paralegal. At the other extreme, paralegals have received calls from clients seeking legal representation in divorce cases. The paralegal then had to explain to the client that although paralegals can work on cases under the supervision of an attorney, they are unable to represent clients themselves.

The purpose of Chapter 1 is to answer many of your questions about the paralegal profession. The chapter will begin by defining paralegal, explaining the type of work paralegals perform, and discussing the skills a person needs to develop to be able to perform this work. Next, the chapter will explore how individuals become paralegals, what professional organizations exist for paralegals, and the licensing and certification of paralegals. Then, we will explain the differences between a paralegal and a secretary, and between a paralegal and a lawyer. Here, we also include a discussion of what constitutes the unauthorized practice of law by lay persons. We finish the chapter by discussing the numerous and varied employment opportunities for paralegals.

Defining the Paralegal Role

What Is a Paralegal?

A **paralegal** is a nonlawyer who has the education, training, and experience to perform legal tasks once performed only by lawyers. Attorneys often divide a case into tasks and then delegate work to the paralegal to perform under the attorney's supervision. By doing this, the lawyer frees himself or herself to concentrate on the tasks requiring more skill, or on making the crucial decisions about the case. Likewise, a doctor delegates to paramedics or nurses the work of gathering the vital signs, administering medications, or giving shots to a patient. In doing so, the doctor frees himself or herself to make major decisions about diagnosis or treatment. The idea of dividing a job into component tasks is also used on assembly lines. Although a worker might lack the knowledge to build an entire car, he or she can become an expert at performing a certain task, such as welding a part onto the car chassis. Likewise, a paralegal can become an expert at preparing cases for trial or at preparing the documents needed to probate a will.

Several paralegal organizations and the American Bar Association have adopted formal definitions for the term *paralegal* or **legal assistant.** For example, the National Federation of Paralegal Associations defined paralegal, or legal assistant, as follows:

> A paralegal/legal assistant is a person, qualified through education, training, or work experience to perform substantive legal work that requires knowledge of legal concepts and is customarily, but not exclusively, performed by a lawyer. This person may be retained or employed by a lawyer, law office, governmental agency, or other entity or may be authorized by administrative, statutory, or court authority to perform this work.

Another paralegal organization, the National Association of Legal Assistants (NALA), also has defined legal assistant or paralegal:

> Legal assistants are a distinguishable group of persons who assist attorneys in the delivery of legal services. Through formal education, training, and experience, legal assistants have knowledge and expertise regarding the legal system and substantive and procedural law which qualify them to do work of a legal nature under the supervision of an attorney.

These definitions indicate that a paralegal, or legal assistant, is an individual who performs legal work under the supervision of an attorney. A paralegal is also known by a number of other names, such as legal assistant, law clerk, legal technician, lay advocate, and lawyer's aide. Regardless of title, paralegals are an important part of the team providing legal services in the law firm, in business, and in government. To understand exactly what you will be doing in your new career field, you need to have a basic understanding of what constitutes legal work.

What Does a Paralegal Do?

Legal work that paralegals perform includes interviewing and maintaining contact with clients, investigation, legal research, legal writing, drafting legal documents, and preparing cases for trial. This list is not exhaustive since there is an infinite variety of duties that paralegals perform.

Interviewing Clients.   One aspect of legal work is interviewing clients and maintaining communication with them. Contact with the client usually begins with an initial interview between the lawyer and the client, with the paralegal sometimes listening and participating in the interview. Some firms even have paralegals conduct initial client interviews without an attorney present. A nationwide survey of paralegals conducted by the National Association of Legal Assistants in 1989 reported that 74 percent of all paralegals participate in attorney-client meetings.

After the initial interview and after the client hires the law firm, the attorney often makes the paralegal a contact person for the client. Consequently, the paralegal is in charge of updating clients on the status of their case and of answering the clients' routine questions. For example, one paralegal, Julie, works for a lawyer who limits her practice to divorce law. Julie's supervising attorney often has her attend and participate in the interview of new divorce clients. After the lawyer ends the interview, Julie often continues interviewing the client to gather the information needed to draft legal documents for their case. Julie is also responsible for taking client calls and keeping clients informed of the status of their divorces. She refers the calls to the attorney when the client has a question requiring legal advice.

4   *Chapter 1*

The 1989 national survey of paralegals conducted by the National Association of Legal Assistants indicated that 57 percent of all paralegals surveyed have daily contact with clients while 79 percent of them have at least weekly contact with clients.

Investigation and the Interview of Witnesses.   Another aspect of legal work is investigation and the interview of witnesses. The first paralegal job for Mark, a recent paralegal graduate, was to interview all witnesses involved in a series of lawsuits filed against an asbestos manufacturer. He was to audiotape or videotape each witness's interview. Mark was also required to summarize each interview for his supervising attorney. Larry, a paralegal who works for an attorney specializing in criminal defense law, is heavily involved in the investigation of crimes such as first-degree murder, rape, and burglary. Larry's good investigative work has been crucial to the success of his supervising attorney in criminal defense work.

Legal Research.   Legal work also involves legal research—a system of looking in law books to find the law on a legal question or legal issue. Legal research is very important because having the most accurate and up-to-date law can greatly influence the outcome of the client's case.

The 1989 nationwide survey of paralegals conducted by the NALA reported that 58 percent of paralegals with less than one year's experience do some legal research. As the number of years of experience increased, the percentage of paralegals doing legal research increased. For example, the survey indicated that 59 percent of paralegals with 1 to 3 years of experience and 68 percent with more than 10 years' experience do some legal research.

The reason only two thirds of paralegals do legal research may be due in part to the type of law practice in which the paralegal works. If a paralegal's primary job is to do real estate closings, it is unlikely that he or she would be given legal research assignments, too. Another reason why only two thirds of all paralegals receive legal research assignments is that some attorneys prefer to do their own legal research.

However, in many law firms, attorneys use paralegals extensively to conduct legal research. For example, Lori, a paralegal working for an attorney specializing in personal injury, spends much of her time researching questions of liability. Lori enjoys researching so much that it has become the most satisfying aspect of her job.

Writing and Legal Writing.   Another important aspect of legal work is writing. A typical paralegal does a lot of everyday writing—that is, writing that contains no reference to legal authority. For example, everyday writing might include a letter to a client informing him or her of a trial date and how to best assist the law firm with trial preparation. Everyday writing might also include a fact interoffice memo summarizing information found through an investigation.

The paralegal also does two other types of writing: legal writing and legal document drafting. Legal writing includes writing anything containing legal authority, such as a letter, an interoffice memo, or a legal brief written for a judge to read. Although new paralegals begin with smaller writing assignments, more experienced paralegals are often assigned to write briefs submitted to the trial judge, and some paralegals even write appellate briefs.

Document drafting is also very important to the practice of law. The 1989 national survey of paralegals conducted by the NALA indicated that 50 percent of all paralegals draft legal documents on a daily basis and 76 percent draft pleadings or documents at least weekly. Paralegals are heavily involved in preparing legal documents because every lawsuit contains many of them. These documents, called *pleadings,* are filed with the court to have a legal effect or to request a judge to make a decision. Someone has to draft these pleadings, and often it is the paralegal who does so. Paralegals are often assigned to draft documents that involve no lawsuit, such as wills, deeds, partnership agreements, and contracts. Fortunately for the paralegal, there are often examples of the documents that he or she can use as guides for creating the new document.

Susan, a paralegal working for an attorney who does a large number of adoptions, often drafts all the documents needed for the adoption. Susan keeps a notebook containing examples of all of the documents needed for an adoption and refers to them when she is working on a new case. The attorney finds Susan's work indispensable since her ability to correctly and accurately draft the documents frees the lawyer to concentrate on other aspects of the adoption case. Susan enjoys her job very much because she is doing almost everything on each adoption case!

Preparing for and Attending Trials.   Another aspect of legal work is preparing for and attending trials. Often, attorneys assign paralegals the task of preparing everything for trial from contacting and interviewing witnesses to preparing documents and exhibits, which are the physical evidence submitted in court. Attorneys often have the paralegal who helped prepare the case assist them with the trial.

What type of legal work you will perform as a paralegal depends upon where you work and for whom you work.

What Skills Are Needed to Perform Legal Work?

To perform legal work, a person needs three basic skills: the ability to organize, to communicate, and to analyze.

Organizational skills are particularly important because attorneys may assign their paralegal numerous projects to do at once. The paralegal must be able to organize his or her work so that projects are completed on time. Timeliness is essential because the practice of law is riddled with deadlines. For example, in one week attorney Alexandra Tolman must file with the court a brief arguing the position of her client, Goldman Chocolate Factory, for a hearing that is to be held in two weeks' time. Her paralegal Megan is assigned the job of researching and writing a rough draft of the brief, which is to be completed within four days. Megan completes the project in four days, and Attorney Tolman spends the next three days reviewing it and redrafting it. She turns the brief in on time. Judge O'Malley reads the brief and on the day of the hearing rules in favor of Goldman Chocolate Factory.

Another paralegal, Zena, who is asked to complete a similar assignment for clients Jim and Hilda Robinson, forgets about the deadline. Zena does the research and brief but turns it in late—in seven days instead of four and only after prompting by her supervising attorney. The attorney, Mary Hooper, does a hurry-up job of reviewing the brief and then files and serves the brief two days after the deadline. At the hearing, the opposing attorney Oran Fisher complains about the late brief and asks for a continuance to reply to the brief. (A continuance means that the hearing will be delayed and heard on another date.) The client, Mr. Robinson, who has had to miss work and drive 50 miles to the hearing, becomes angry after the continuance is granted and yells at Ms. Hooper, the attorney. Ms. Hooper then expresses concern to Zena about not completing projects on time.

Organizing your time is important, but easy, if you have developed a system to follow. Chapter 2 includes a discussion of techniques recommended by time-management experts for organizing your time.

Paralegals also use organizational skills to prepare cases for trial and to organize documents and exhibits. (Exhibits are items such as clothing, a weapon, or photographs used as evidence in a trial.) Because legal secretaries may be unaware of what certain documents are, attorneys often rely on paralegals to organize cases for them. A lawyer who has a well-organized case has a better chance to win at trial.

Communication skills are important to a paralegal because of the constant need to communicate with clients, attorneys, and other legal staff members. Oral communication and the ability to work well as a member of a team are important. A paralegal needs to be able to get along well with others.

Of even greater importance are writing skills. Writing permeates every aspect of the practice of law, from writing a simple letter to

The Paralegal Profession

7

Figure 1
Duties of Paralegals

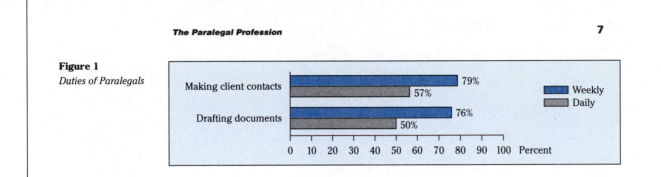

Figure 2

*Type of Education
Completed by Paralegals*

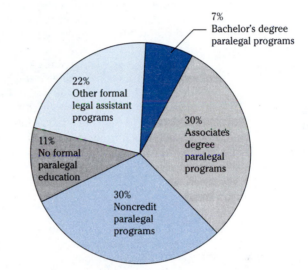

Source: 1989 National survey of Paralegals conducted by the National Association of Legal Assistants.

Figure 3

Growth in Formal Paralegal Education

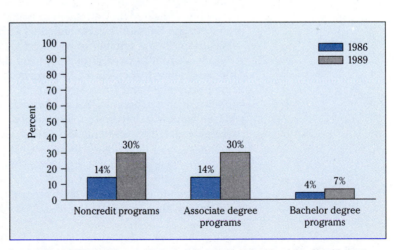

Source: 1986 and 1989 National Surveys of Paralegals conducted by the Nationsl Association of Legal Assistants.

creating an appellate brief. A paralegal who can write well will be indispensable to his or her supervising attorney. If you feel that you do not write well, take a basic writing course at your college; practice your writing in this course and in other paralegal courses in order to improve your skills.

Writing well is like playing a sport well or like playing a musical instrument well. Imagine the situation of your not having played your flute since high school, which was 10 years ago. Your playing would be rusty! The same is true with writing. If you have written very little in the last few years, or have not reviewed the basic tenets of good writing recently, your writing might be rusty, too. The more you practice and the more you concentrate on mastering basic skills, the better your writing will be. Because writing can be improved with practice, one of the goals of this book is to provide you with the opportunity to begin polishing your writing skills.

Analytical skills are also important to success in the paralegal profession. They involve the ability to research both law and factual information, and then to apply this information to the client's case. The capability to find and analyze law and facts improves with practice. This course will introduce you to the analytical process involved in the legal profession.

How Do People Become Paralegals?

People become paralegals in two ways: they take courses (or earn a degree) in paralegal studies, or they work into the position from a legal secretarial or clerical job.

Although there are two ways to become a paralegal, a growing number of paralegals working in the legal profession have some formal paralegal education. In the 1989 NALA survey, 89 percent of those responding indicated they attended or completed a formal legal assistant program. The 1989 survey also indicated a significant increase, since the 1986 survey, in the number of paralegals attending paralegal education programs—from 14 percent to 30 percent for those attending noncredit programs, from 14 percent to 30 percent for those attending associate degree programs, and from 4 percent to 7 percent for those attending bachelor degree programs. These statistics indicate that receiving paralegal education is becoming increasingly common even among those paralegals already working in the field.

Colleges and universities throughout the United States offer a variety of paralegal programs, lasting from three months to four years. In shorter programs, the student attends classes for three months to two years, depending on the college program. Often individuals earn a certificate at the end of their course of study.

Colleges and universities also offer paralegal programs in which the student earns an associate degree after two years or a bachelor's degree after four years of study. Many paralegal programs require the student to complete an internship before graduation. Internships provide the student with valuable work experience.

The American Bar Association (ABA) has established a committee that sets forth standards for paralegal programs and has a commission that approves programs. To gain approval, a program must follow strict guidelines regarding the types of classes and the number of semester or quarter hours needed to complete the certificate or degree. By 1990, the ABA had approved only 134 of the 500 paralegal programs in existence in the United States, or about 23 percent. For either economic or philosophical reasons, many schools have never sought approval by the ABA even though many of these programs closely follow the guidelines given by the ABA. Instead, many programs rely on their college accreditation granted through college accreditation bodies. Whether or not ABA approval is important in a hiring decision depends upon the general philosophy of the law firm or business involved. To some employers, ABA approval is important. To other employers, the qualifications of the applicant are paramount regardless of whether or not the paralegal attended an ABA approved school.

Many of the paralegal programs in existence today were started recently. Some may not have gained ABA approval because they have been in existence for only a short time. Prior to the 1970s, no formal education programs existed for paralegals anywhere in the United States. During the 1980s, many colleges and universities started paralegal programs.

Surveys show that paralegals who have more paralegal education generally start at a higher salary than those attending a shorter course of study. However, the choice on the length of an educational course must be geared to the student's individual life situation.

Legal Secretary to Paralegal.   Some individuals become paralegals by working into the position from the job of legal secretary. Often, by virtue of their experience, these persons are given paralegal duties in addition to their secretarial duties. One advantage to becoming a paralegal after being a legal secretary is the valuable experience that has been gained. However, one of the disadvantages to entering the profession this way is that the attorneys may still perceive the paralegal as a secretary and continue to assign clerical duties such as typing, filing, and answering the phone. In this situation, the paralegal may feel a frustrating underutilization of her skills. This method of becoming a paralegal can work for both the secretary and the law firm if the law firm allows the secretary to move into a paralegal position and perform fewer clerical duties. Legal secretaries who want to work into a paralegal position with their current employer will find that they have more opportunity to do so if they also complete some type of paralegal education.

Certified Legal Assistant Designation.   Legal secretaries who have much experience but no formal paralegal education may seek to gain more recognition of their abilities by taking the certified legal assistant exam administered by the National Association of Legal Assistants. This program is also helpful for the paralegal who has a bachelor's degree in another subject but has little formal paralegal education.

By passing this exam, the paralegal may call himself or herself a **certified legal assistant,** abbreviated as **CLA.** To sit for the certified legal assistant exam, the paralegal is not required to take any classes. Instead, the CLA applicant must study on his own the material tested in the examination. To be eligible to sit for the CLA exam, the paralegal must meet one of the requirements listed below (requirements effective January 1, 1991):

1. Graduation from a legal assistant program that is:
   a. Approved by the American Bar Association.
   b. An associate degree program.
   c. A post-baccalaureate certificate program in legal assistant studies.
   d. A bachelor's degree program in legal assistant studies.
   e. A legal assistant program that consists of a minimum of 60 semester hours (or equivalent quarter hours) of which at least 15 semester hours (or equivalent quarter hours) are substantive legal courses.
2. A bachelor's degree in any field plus one year's experience as a legal assistant.
3. A high school diploma or equivalent plus seven years' experience as a legal assistant under the supervision of a member of the bar, plus evidence of a minimum of 20 hours of continuing legal education credit to have been completed within a two-year period prior to the examination date.

The CLA examination, which is a two-day written test, is given three times a year in major cities throughout the United States, including once a year at the national NALA convention. The exam tests English skills, such as word usage, grammar, and sentence structure, as well as legal ethics, human relations and interviewing techniques, judgment and analytical ability, and legal research and terminology. The exam also includes a substantive law section in which the applicant chooses to be examined in four of eight specialty law areas. After an individual has passed the two-day exam and has become a CLA, he or she may apply for and test for specialty certification in several areas, such as civil litigation, probate and estate planning, corporate and business law, criminal law and procedure, and real estate. The specialty certification test is a four-hour exam.

Students often wonder whether they need to go to school to be a paralegal if they can just take the CLA exam. According to individuals who have taken it, the exam is difficult and required months of study; some individuals had to retake several sections of the exam in order to pass. Also, the danger with the CLA program is that it is not universally accepted or even acknowledged by attorneys. Some attorneys who have worked with CLA paralegals have a good opinion of the program because of the quality of the individual paralegal. However, there is more recognition for the program in some parts of the country than in others.

When employers advertise for a person with a paralegal certificate, they are usually referring to a certificate awarded by a college or university, not the CLA designation.

SUMMARY

Legal work performed by paralegals includes
- Interviewing and maintaining contact with clients.
- Investiation.
- Legal research.
- Legal writing.
- Drafting legal documents.
- Preparing cases for trial.

To perform legal work, a paralegal needs the ability to
- Organize.
- Communicate.
- Analyze.

Paralegals prepare for the profession by
- Taking courses in the field.
- Earning a degree in paralegal studies.
- Working first in a secretarial or clerical job.

Exercise 2

Directions: Use your word meaning techniques: word parts, context clues, and dictionary to define each of these words from the sample chapter. Find and define these words, then use each word in an original sentence. The number following each word indicates the page on which you can find it in the sample reading.

lay (p. 1) _____

_____

_____

delegate (p. 2) _____

_____

_____

entity (p. 2) _____

_____

_____

riddled (p. 6) _____

_____

_____

permeates (p. 6) _____

_____

_____

accreditation (p. 9) _____

_____

_____

paramount (p. 9) _____

_____

_____

perceive (p. 9) _____

_____

_____

underutilization (p. 9) _____

_____

_____

universally (p. 11) _____

_____

_____

TAKE ACTION

Exercise 3

Directions: Answer each of the following questions about the sample reading.

1.   Identify the four major topics of this chapter section.

_____

_____

_____

2.   Define in your own words the term *paralegal.* Give a synonym for *paralegal.*

_____

_____

_____

3.   Study the graphs in Figures 1 to 3 on page 7 of the sample reading and circle the letters of the statements that can logically be inferred from the data presented.

Figure 1
A.   Of the paralegals surveyed, 21 percent *do not* meet with clients during the workweek.
B.   Drafting legal documents occupies 76 percent of most paralegals' time.
C.   One in two paralegals drafts documents daily.

Figure 2
A.   89 percent of paralegals have completed formal training in the field.
B.   Degree programs are more popular than noncredit programs.
C.   Most attorneys prefer to hire paralegals with formal training.

Figure 3
A.   Between 1986 and 1989, the number of paralegals attending noncredit programs more than doubled.
B.   Associate degree programs in paralegalism grew at the same rate as noncredit programs.
C.   Bachelor degree programs are increasing at a slower rate than the other two categories.

Exercise 4

Directions: Prepare the significant information from this chapter for self-quizzing. Make a study card for each of these terms: *paralegal, NALA,* and *CLA.*

FRONT

BACK

FRONT

BACK

FRONT

BACK

Exercise 5

Directions: Write a brief summary for each of the four major headings in the sample chapter. Do not refer to the text to make your summary. Instead, practice quizzing yourself on the section. When you have achieved mastery, write your summary here.

1. _____

_____

_____

_____

_____

_____

_____

_____

_____

2. _____

_____

3. _____

4. _____

CHECK YOUR PROGRESS

Directions: Put into action the principles of reading for retention! At the end of one week, use this checklist to evaluate your progress. Then use the space that follows to analyze your growth.

PROGRESS CHECKLIST: Improving Reading Retention

Yes   Usually   No

___ ___ ___ **1.** I use strategies to improve my basic comprehension and reduce my frustrations when reading textbooks.

___ ___ ___ **2.** I look for informational patterns when reading textbooks in mathematics, social sciences, science, and skill courses.

___ ___ ___ **3.** I have established a reading/note-taking cycle in each of my courses to improve the learning process.

___ ___ ___ **4.** I read my chapters using the three reading phases.

A. Discuss the ways in which you have changed your approach to reading textbook chapters. Explain the strategies that have reduced your frustrations and improved your comprehension and retention.

B. Identify the courses in which you would like to improve further your reading strategies and discuss ways you might accomplish those goals.

You Be the Critic.   Describe in a line or two what you enjoy reading and why you find it enjoyable. Make a quick list of recommended readings and exchange with a classmate. You may learn about different and exciting sources for pleasure reading.

Building Listening and Note-Taking Skills

THE SKILL THAT GETS THE JOB

Order Desk Clerk.
For a busy wholesaler. We are looking for a good listener with excellent interpersonal skills and the ability to handle telephone orders with accuracy and speed. Opportunities for advancement.

WHAT'S YOUR EXPERIENCE?

The old expression "I'm all ears" explains just part of listening dynamics. What elements of effective listening do you think are missing from that saying? How do you rate your listening and note-taking abilities? What would you like to learn about these very important skills? Use the space below to explore your skill, your knowledge, and any questions you have about this chapter's topic.

_____

_____

_____

_____

_____

_____

_____

_____

_____

_____

_____

In this chapter you will learn to

»»»   **Listen actively.**

»»»   **Change ineffective listening habits.**

»»»   **Prepare for note taking.**

»»»   **Select and organize information.**

»»»   **Keep pace with time savers.**

»»»   **Review and practice notes to increase understanding.**

BUILDING LISTENING AND NOTE-TAKING SKILLS

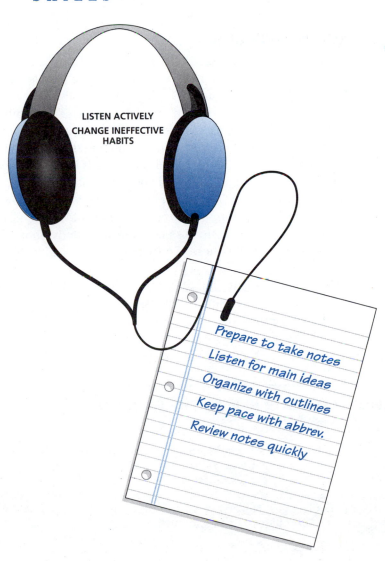

Do you sometimes wish for a silent world—no car horns, no noisy children, no 50-minute lectures? Amid the buzz of signals and voices that people hear each day are vital messages and information that they must receive, comprehend, and retain. Experts estimate that almost half of your communication time is spent listening. Is it time well spent? Studies indicate that listening accuracy is limited and that people quickly forget much of what they have heard. Most poor listening stems from a lack of involvement in the communication process.

Developing your listening skills is important for understanding your lectures and, consequently, for taking good lecture notes. Business and industry also value listening as an employee skill. The Sperry Corporation offers their employees listening training. Why? Poor listening is costly to business. When an employee does not use good listening skills, the result can be poor customer relationships, delay in services, and loss of profits. This chapter will guide you in

- Becoming an active listener in common listening situations.

- Overcoming ineffective listening habits.

- Taking useful notes while listening.

ACTIVE LISTENING

You can use just your ears to listen for the whistling signal of a tea kettle, but you need what's between your ears when listening to people and complex information. **Active listening** is the process of being personally involved in the communication process through observing the speaker and thinking about the message at an inferential level as well as a literal level. When you are listening actively, your ears, mind, and eyes are engaged in understanding the information and the nuances of how the information is communicated. Much listening is passive rather than active. Passive listeners listen out of obligation rather than personal interest and hear just a basic message. They often hear partial statements because they are waiting for the speaker to stop so they can go on to something else or so they can speak themselves. These passive listeners are frequently short-changed. Compare the knowledge gained by these two students in a typical lecture situation:

nuances

> *Instructor:* "The further globalization of markets is the wave of the future. This important and interesting issue affects not just our field of study but all areas of business."

INFORMATION FILE: PUT YOUR EAR TO THE GROUND

Listening to Heavenly Bodies . . .

The American space agency, NASA, has been listening to the heavens. What do they hope to hear? They scan the skies day and night with special telescopes in Puerto Rico and California to detect signs of intelligent life from outer space. These scientists reason that an intelligent life form would develop principles of math and science similar to ours. Thus, these beings could communicate with us through radio waves. Other scientists disagree. Nevertheless, the program will continue for approximately 10 years at an estimated cost of $100 million. Get your welcome mat ready.

Student 1: "Globalization will continue in the future."

Student 2: "In the future even more markets will be globalized, affecting all areas of business. Mrs. D. thinks this is important—probably a big test question! Could I use it for my paper topic?"

The first student passively picked up just the basic information presented in the first sentence and completely missed the valuable learning the second student received through active listening. Active listening is essential when you want to

- Build a relationship with the speaker.
- Acquire useful information.
- Accomplish an important task.

Often these are simultaneous goals, making active listening strategies a high priority. How you apply active listening strategies will vary with your role in the communication flow. The most common listening roles for students are as listener-copartner and as listener-observer.

Listener-Copartner

As a **listener-copartner** you are actively engaged in both listening and speaking with the other people involved. This is your role in most classes, many family settings, and work situations. Typically, students do not think of themselves as copartners in the classroom communication process. Avoid that passive approach to your learning and your relationships. Try out these strategies for being an effective copartner in the classroom, during discussions, or in meetings.

1. **Understand what is expected of you as a listener in each situation.** In your classes your instructors expect you to
    - Be on time.
    - Read and prepare before class.
    - Take notes from lectures.

   In meetings you may be asked to follow a specific agenda for discussing topics. Usually business meetings address old topics first, then listen to committee reports, and finally ask for new topics of discussion.

2. **Really listen to what the speaker is saying.** Often people just listen for a break in the conversation so they can speak. Frequently their comments are inappropriate because their ideas are not linked to what was previously said. In that case the conversation becomes a contest for who will continue to speak, and useful communication breaks down.

3. **Maintain good eye contact with the speaker.** In doing so, you signal to the speaker that you are truly listening, and you also maintain your concentration. The supportive link you establish with the speaker can be helpful to you when you want a turn as speaker or when you want to ask a question in the classroom.

empathic

WITH A LITTLE HELP FROM MY FRIENDS

Listening to help others is an important part of personal relationships. In this capacity the effective listener uses empathic listening strategies to understand the speaker's needs. Here are some tips you can use when you're called upon to be that understanding friend.

- **Let your friend express his or her thoughts and needs.** Keep your talking to a minimum, and don't rush in with "helpful suggestions."

- **Keep good eye contact with your friend and observe body language and speech patterns for subtle messages.** Your friend's movements and facial expressions can alert you to feelings of confusion, embarrassment, or anger. You can detect similar messages in the pace of someone's speech and tone of voice. A high-pitched voice often signals nervousness; gaps in speech might indicate uncertainty or fear.

- **Give your friend a nod of the head or an encouraging word to signal that you are listening and that you understand.**

- **Encourage your friend to continue speaking by paraphrasing what has been said or mirroring the feelings expressed.** You might say, for example, "So the test grade came as a complete shock, and you're feeling really discouraged."

- **Extend your feelings to the other person when appropriate, but remember to focus on that individual's needs.**

- **Maintain confidentiality at all times.** Often friends indicate that a conversation should be held in confidence. At other times, people do not specifically indicate that the information is private. To avoid misunderstanding, treat every serious personal conversation as confidential.

P.S. You can listen and help, but you don't have to *solve* another person's problem.

INFORMATION FILE: PUT YOUR EAR TO THE GROUND

Listening for Fetal Bodies . . .

In an effort to provide their children with an early advantage in life, some mothers are sending messages to their children before they are born. These women are wearing an electronic belt that transmits sounds similar to the human heart beat to the womb. The device is marketed by the Prelearning Research Institute, which claims that children who have listened to the "cardiac curriculum" scored 25 percent higher on standardized tests. Many moms are also enthusiastic about their children's development. However, some experts are doubtful of the results and are concerned about potential harm to the fetus.

4. **Use your eye contact to observe the speaker's nonverbal communication so you can fully understand her or his message.** Nonverbal communication includes the messages people convey through

- Eye contact.
- Body posture and movements.
- Facial expressions.
- Speech patterns.

These signals are particularly important in classroom settings because an instructor's body movements can provide you with clues to the information that is important for exams. Some teachers will use emphatic hand motions or write information on the chalkboard when making an important point. Often, body language is accompanied by changes in speech patterns. Usually when instructors speed up the pace of their sentences and speak in a higher pitch, they are excited. Sometimes instructors intentionally slow down the speed of their delivery to provide emphasis for important information.

5. **Paraphrase what the speaker is saying and take notes if the information is to be used at a later date.** The average speaker communicates about 150 words per minute whereas the listener is capable of hearing approximately 300 words each minute. If you are alert, you can use that gap to paraphrase the words of the speaker. Figure 9–1 demonstrates the dynamics between a lecturer and a "silent" participant in class. Notice how the student follows the speaker's logic at each step and makes the information personal.

6. **Provide feedback to the speaker and group when appropriate.** Actively participate to give others the benefit of your thinking and experience by

- Asking questions.
- Providing agreement.
- Suggesting alternatives.

Often when students are dissatisfied with a lecture or a discussion, they simply wait for it to end instead of trying to improve communication. By doing so they relinquish their power to others and actually contribute to the *status quo*. Chapter 1 introduced techniques for asking clear and concise questions. Review them now if you have been hesitant to ask questions in your classes. You *can* improve the quality of your learning experiences.

status quo

Be a full copartner in group situations by listening actively, taking notes, and providing helpful feedback.

Listener-Observer

Copartner listening situations are ideal for learning and developing relationships. Sometimes, however, a full exchange between the speaker and the listener is not practical. During formal speeches, in large lecture settings, and for audiovisual presentations, you become a listener-observer with less open participation. These are some of the most difficult listening situations because they provide few opportunities for you to interact with the speaker. Some students actually view these situations as opportunities to completely disengage from the communication process. While grabbing a quick nap, the student loses valuable information—a

FIGURE 9–1   *Paraphrasing the Lecture Message*

review of all formulas required for the upcoming test, an interesting issue that could be used as a paper topic. To make the most of listener-observer situations, use these strategies.

1. **Set a personal learning goal by choosing something you would like to learn from this listening experience.** A goal will help you focus your attention. While waiting for the presentation, you can formulate one or two broad questions that you expect to be answered. For example, your merchandising instructor has indicated you will have a video presentation on methods of discounting merchandise. You can quickly brainstorm questions such as these:

    How is merchandise discounted?

    What are the advantages of discounting merchandise?

    Are there times when discounts do not help profits?

    Now you have three specific reasons to stay awake in a dark room at 3 in the afternoon.

2. **Closely watch the visual aids used in the presentation.** In large lecture settings, instructors often employ overhead transparencies or slides to display important and complex information such as examples, summaries, and analytical data. Since you will not be able to establish eye contact or observe nonverbal forms of communication firsthand in these classes, focus on the visual aids to maintain concentration and enhance comprehension. Challenge yourself to understand and record in your notes each concept presented through visual aids.

overt

3. **Actively engage your mind in processing the information you are hearing.** Since overt participation is minimal in listener-observer situations, your mental involvement is very important. Listen, paraphrase the main concepts, and critically analyze what is being said. Often in listener-observer situations, people do not evaluate the logic or accuracy of the message. Because they are not actively engaged in a discussion format, people take a passive approach and simply accept what they are hearing. This can be a dangerous approach. Sales presentations and political speeches often contain highly emotional information that is not logical or factual and is intended to sway the listener. For example, the following advertisement suggests that a large majority of citizens favor one candidate and that he is unbeatable, but no specific facts are given to support those suggestions.

Over 70 percent of the people voted Bob Burns most qualified for the position of school board president. Bob Burns and the people of Sherbrooke County—an unbeatable combination for the future of our children!

This ad is designed to sway the voter without really informing. Resist the sway of speeches and advertisements by engaging all your listening powers for maximum learning in listener-observer situations.

INEFFECTIVE LISTENING HABITS

Most likely your effectiveness as a listener-copartner or a listener-observer varies with your interest and concentration. In one course you might fulfill each step effortlessly, whereas in another you struggle to focus on the speaker's words. People seek diversion to escape from an uninteresting or negative listening situation. With repeated use of escape behavior, they develop ineffective listening habits. What are your ineffective listening habits? If you recognize your negative habits, you can strive to replace them with your active listening skills.

Daydreaming and Other Pastimes

Daydreaming is a typical way people escape from a listening situation. Students plan trips, think about new dates, and attempt to solve problems as important information passes them by. Some daydreamers add **doodling** to their escapes strategies. Where valuable notes should be written, flowers bloom and comic book heroes emerge. Most daydreamers are minimally entertained by their activities, so

INFORMATION FILE: PUT YOUR EAR TO THE GROUND

Listening with an Accent . . .

A biologist in England has discovered that birds of the same species sing differently in different regions of the country. By recording the songs of birds in the south of England and their cousins in Wales, the scientist was able to detect distinct patterns for each group. In other words, the birds had regional accents, just as humans do. When he played the songs of one group to the other birds, they reacted much like humans who hear an unfamiliar accent. The birds sang louder, puffed their feathers, and even tried to peck something.

they **watch the clock,** noting the minutes as they go by instead of recording the homework instructions. **Avoid daydreaming by actively taking notes and joining in discussion groups.**

Negative Listening

During your lifetime you are sure to encounter speakers who are entertaining and can teach with great ease. You will also encounter many who are difficult to follow and "turn you off." Some people escape from these situations by **focusing on negative characteristics** of the speaker. Instead of listening more intently to overcome the difficulty, these escape artists count the number of *ums* the speaker utters or criticize a physical aspect of the speaker, such as wardrobe. Although some students might find this pastime entertaining, they are losing valuable information and establishing a negative learning cycle. **Focus on the content of the lecture with strong, specific listening goals to overcome the negative aspects of a speaker.**

In other situations, people react negatively to the message, not the speaker. Ironically, people are often negative listeners when the topic is very important to them. They reject all viewpoints and information that do not coincide with their own positions. Filtering out information in this way limits the listener to her or his own experience and prevents growth. **Learn about the ideas of others as a means to maintain and strengthen your own beliefs.**

Distractions

covert

Listeners may also have limited concentration because they are frequently distracted by events around them. When boredom sets in, they count cars passing by the window or engage a neighbor in a covert conversation. Then they are lost when they attempt to focus on the speaker again, so they turn to the next convenient distraction. Typically three positions in a room are sources of distractions: seats near windows, seats near doors, and seats in the back of a room. The last position is a source of distraction because students who are not serious about listening often sit as far away from the instructor as possible. By sitting there yourself, you make it possible to be distracted and take the risk of associating with less serious listeners. **Position yourself for learning and a positive relationship with the speaker by choosing a seat away from most distractions in the room.**

Pretending to Listen

Pretending to listen is used as a cover by daydreamers, negative listeners, and people who are distracted. These people attempt to give the *appearance* of listening by periodically making good eye contact with the speaker and occasionally providing a positive nod of the head. Usually these listeners believe they have duped or tricked the speaker and the rest of the group. Oddly, they sometimes trick themselves into thinking that their outward signs of active listening equal good listening. Pretending to listen is a detrimental habit because it leads to missing valuable information and misleading the speaker. As a result, true communication does not occur. **Engage in genuine active listening to gain valuable information and maintain positive listening relationships.**

detrimental

CHANGING INEFFECTIVE HABITS

Changing these ineffective listening habits takes more than a resolve to listen actively or to keep an open mind. If you saw yourself in these descriptions of negative listening, you need to reevaluate your basic concentration strategies and strengthen your interest in the subject area.

Concentration

Be sure that you are in top condition for concentrating by double-checking each of these factors. Are you

Managing stress?

Keeping physically fit?

Focusing on your semester goals?

Begin working today on any of these factors that distract from your listening concentration. If necessary, review Chapter 4. When concentration factors are not a problem, ineffective listening usually stems from a lack of interest in the subject area.

Personal Interest

Few people can maintain a high interest level in all topics they encounter. Nevertheless, in many situations, academic and professional obligations require people to overcome their disinterest and perform as active listeners. If you are disinterested in one of your subjects, examine the reasons why. Disinterest typically stems from one of these sources.

1. **The purpose of the information is not fully understood.** Students frequently take courses as part of their program without really knowing why the course is important to school or work. You can better understand the purpose of a course by reading the preface to your textbook and any introductory materials your instructor gave you at the beginning of the semester. Your academic advisor or the course instructor can also help you understand how all your courses fit together and apply to the world of work.

INFORMATION FILE: PUT YOUR EAR TO THE GROUND

Body Language with an Accent . . .

Even if you learn the language of a country, you might be unsuccessful in correctly communicating your message in that culture. Why? If you send the wrong message through body language, you could confuse or possibly offend your host. Here are a few examples of the complexity of body language around the world. In Arab countries, it's rude to stand with your hands in your pockets or to touch someone with your left hand because that hand is considered unclean. In South Korea, moving your arm and hand in a circling motion toward the shoulder is used only to encourage dogs to come forward—*not* people. When a Brazilian pinches her earlobe, she is not confused, she is expressing appreciation. But don't be discouraged by these vast differences in communication. There is one universally used and understood form of body language—YOUR SMILE.

compromised

2. **The material is difficult to understand.** Listening ability can be compromised when people have difficulty understanding the ideas presented by a speaker. If this is your situation, put these corrective steps into action today:

   - Devote more study time to this subject.
   - Make greater use of your textbook, study guides, and any additional materials you can find in your library.
   - Seek help from a study partner, your study group, your instructor, or a tutor.

   If your progress stalls because the subject is difficult, don't allow ineffective listening habits to take hold. Seek ways to master the information and maintain your listening efficiency.

3. **Personal involvement in the topic is lacking.** Sometimes no matter how hard you try to understand the information in and purpose of a course, your negative feelings continue. In these situations, you must discipline yourself to create daily motivation despite your feelings. Each day before class begins, establish a positive mental set with some informal objectives such as these:

   I'll take notes throughout the lecture.

   From last night's reading, I'll listen for these topics:

   - *the state court system*
   - *the federal court system*

   No clock watching!

   When you overcome your negative feelings and see results in your listening and learning, be sure to reward yourself. Then you will be motivated to go in there and try again the next class. This one-day-at-a-time approach slowly builds personal strength and removes some of the frustration that comes with difficult listening situations.

   Cast off the labels that characterize you as a good or bad listener because no one label can describe your abilities in *all* situations. In each listener role, maximize your listening performance by avoiding escape behaviors and emphasizing active listening activities such as paraphrasing, analyzing, and note taking.

TO TAPE OR NOT TO TAPE

Students often ask about taping a lecture rather than taking notes. Taping a lecture has advantages and disadvantages. You can make your own decision, based on your learning style, your class setting, and the common advantages and disadvantages listed below. Before you do use a tape recorder in any class, be sure the instructor approves.

ADVANTAGES

- You have a complete record of the lecture.

- You can review the information multiple times.

- You can develop a strong auditory memory record by listening to the recording.

DISADVANTAGES

- Reviewing with a taped lecture is very, very time consuming. It will take you 50 minutes to review a 50-minute lecture!

- A recording does not give you the visual messages that are so important to communication and the memory process.

- By taping lectures, you are not challenging yourself to improve your note-taking skills.

- You cannot quiz yourself by listening to a taped lecture.

Some students have devised creative ways to study with lecture tapes while accomplishing other tasks. Commuters review their lessons while waiting for traffic to move, walkers and runners put on their headphones and exercise their minds along with their bodies, and others take the boredom out of everyday chores by listening and working at the same time.

NOTE TAKING

Would you like to buy an inexpensive, handy device that can enhance your concentration, improve lecture comprehension, and produce a study guide for exams? Put away your wallet. This "device" is already yours: Your note-taking skills can give you all these important learning benefits. Note taking is such a powerful learning strategy because it engages you directly in the memory process. While taking lecture notes, you are cooperating with the instructor to encode the material. Because instructors rely heavily on their lecture material for test questions, your notes are often a direct line to tests as well. The better your note-taking abilities, the greater your learning benefits. A skilled note taker

FIGURE 9–2   *The Reading/Note-Taking Cycle*

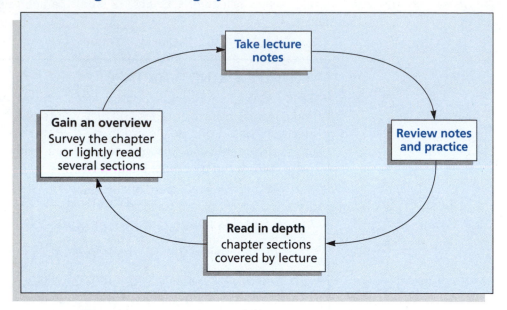

Prepares beforehand.

Selects significant information.

Organizes the notes in a streamlined format.

Uses time-saving strategies.

Reviews and practices the information.

You can easily accomplish these five steps with daily effort and practice.

---

1. Be prepared with

    A good notebook system.

    Your reading assignment.

    Labeled paper and a pen for each class session.

---

1. Be Prepared for Note Taking

Double-Check that Your Notebook System Is Working Well.   If you have lost papers or your notes have become mixed up, review the suggestions for paper management in Chapter 1.

Read Your Textbook Assignment to Prepare for the Lecture.   In Chapter 8, you saw the value of pacing your readings and reviewing your lecture notes to improve text comprehension. Your reading and comprehension of the text *before* class will also improve your ability to follow the lecture and take notes. Figure 9–2 gives you the reading/note-taking cycle again.

When you set this cycle in motion, you maximize learning because rapid reading prepares you for note taking, and reviewing your notes prepares you for in-depth reading. If you are unsure of any reading techniques, you can review them in Chapters 7 and 8. As you analyze how each instructor paces a chapter, you will become confident in pacing your own reading to prepare for each lecture.

Have Labeled Paper and a Pen Ready for Every Class. Some students wait until the teacher begins the lecture to get out their materials. They lose valuable time and disrupt the concentration of others. Always assume that a lecture will be given and that you should take notes. Date and label your paper with a course reference, and if you can, the topic of the notes. Be ready for note taking by assembling the appropriate materials and previewing related textbook topics. Good preparation will make listening for the important ideas easier.

2. Focus on

Reviewing information at the start of class.

Identifying the message *before* you write.

Selecting main ideas and supporting details.

Identifying organizational patterns.

2. Focus on Selecting the Significant Information

Your next challenge is to select the significant information and put it in order while keeping pace with the instructor. Sometimes students attempt to record everything the instructor says, but they quickly become frustrated. Take the pressure off your note taking by focusing on the most important information. Follow these guidelines for selecting the significant information.

Be Alert for Review Information at the Beginning of Class. If your instructor begins with a review of previous topics, don't feverishly copy everything again. Instead, refer to the appropriate set of notes. (That will be easy if you've dated and labeled each set.) Then you can fill in any gaps or insert additional interesting information as the review progresses. In this way, you'll keep your notes cohesive and make it easier to comprehend them. Once you've begun to take notes, relax just a bit. You'll be able to concentrate and listen better.

cohesive

Focus on Understanding the Information *Before* **You Write.**   Remember that speaking occurs much more slowly than listening. Use that time gap to grasp the flow of ideas. Be especially careful to listen when your instructors use visual aids. Sometimes students focus on copying a diagram or an outline and forget to listen to the instructor. Later on they have a complete replica of the visual, but they don't have a clue to what it means. You can always ask instructors to show visual aids for a longer period of time, or you can speak with them after class.

Select the Main ideas and the Supporting Details.   Remember main ideas are general concepts that are explained by specific descriptions, reasons, or examples. Identifying general concepts in the middle of lecture material can be challenging. Can you pick out the general concepts in this list of statements?

1. Investors commonly purchase four types of bonds.

2. Approximately 500 milliliters of air are inhaled in a normal breath.

3. Attitudes about lifestyle and gender roles have changed.

4. Municipal bonds are purchased from state and local governments.

5. The breathing process involves inhalation and exhalation phases.

6. From 1974 to 1985 the number of women choosing to work outside the home grew by more than 10 percent.

Items 1, 3, and 5 present the general concepts or the main ideas. Once you have identified the main ideas in a lecture, you have a framework for the rest of the information you select. If you want to review information about general concepts and main ideas, consult Chapters 5 and 7.

Listen for the Signal Words of the Four Basic Thinking Patterns.   When you recognize one of the thinking patterns, you can anticipate how the teacher will structure the information. The three general concepts in the previous list also signal organizational patterns with which you are familiar. Reread the odd-numbered items in that list and identify the probable organizational pattern for each. Did you predict these patterns?

1. General and specific classification.

3. Comparison and contrast, possibly cause and effect.

5. Time order process.

Once you recognize the organization the lecturer is using, you can begin to order the information as you record it.

---

3.   Organize your notes into

    A simplified outline.

    Maps using thinking patterns.

---

3. Organize Your Notes

Organize Your Notes as a Simplified Outline.   Don't try to make a formal outline. While you are deciding between using a III and a 3, an important concept will slip by. Usually, identing specific information will suffice. Study this simplified outline for the topic of changes in lifestyle and gender roles.

Chngs. in think. abt. lifestyle & gend. roles
   traditional—   husband provides for fam.
                   wife manages home & kids
                   '74—50% women wanted this life
                   women spend 26 hrs. on chores, men 8 hrs.

   modern—   husb. & wife share all responsib.
                       work
                       home
                       kids
                   '85—57% women wanted this life
                   women spend 18 hrs. on chores, men less than
                   10 hrs.

These notes clearly identify the two types of lifestyles—traditional and modern—that are being compared. The specific data for each is indented and grouped beneath the lifestyle type.

Organize Your Notes into Diagrams.   The mapping techniques described in Chapter 5 are an excellent way to record and organize your notes. This approach is fast, and the relationships among ideas are easy to see. Here are the previous notes arranged as a T-chart.

Chngs. in think. abt. lifestyle & gend. roles

traditional—husband provides for fam. *wife manages home & kids*	*modern—husb & wife share all responsib:* *work, home, kids*
'74—50% women wanted this life *women spend 26 hrs on chores,*	*'85—57% women wanted this life* *women spend 18 hrs on chores,*
men 8 hrs.	*men less than 10 hrs*

A T-chart can be particularly useful when the information is in the comparison and contrast thinking pattern because the instructor may give alternating descriptions that can make it very difficult to set up notes in the simplified outline form

FIGURE 9-3	*Common Abbreviations*

concl = conclusion	$\times$ = times
gov't = government	$\div$ = divided by
info = information	> = greater than
intro = introduction	< = less than
max = maximum	↑ = increase
min = minimum	↓ = decrease
vs = versus	∴ = therefore
w/ = with	∵ = because
w/o = without	♂ = male
@ = at	♀ = female
? = question	→ = results in, yields
& = and	# = number
− = minus	+ = plus

previously shown. With the T-chart format, you can move with ease from side to side adding information. Webs, numbered processes, and cause and effect diagrams can be equally useful for note taking.

As you experiment with different ways to organize lecture information, you will develop your own strategies for each course and type of the material, and you'll be surprised by the speed you develop.

> 4. To save time and keep pace with your instructors, use
>
> Brief phrases instead of full sentences.
>
> Abbreviations.

4. Keep Pace with Your Instructor

Besides the organizational strategies used with the previous notes, did you notice any other distinctive features? These notes also model two other efficient note-taking strategies that will help you keep pace.

Write in Brief Phrases.   Instead of writing in full sentences, write just the essential words as in a classified advertisement. Sometimes students think they can eliminate small words; however, these are often critical to the meaning. Can you interpret this phrase, "air moves lung"? What is the crucial missing word: *into, from, within, through?* Play it safe. Always include words that denote location, direction, quantity, or negation.

crucial

Use Abbreviations to Save Time.   You are already familiar with many abbreviations you can apply to your note taking. Make use of them from all areas of your knowledge—mathematics, geography, science. Read the abbreviations listed in Figure 9–3. You'll be surprised how many are part of your vocabulary.

Taking notes is a complex process, but you don't need a stenographer's skill to be successful at the task. With practice and patience, you will begin to see your own notes take shape, much like the sample notes in Figure 9–4. These notes are not a perfect transcription of the teacher's words, but they do provide the student with an organized, understandable record of the major concepts. These notes will be a definite plus to this student as she studies for her test.

CRACKING THE ABBREVIATION CODE

In addition to using standard symbols, you can abbreviate less common words yourself. Several guidelines, however, should be followed to prevent confusion later on.

1. Limit an abbreviation to just one meaning to avoid confusion. For example, if you use " to mean inches, do not also use it to indicate seconds.

2. Use more than an initial prefix as an abbreviation. If you use *inter*, as your abbreviation for *international,* you could later confuse it with such words as *internal* and *intermediate. Internat.* still eliminates half the word and is precise.

3. Save time by abbreviating names, but be sure that you use the full name at least once so you have a point of reference. For example, Sigmund Freud could simply become *S.F.* once you have written the complete name.

5. Review and Practice Your Notes

From several chapters in ASAP, you know that you can lose large amounts of information if you do not review quickly. If you haven't scheduled review time for your lecture notes into your daily schedule, do it now. Remember, you don't need large blocks of time, just 10 to 15 minutes as soon after your class as possible. Read over your notes to consolidate your learning and then revise them for correctness, clarity, and conciseness.

FIGURE 9–4   *Sample Notes*

BIO. Chpt. 23   2/10

<u>Skin in Vertebrates</u>

Composition
    <u>Made up of tissue</u>
    <u>Lgst. organ of body</u>
    Cells vary in animals
        fish - scales
        birds - feathers
        mam. - hair

Structure
    <u>2 layers of skin cover 3rd lay. of deep tissue</u>
    1. Epidermis
        <u>thin outer layer</u>
        <u>contains keratin and melanin</u>
          prevents dehydr.
          blocks invasion of microbes
          helps repair wounds w/ new skin
          melanin gives skin color & protect.
            from sun

    2. Dermas
        <u>thick middle layer</u>
        <u>made up of connective tissue</u>
        <u>provides structure for</u>
          <u>hair roots</u>
          <u>sweat glands</u>
          <u>nerve endings</u>

Revisions.   Figure 9–5 demonstrates how the student later improved the sample notes. Notice how she has made major concepts stand out and has corrected problems in organization and spelling. Finally, she drew a small diagram to visualize and summarize the information. As you read over your notes, improve them by

- Correcting errors in names and terminology.

- Filling in gaps where you became lost.

- Clarifying logic and organization.

- Noting possible test information and areas of confusion.

FIGURE 9–4	*Concluded*

Skin   *2/10*
                                                                          cont'd

   3. Deep tissue
        Called subcutaneous layer
              Contains
                 H_2O
                 adipose tissue
                 muscle
        Helps protect body by
              storing energy
              insulat. against cold
              muscle helps skin move

Sometimes students work together after class to improve their notes in especially difficult courses. If you are well matched with another student, this kind of collaborative learning is excellent. In independent situations, rely on your textbook and handouts to improve your lecture notes. Avoid rewriting all your lecture notes, because the process is too time consuming. If your notes are so messy they are

unintelligible

unintelligible, be sure that you are leaving plenty of white space between ideas and are deleting mistakes with a simple horizontal line. When you have your notes in top order, you are ready to practice them briefly.

Practice with Self-Quizzing.   Don't lose your momentum now. Practice is the key to mastery and high exam marks. For self-quizzing, follow these simple steps and the sample notes in Figure 9–5.

FIGURE 9–5   **Revised Sample Notes**

> BIO. Chpt. 23   2/10
>
> <u>Skin in Vertebrates</u>
>
> | | |
> |---|---|
> | | <u>Composition</u> |
> | <u>Composition</u> | Made up of tissue |
> | of skin | ☆ <u>Lgst. organ of body</u> |
> | examples | Cells vary in animals |
> | | fish - scales |
> | | birds - feathers |
> | | mam. - hair |
> | | |
> | <u>Structure</u> | Structure |
> | | 2 layers of skin cover 3rd lay. of deep tissue |
> | 1st layer | 1. Epidermis |
> | | thin <u>outer layer</u> |
> | Keratin | contains <u>keratin and melanin</u> |
> | 2 jobs | ⌠ prevents dehydr. |
> | | ⎨ blocks invasion of microbes = germs |
> | | ⌡ helps repair wounds w/ new skin |
> | Melanin | ⌠ melanin gives skin color & protect. |
> | 2 jobs | ⌡ from sun |
> | | |
> | 2nd layer | 2. ~~Dermas~~ Dermis |
> | | thick <u>middle layer</u> |
> | composition | made up of connective tissue |
> | job | provides structure for |
> | | ⌠ hair roots - follicle |
> | | ⎨ sweat glands |
> | | ⌡ nerve endings |

1. **Place a key term or phrase in the left margin for each major topic.** Remember, key terms are general and encompass the more specific information. Draw a vertical line to separate your terms from the body of notes.

2. **Cover the notes and quiz yourself through recitation or in writing, using the key terms as your cues.** Continue practicing for your desired mastery level. For example, the student might quiz herself in this fashion.

> *Key word*—composition of the skin
> *Recitation*—"Skin is made up of tissue cells. It's the largest organ of the body."
> *Key word*—examples
> *Recitation*—"Three varying forms of skin in animals are birds' feathers, fish's scales, and mammals' hair."

FIGURE 9–5   *Concluded*

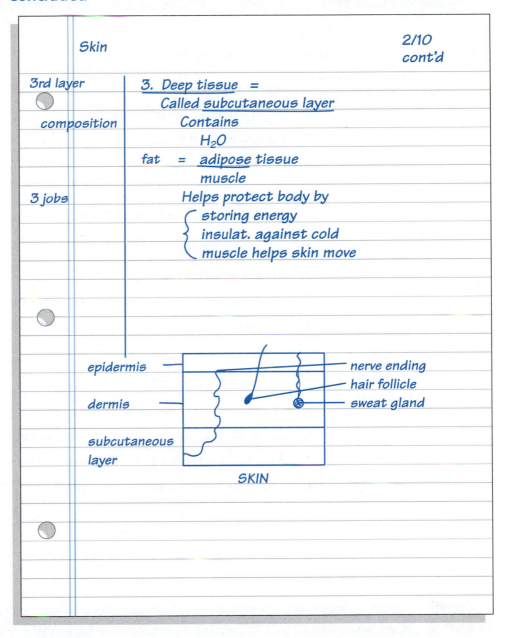

Any learning system can be adjusted to meet your own needs and learning style. Perhaps you already use a note-taking system that differs from the one presented here. The steps of this system are based on the Cornell note-taking system originated by Dr. Walter Pauk. Many students have used the system successfully. Monitor what is effective for you when you take notes and capitalize on those strategies. Soon you will have your own tailor-made note-taking system.

Note taking demonstrates the remarkable capabilities of the human mind. While listening actively, you are able to identify important information and record it in a useful format, all within a matter of seconds. Like the skill of a magician, much advance work and follow-up go into the wizardry of note taking. Step by step, you can master this skill that will lead you to academic excellence and give you an edge in professional achievement.

THE ASAP REWIND «« «« ««

How can I learn more in my lectures?

Use these active listening strategies:

1. Focus on the speaker's message.
2. Observe nonverbal communication.
3. Paraphrase what is said.
4. Contribute to discussions.

What can I do about my bad listening habits?

Follow these steps to establish new habits:

1. Set specific listening goals.
2. Avoid distractions.
3. Focus on the message, not the speaker's shortcomings.
4. Take notes.

How can I take meaningful, useful notes?

Use these steps for good notes:

1. Be prepared every day to take notes.
2. Listen, then record the important information in an organized format.
3. Write in brief phrases and with abbreviations.
4. Review and practice your notes regularly.

 WORD POWER

Exercise 1

Directions: Your ability to listen well can be directly affected by your vocabulary. Strengthen your vocabulary and your listening skill by mastering the following words. Define each word using the word meaning techniques: word parts, context, and dictionary. Then put your new word to work in an original sentence.

nuances _____

_____

_____

empathic _____

_____

_____

status quo _____

_____

_____

overt _____

_____

_____

covert _____

_____

_____

detrimental _____

_____

_____

compromised _____

_____

_____

cohesive _____

_____

_____

crucial _____

_____

_____

unintelligible _____

_____

_____

TAKE ACTION

Exercise 2

Directions: Your boss is displeased with how staff members listen and participate in your bimonthly meetings. She has asked staff to submit suggestions that could be given to the entire work team to improve the communication process. Based on your knowledge of active listening, write a brief memo to your boss in which you make a minimum of four suggestions. Use your own paper to write your memo.

Exercise 3

Directions: A friend boasts that he's never taken a lecture note and never will. Can you convince him that note taking is worth his effort? Your friend doesn't listen very well, so make just three concise points that will change his mind.

_____

_____

_____

_____

_____

Exercise 4

Directions: Examine the following sample notes. How do you think the student could improve? Make a minimum of four suggestions, giving the student specific directions for improvement.

> 11/18
>
> Input equip—used to enter information into the computer.
> Several types—The keyboard differs from type. It has movement and function keys.
>   A mouse is a small hand oper. input attachment. Acts as pointer to move without keyboard. Optical Character Read (OCR)
>   is a machine connected to the computer. It scans documents and makes magnetic form. Sent to computer. Can be created.

_____

_____

_____

_____

_____

_____

_____

Exercise 5

Directions: Give your own note taking a boost—and your current affairs knowledge too. Take notes while listening to a television or radio news program for at least 15 minutes. You'll find this a challenging assignment because newscasters use prepared scripts and speak quite fast. If you get lost, don't give up. Start in again with the next topic. *Be sure you review and revise your notes immediately afterward.* You'll be surprised how much of the missing information you'll be able to fill in. This mental workout will expand your note-taking capabilities. Use your own paper for this assignment.

Exercise 6

Directions: Revising notes and creating key words for self-quizzing are challenging note-taking skills. Prepare the practice notes in Figure 9–6 for self quizzing. Use this chapter to help you complete the following.

1. Add any missing significant information.

2. Make major concepts stand out. You can number them, underline them, put them in boxes—whatever is the best method for you.

3. Identify key words for each major concept and its supporting details. Put your key words in the corresponding area of the left-hand column. Use Figure 9–5 to help you create your key words.

4. Can you encode *all* the information as a whole? Make a diagram or write a summary.

FIGURE 9–6   *Practice Notes*

St. Skills   Mar. 8

                        Active Listen.

2   Common listen. roles for students
        Listener co-partner—share spkg
                                & listening
            Be on time
            Read & prepare before class
            Take notes
            Really listen to message
            Keep good eye contact
            Watch nonverb. commun.
                eye contact
                body move.
                expression
                speech patterns
            Paraphrase spkr. & take notes
            Give feedback
                ques.
                agreement
                suggestions
        Listener observer—mostly listen
            Set learn. goal—brainstorm
            Watch visual aids
            Process & encode enfo

Directions: Put into action the principles of listening and note taking! At the end of one week, use this checklist to evaluate your progress. Then use the space that follows to analyze your growth.

PROGRESS CHECKLIST: Listening and Note Taking

Yes   Usually   No

___ ___ ___   **1.** I use active listening strategies to maximize my communications.

___ ___ ___   **2.** I use concentration strategies and specific listening goals to overcome ineffective listening habits.

___ ___ ___   **3.** I prepare the assigned reading and all the necessary materials before a lecture.

___ ___ ___   **4.** During a lecture, I listen for main ideas, significant details, and thinking patterns.

___ ___ ___   **5.** I organize my notes in a simplified outline or use mapping diagrams.

___ ___ ___   **6.** To save time, I write in brief phrases and use abbreviations.

___ ___ ___   **7.** I review my notes soon after class to clarify the information.

___ ___ ___   **8.** I practice the information in my notes by quizzing myself.

A. Describe the listening and note-taking strategies that are bringing you classroom success. Explain how you have been able to avoid or overcome ineffective listening habits.

B. Identify the classes in which you find listening and note taking more difficult. Explain what you think are the causes of your difficulty and how you might use the strategies of this chapter to improve the situation.

Do You Have a Listening Wish List?   If so, take some time and space to explore how others can listen better to YOU. Use the power of your pen and mind to tap your communication potential and the potential of others. Remember, anything is possible.

DEVELOPING PERFORMANCE SKILLS

CHAPTER

10

Preparing for Tests

THE SKILL THAT GETS THE JOB

Legal Assistant.
For high-powered firm. The ideal candidate will be a CLA with speciality certification in criminal law. Duties include trial preparations. Must be results-oriented.

WHAT'S YOUR EXPERIENCE?

A play-off game, a job interview, or a test at school—everyone talks RESULTS. However, results should be the number 2 topic—behind PREPARATION. How do you prepare for tests? Do you feel your preparation pays off with good results? Use the space below to explore your skill, your knowledge, and your questions about this chapter's topic.

_____

_____

_____

_____

_____

_____

_____

_____

_____

_____

_____

In this chapter you will learn to

»»» *Focus on doing your best.*

»»» *Build strength through personal support and stress management.*

»»» *Build a study schedule.*

»»» *Achieve mastery at the recall and analysis level.*

PREPARING FOR TESTS

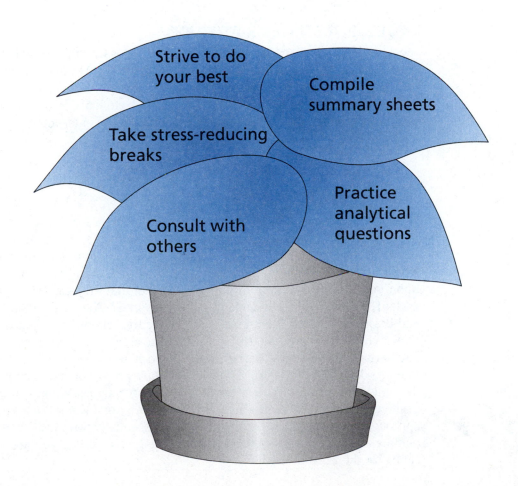

Let's play a quick association game. As you read each of the following words, jot next to it the first word that comes into your mind. For example, the word *peanut butter* might be associated with *jelly.* Okay, let's see what's on your mind.

Friday

sports

bills

number 2 pencil

grade

Did you associate *number 2 pencil* with *test?* What association did you make with *grade?* Did you immediately think *100?* Most people can remember the testing process from a young age—Friday spelling quizzes, final exams, college entrance tests. With each testing experience you have developed a mental set and habits that now affect your test preparation and your test taking. This chapter discusses how to achieve a positive mental set, how to prepare academically, and how to maintain your physical fitness. The aim is to make new associations and new habits in order to achieve on exams with less stress. You will be able to use your new set of skills beyond school too, as you strive to meet the challenges of job placement exams and job interviews.

DEVELOP A STRIVER'S ATTITUDE

Most people understand the need for creating a positive attitude before accomplishing a difficult task. There is even a slang term for creating a positive mental set, "psyching yourself up." *Psych* is a prefix meaning mind or mental; thus, the phrase means getting one's mind up. Even though students understand the importance of a positive mental set, they often unthinkingly enter into a negative psychological cycle when a test is announced.

Resist Negative Thinking

Negative thinking usually begins with these four simple words: "I'm going to fail." If students understand the power of a positive mental set, why do they actually create negative momentum? One explanation is that out of fear, they predict the worst, hoping to cushion the actual "blow" later on. Another is that they dwell upon poor performances from the past and feel that they can't break out of the cycle. Have you had these feelings or similar ones? The very fact that you care and desire to succeed has caused you to place tremendous pressure on yourself. If not channeled properly, that pressure can create negative associations and

counterprodutive

counterproductive stress. Harnessing your positive power can begin with these four words, "I'll try my best." Figure 10–1 shows how you can change negative thoughts into actions that aim for your best performance. When you establish a positive mental set this way, you become a striver, not a winner or a loser. People approach the challenge of doing their best in essentially two ways: Some are competitors and others are producers. Identify the type of striver you are so you can capitalize on those strengths.

FIGURE 10–1   *Striving to Overcome Negative Thoughts*

INFORMATION FILE: MEETING THE CHALLENGE

The Meaning of Pressure . . .
The next time you feel pressured by midterms or final exams, remember that things could be worse. If you were a college preparatory student in Germany, you would probably take 13 classes each week, 2 in your major and 11 others in a variety of subjects. In at least five of your courses you would take exams twice a semester. Each exam would be a written test lasting approximately five hours.

Identify Your Achievement Style

Many people get their positive energy from building something over an extended period of time. These people are **producers** who enjoy a variety of hobbies and pastimes—gardening, mastering computer software. They work toward a product that is finished when the last piece falls in place. Is this your style? Then you possess the producer's invaluable patience and ability to set interim goals. You can approach each test as a problem that will be solved with specially acquired knowledge. Use your long-range vision to treat each test as one part of your larger goals—your course grade, your G.P.A., and your professional skills.

Competitors approach an exam and most challenges as a fight—they have a me-against-it attitude. If you've competed in sports or music competitions, you know this type of challenge. It creates the positive stress needed to tackle the skill workouts and the actual contest. Does this approach excite you? Then channel your energies into the contest of the exam. Use your knowledge of competition to create your academic edge and positive flow of energy.

requisite

All people, competitors and producers, sometimes find themselves short of the requisite skills or the correct solutions. The consequences can be failed projects or disappointing test grades. Ironically, an important part of your positive mental set is knowing that you can cope with setbacks.

⊘ STRESSBUSTER

PASS THE WORD. Let others know when you are going through a particularly stressful time, like final exams. Maybe they won't be able to give you direct help, but they can understand your tension and your preoccupation with other matters.

BUILD PERSONAL STRENGTH

How have you dealt with disappointment in the past? Most often three strategies help strivers over the hurdle of disappointment.

FEEL—don't hide. When a setback occurs, feelings of anger and frustration are natural. If you suppress or try to deny those feelings, they will remain with you longer and affect your ability to view other challenges positively. Take time now to put past failures behind you and to accept that some difficulties will arise in the future.

LEARN—don't blame. Sometimes peoples' feelings of frustration cause them to place blame on themselves or others. Instead of blaming, analyze how you can do better. This kind of positive behavior will help you strive in all aspects of your life.

perseverance

TRY AGAIN—don't quit. Perseverance is a key behavior for strivers.Without it, your positive mental set will remain weak. Begin each challenge knowing you won't give up.

Does such a high level of resolve and confidence seem superhuman to you? People who strive—whether they are Olympic athletes or sandlot competitors,

Nobel scientists or basement hobbyists—derive motivation and strength from other people.

Gaining Strength from Others

Athletes work closely with a coach and their teammates to develop their skills and maintain their outlook. Scientists look to a mentor and colleagues for support. You can gain the same kind of strength for the rigor of exams by tapping the personal support network you built in Chapter 2. Your coach or mentor may come from a variety of places:

- **Classmates** who want to work together for achievement.

- An **instructor or tutor** who provides extra skill, knowledge, and support.

- A **family member or friend** who listens and reminds you of your personal strength.

Don't walk the testing path alone. Along the way, discouragement could overtake you.

The power of the company you keep also extends to your friends and casual school acquaintances. How often have you heard small groups of students complaining that the test will be impossible to pass or that their last test grades doom them for the rest of the term? Attitudes, both negative and positive, are contagious. Position yourself to catch the positive attitude of the strivers in your classes.

Often students who are positive about preparing for exams organize themselves into study groups. When a study group is well organized, participants benefit because

- Boredom decreases.

- Morale improves.

- Learning is in greater depth.

If you want to create or join a study group, consider these organizational factors.

1. The group should have three to six participants. Larger groups are difficult to keep organized and often become social gatherings.

2. The group should have a specific plan for studying the test material. For example, each member might be assigned a chapter section or several discussion questions to present to the group. Assigning two people to prepare the same material is also a good strategy because it reduces the chance of the entire group learning incorrect information.

3. The group should set specific times for study and certain times for breaks. Setting a work policy will help your group stick to its objectives and avoid aimless conversations. Some groups ban certain topics—dating, television programs and movies, other friends—in an effort to maintain a work atmosphere.

INFORMATION FILE: MEETING THE CHALLENGE

The Champion's Approach . . .

According to David D. Burns, M.D., anxiety level does not separate the winners from the losers. In a study of Olympic gymnasts, researchers found that high and low performers had equal stress levels before events. Where the two groups of competitors differed was in their approach to handling the stress. The Olympic winners shut anxiety out of their minds by concentrating on accomplishing small aspects of their gymnastic routines one step at a time. In doing so, they kept control of their anxiety *and* performed with focused skill.

4. The group should set new objectives and make plans for the next meeting at the end of the current study session. Sometimes groups work well for several sessions and then deteriorate. Members come unprepared or miss sessions because they are busy with other assignments. Making plans for the next session will maintain your group's sense of purpose.

dynamics

These suggestions make no mention of leadership because group dynamics vary greatly from one situation to another. Some study groups work very well with shared leadership. Sometimes one person keeps the study activities moving along while someone else sees that each person fully understands the information; in other situations, one person is in the primary leadership role.

When you feel that you are learning the required information and that you have the support of others, you have taken the first step toward managing the stress related to test preparations.

Using Stress Management Techniques

Once you've established the momentum of a positive mental set, move quickly to keep your stress level in the positive, motivational range. Stress builds even when you have no immediate problems. Exam preparation is stressful because it is an *counterbalance* added responsibility and because studying is a solitary activity. Counterbalance these added stresses by using the stressbusters at the end of each ASAP chapter or the stress management techniques from Chapter 3. Unwind with a short music fest or some recreational reading. If you feel the need to "blow off some steam," keep an exam journal in which you can express your anxieties, or call a friend to talk about anything—anything but school! Finally, never, never say, "I'm going to fail."

dispel

When is your next test? Begin today to dispel a negative mental set. Construct a positive mental set for exams by striving to do your best with the support of others and stress management strategies.

PREPARE ACADEMICALLY

A key to maintaining a positive stress level is your preparation for an exam. Some people wait until the night before, trying to cram all the knowledge and skill into their minds at the last minute. Some of these individuals are disorganized, but others claim that they think better under extreme pressure. When you begin

---

THE $$$ IN STRESS

Every student knows the cost of excessive stress in test situations, but have you ever thought about the cost of stress in other daily situations? According to Dan Costley and Ralph Todd, authors of *Human Relations in Organizations,* stress-related problems in the United States cost approximately $75 to $90 billion each year. Much of this expense occurs in the workplace, where employee stress results in accidents, job turnover, lowered productivity, and absenteeism. To combat the high cost of stress, companies like Johnson & Johnson, Xerox, and AT&T have launched stress management programs and studies. The results of one study provide the key to stress management in the office OR in the classroom: work smarter instead of harder. How can you work smarter? The strategies are at your fingertips—in the pages of ASAP.

STRESSBUSTER

Want to take a shortcut? Look at today's to-do list and remove the *least* important item. Tomorrow will be soon enough to accomplish that task. Now you can breathe easier and enjoy the rest of the day.

---

studying at the last minute, you have inadequate time for the memory process to work fully. In addition, you run the risk of shifting from the benefits of positive stress into the negative effects of anxiety. Other students begin studying well in advance of the exam and devote all their energies to studying and excelling. While such dedication is admirable, it too can be counterproductive. If you study too intensely, you can neglect important tasks in other subjects and forget to take the stress management breaks necessary for maintaining your positive mental set. Avoid either of these extremes. Instead, establish a study schedule for the exam so you can use each stage of the memory process and stress-reducing activities.

Plan Ahead

You should start studying for a typical test at least one week in advance. The scope and complexity of most tests require a high skill level and a thorough understanding of the material. Your exam study schedule can be constructed in much the same way as you constructed a project schedule in Chapter 3.

First, divide the test material into logical segments that can be reviewed and rehearsed over one or two days. In most courses the simplest way is to use a textbook chapter as the basic study unit. For a test in an introduction to computers course covering three chapters, you would have three basic study units. When doing your weekly planning, you could set a schedule like this:

Sunday:	*gather background information*
Mon. & Tues.:	*review Chapter 9*
Wed. & Thurs.:	*review Chapter 10*

Friday: review Chapter 11

Sunday: overall review

This simple schedule provides adequate preparation time spaced over a week so you would be able to meet your other obligations without mounting negative stress. An effective schedule includes:

- Time for gathering background information about the test.

- A sequential arrangement of chapters so skills can be mastered in a logical order.

- Study time for chapters adjusted for the complexity of the material, performance on previous quizzes, and the freshness of the material.

- An overall review session to fully test mastery.

THE MYTH OF CRAMMING

People hate to be crammed on an elevator or at a small restaurant table. They dread days that are packed with appointments and responsibilities, but when test time arrives, students cram their studies into one or two hectic, stress-filled sessions. Why? Some students cram because they think "all-nighters" are the thing to do. Some are forced into cram sessions because they do not record test dates and then are caught at the last minute. Many students believe that they do their best learning under pressure. Learning studies would contradict them. Because the information learned in cramming sessions is not practiced over a period of time, the information does not remain in long-term memory or it is easily confused with other information and cannot be recalled. The cramming myth continues because some students do make good test grades when they have crammed their studies. What students do not realize, however, is that in just a short period of time, their learning is dramatically reduced. As a result, they will have greater difficulty reading the next chapter and studying for the next test—especially if they cram again.

Gathering Background Information

In their eagerness to master information for a test, many students do not take time to educate themselves about the test itself. Athletes spend a large part of their training time watching film footage of opposing teams and previous games. Begin your test training by gathering all possible information about the upcoming test so you focus your study in the right direction.

1. **Review any information about the test provided by your instructor.** Most instructors give students considerable advance information about the nature of their exams. Some instructors provide review guidelines; others note specific course objectives that they will emphasize; some discuss the type of

questions they will use. Always be alert for this kind of information, and be sure you put it in writing because your memory will be neither complete nor accurate.

2. **Analyze previous tests and quizzes from the course.** You should keep all your previous tests and quizzes for this purpose. Sometimes you can ask your instructor to examine old tests. Look for these patterns so you can maximize your study:

   - The types of questions the instructor most often uses.
   - Areas in which you seem to have problems.
   - Quiz topics that might be expanded on the test.

   Armed with this information, you can adjust your study to meet the demands of that particular course. For example, if you see that the instructor usually includes a multiple choice section that requires you to choose *all* the correct answers, you can be sure to study all possible answers, such as a complete numbered list in your textbook. If you realize that you are having difficulty with one type of question, you can consult Chapter 11, which gives tips for answering most types of test questions. Your most current quizzes also can give you advance notice of information that will be covered in depth on the test because instructors often test major concepts on quizzes before fully testing them on an exam.

Of course, you cannot rely on past exams with 100 percent certainty. Instructors may change their testing strategies because the material is significantly different or because they wish to challenge students in new ways. Usually instructors will indicate to students that their testing format is changing. Then you can adjust your study strategies accordingly.

MASTER EACH STUDY UNIT

If gathering background information about the test increases your anxiety level, be sure to take a stress-reducing break. When your positive motivation is renewed, turn your energies to mastering the material in the study units you established in your study plan. To be fully prepared for an exam, you should master the information at two levels: recall and analysis. Many students have difficulty with exams because they are prepared only to recall or identify facts and concepts. Most college exams, however, require students to use their basic knowledge to solve problems, analyze case studies, and synthesize ideas.

Studying to Recall Information

The recall mastery level provides a foundation of knowledge that you will draw upon for the more sophisticated tasks required at the analytical level. In order to **recall or identify information,** Dr. Walter Pauk of Cornell University recommends compiling **summary sheets** for each study unit. This is an excellent study technique because it incorporates all the phases of the memory process as discussed in Chapter 6. The following steps are a variation of the process described by Dr. Pauk. As you read them, see if you can identify each step in the memory process.

pertinent

1. **Select the major topics that you will master in the study unit.** Consult all your pertinent learning materials: lecture notes, textbook, handouts, and outside readings. Be sure you also use your valuable background information about the test as you make your selections.

2. **Carefully condense the information so you can arrange it on just one or two sheets of standard paper.** Work first from either lecture notes or your textbook, whichever you find easier. Then turn to the other source, adding only significant information. Remember, don't duplicate information; you want a condensed version. Lastly, consult your handouts and outside readings. Often these can provide illustrative examples and contrasting viewpoints to round out your summary of a major point.

3. **Arrange the information by major topic headings so that you can do self-quizzing.** Draw upon your organizational patterns from Chapter 5, and arrange the information in ways that help you make associations and visualizations. Figure 10–2 shows summaries that use a variety of mapping techniques for different subject areas. You could use a summary like these for self-quizzing (either oral or in writing) by covering the detailed information and leaving the heading visible as a quizzing cue. Notice that many of the headings include a number: 3 types of bonds, circulatory cycle—6 steps. Using totals in your headings will help you practice all the important details or concepts.

4. **Rehearse the information on your summary sheets for one study unit until you have achieved recall mastery in the 90 percent range.** When your level of understanding and remembering basic information is high, you will be well prepared for typical objective test questions. Your knowledge will also give you a firm basis for problem solving and analytical questions.

Does compiling summary sheets seem too time consuming to you? Actually, studying from summary sheets will save you time because you will not be duplicating your efforts as you work from your lecture notes, then your textbook, then your other sources. In compiling a summary sheet, you are fulfilling each of the memory steps—selecting, encoding, and rehearsing the significant information. Don't discard your summary sheets after the test. You can use them again for your final exam review. Of course, like any summary, your summary sheets must be correct and clear as well as concise. When you gather background information for the test, be sure to find out if your instructor will accept paraphrased answers or if you must be able to duplicate the information exactly.

Studying to Analyze Information

When you are certain of your basic knowledge, you are ready to practice the information in situations similar to those used on your exams. In math, accounting, and computer programming courses, you will be asked to use your basic knowledge to solve problems. In courses such as business law, office procedures, and health and child care, you will be expected to apply your knowledge to case studies or hypothetical situations. Exams in courses such as psychology, biology, history, and literature will test your ability to combine information from many sources to analytically discuss ideas.

Practicing questions at the analytical level is not intended to second-guess the instructor or predict specific exam items. Rather, practicing questions will develop

FIGURE 10–2   *Summary Sheets*

Bus. Math	*Summary Sheet*	CHPT. 16 Investments

Definition of bond
  long-term promissory note with payment due within
  a specific number of years (10 or more). Amount paid
  = face value or amnt. printed on certificate. Interest
  paid periodically. ✭ Exception – Savings Bonds

3 Types of bonds
  registered bond – owner's name registered w/ issuer
     coupon bond – not registered, owned by holder;
              coupons attached to bond – are
              sent to issuer as interest
              payment comes due
  municipal bond – issued by state & local gov't. for
              public projects   ex. new school

BUYING BONDS	SELLING BONDS
Mkt. Accrued Com- Total Value + Interest ⊕ mission = Exp.	Mkt. Accrued Com. Net Value + Interest ⊖ & = Pro- sec ceeds fee

the necessary thinking skills. As you see your skill developing, you will also feel your confidence in your knowledge and abilities increase. Let's look at ways to prepare for the most common types of exam questions.

Solving Quantitative Problems.   Prepare for solving quantitative problems on your exams by working problems in your textbook or study guide. Quantitative problems are most common in math, science, and applied business courses. Be sure that you are choosing problems for which answers are provided so you can check your accuracy. When you find that your answers don't match up with those provided, begin troubleshooting your work. Don't just accept the answer given by the text, but actually determine where you made errors in logic or computation.

FIGURE 10–2   **Concluded**

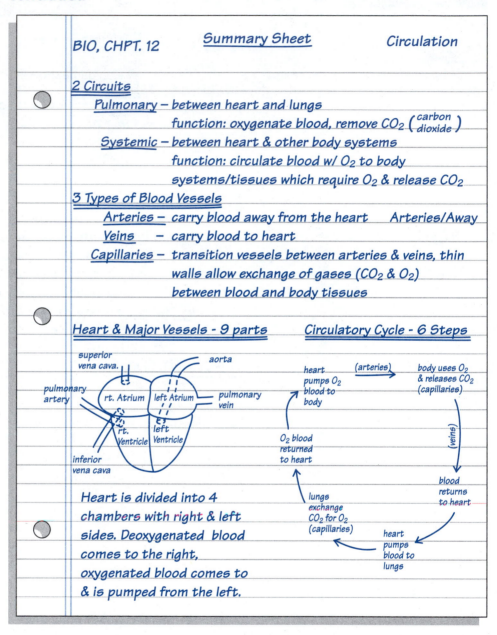

Keep working problems until you are achieving accuracy in the 90 percent range. Don't fall into the trap of simply copying solutions as patterns to be memorized. On the exam you could use the wrong solution for problems because you lack a true understanding of the solution steps. If you find yourself stumped, don't panic. Because you have begun your exam studies early, you have sufficient time to ask one of your resources—a classmate, your instructor, a tutor—to help you understand how to solve the problems.

conceptual   **Solving Conceptual Problems.** In many courses instructors want to test your ability to apply principles, laws, or procedures to real case studies and hypothetical situations. These are conceptual problems rather than quantitative problems, and

INFORMATION FILE: MEETING THE CHALLENGE

The Password is CHEATING . . .

Some people like tests, even enough to participate on television game shows. In the 1950s, game shows reached their peak of popularity, bringing big money and status to television producers, advertisers, and contestants. Overnight, through the testimony of an unhappy contestant, these same people were publicly branded as cheats. An investigation by Congress revealed that contestants who won prizes ranging from $64,000 to $129,000 were coached on specific answers before the program. As a result of this scandal, the television game shows you watch today must adhere to strict regulations and limit the size of the prizes they award.

sometimes solutions to them are less well defined. In some instances, there are several acceptable answers. To prepare yourself for such exercises on exams, first study any model studies or situations you have been given. Use your knowledge of cause and effect to understand how each problem was defined and how appropriate solutions were chosen. To practice your skill, answer any other case studies or hypothetical situations that are provided in your textbook or study guide. If you need more samples than these sources provide to achieve mastery, check in the library for alternative textbooks that use similar exercises. Whenever possible, check your answers to the exercises in the answer key or with your instructor. If you are having difficulty with this type of question, check into these factors:

- Do you have a firm understanding of the laws, principles, and procedures that are being used?

- Are you reading the study or situation very carefully, identifying the problem or problems and all corresponding effects?

synthesize

Discussion Problems.   These test questions, often called essay questions, are the broadest of all. They require you to connect or synthesize ideas to produce

- Proof.

- Relationships.

- Explanations.

- Evaluations.

The discussion questions provided in your text or study guide are an excellent source of practice material for this type of question. Write out your answers, using organizational patterns to organize your thoughts. Usually textbooks do not provide answers to these questions, so you will have to compare your answers with those of study partners or ask your instructor to review them with you. If the questions in your text are limited, consult the library or create your own. Challenge yourself to develop questions that combine two or more headings from your summary sheets. When you have finished answering your questions, exchange with friends. With consistent practice, you are sure to develop your skill and confidence in answering essay questions.

Give yourself a well-deserved reward each time you score a victory with the mastery of a study unit at both the recall and analysis levels—then schedule one final review.

Schedule One Final Review

When all study units are complete, you are ready to stage a quick, overall study session. This activity is to assure that you can recall information when questions are asked in a random order. This means combining the terminology, formulas, laws or principles, and facts from all the chapters. An easy way to accomplish this is to expand your use of study cards. In Chapter 8, you learned how to use study cards to master terminology. Figure 10–3 illustrates how you can use study cards for concepts. The cards are handy because you can mix them up and practice the information in a variety of ways. Since you have practiced the material extensively for a week, you should need just a few self-quizzes covering all the information. As you quiz yourself, keep two piles of cards, those you know with ease and those that require more study. Spend your remaining study time just on the material that is still difficult. Conclude your exam studies at a time that allows you to manage your stress level and take care of your physical needs.

Academic preparation, when done the right way, is far more than what happens the night before the exam. Be academically prepared for your exams by studying systematically over a period of time, mastering the material at the recall and analytical levels.

WHEN IS ENOUGH, ENOUGH?

It is important for you to decide when you will stop your test preparations. Some students are peering over notes as the instructor readies to pass out the exams. Other students end their academic preparations early the day before. Even if you are still unsure of some material, you might decide to end your study efforts. Base your decision on how well you handle stress near the actual time of the test. If your anxiety begins to mount, end your studies early so you do not begin to confuse material that you have mastered. A good strategy is to avoid the self-quizzing method in your final study hours because it can produce stress if you make mistakes. Simply read over your summary sheets for a general review. Some students find that studying exam material before going to sleep is especially stressful because they become keyed up and cannot fall asleep. Have confidence in yourself and all the effort you have put forth. You've come into the homestretch. Don't stretch yourself too far.

KEEP PHYSICALLY FIT

Chapter 3 discussed the importance of caring for your body's basic needs as part of your lifestyle. At no time is your physical condition more important than exam time. Even students who regularly schedule adequate sleep, exercise, and meals find themselves taking shortcuts while studying for exams. Unthinkingly they are expecting their bodies to perform longer and better with less resources. In actuality, the opposite will happen. People who push their bodies without providing sufficient sleep, nutrition, or activity

FIGURE 10–3   *Study Cards*

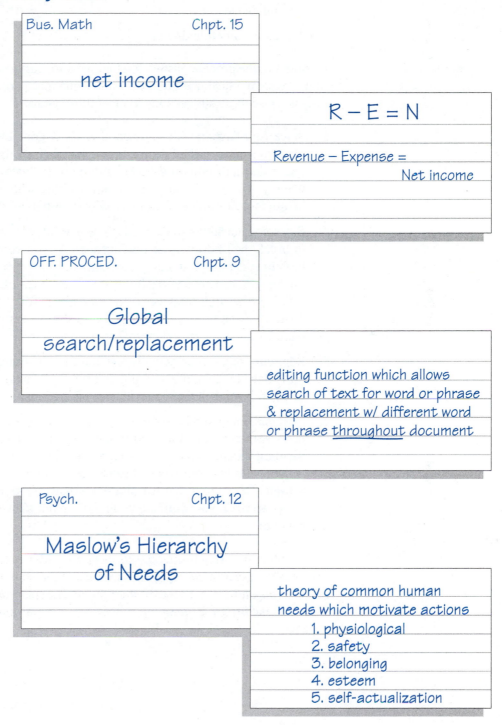

- Become moody.

- Are unable to concentrate.

- Have difficulty thinking clearly.

augment

Throughout the process of studying for an exam, augment your progress by maintaining your physical condition with nutritious meals, regular sleep, and frequent exercise. Use these suggestions to meet those goals.

1. Stock your kitchen with some good foods. A good time to do this is when you plan your study schedule for the exam. Buy all the ingredients for several quick and nutritious meals. Make large quantities so you can eat leftovers when you really get busy. If you are working with a study group, you might be able to coordinate your meals with members of the group too.

2. Buy some nutritious snack foods as well. While studying, students often nibble to break their boredom or nervousness. As you know, many snack foods are high in sugar and salt, and you could create an imbalance in your nutritional intake. You can review healthful snack options in Chapter 3. Some students also increase their intake of coffee and tea or soft drinks while studying. As a result, they find themselves keyed up from excessive caffeine and unable to concentrate or sleep. Try herbal tea or a fruit juice with your snack instead.

3. Remember that sleep actually facilitates the learning process. Therefore, you don't have to feel guilty about going to bed because you still have more work to do. Tell yourself that you will be studying in your sleep—SWEET DREAMS.

4. Maintain your exercise routine as a means of reducing stress. Students quickly drop exercise from their priorities when they feel the pressure of an impending exam. Avoid such a hasty decision by arranging specific exercise activities during your week of exam preparation or as breaks from your study routine. Remember that learning takes place gradually over time. When you are exercising, you won't be wasting time but allowing your learning to consolidate.

Situations that require people to perform under pressure abound in life. For students the greatest challenge lies in tests. Often students have formed negative associations and habits based on their previous experiences. You can change negative test factors by developing a striver's attitude and studying adequately in advance.

THE ASAP REWIND «« «« ««

What can I do to be more positive about tests?

Develop a striver's attitude by

- Aiming for your best effort.
- Using other people for personal support.

How can I reduce the stress when I study for a test?

Use these stress management strategies:

1. Make a schedule for your test studies.
2. Take regular breaks.
3. Maintain your physical fitness.

How can I be sure I've studied the right material?

Follow these steps for comprehensive study:

1. Analyze previous tests and quizzes.
2. Master the information at the recall level.
3. Practice answering quantitative, conceptual, and discussion problems.

 ## WORD POWER

Exercise 1

Directions: Understanding vocabulary is essential to test performance. Make the words listed below part of your vocabulary. Define each word using the word meaning techniques: word parts, context, and dictionary. Then use it in an original sentence.

counterproductive _____

_____

_____

requisite _____

_____

_____

perseverance _____

_____

_____

dynamics _____

_____

_____

counterbalance _____

_____

_____

dispel _____

_____

_____

pertinent _____

_____

_____

conceptual _____

_____

_____

synthesize _____

_____

_____

augment _____

_____

_____

TAKE ACTION

Exercise 2

Directions: Have you heard the expression "Experience is the best teacher"? Use the experiences of your life to build a positive mental set for exams. Describe in three paragraphs:

1. Your current attitude about exams.

2. A situation in your life when you overcame disappointment or achieved beyond your expectations.

3. How you can use that experience to improve your mental set about tests.

_____

_____

_____

_____

_____

_____

_____

_____

_____

_____

_____

_____

_____

Exercise 3

Directions: As a tutor, you have been assigned a new student who is having difficulty concentrating while studying because of test-related stress. In a paragraph, give the student three specific strategies for test preparation and explain each. Keep your recommendations simple so you do not increase the student's stress.

_____

_____

_____

_____

_____

_____

_____

Exercise 4

Directions: Practice making study questions from chapter headings. Make a question for each of the three major headings in Chapter 6. Then briefly answer the questions you have posed.

_____

_____

_____

_____

_____

_____

_____

_____

_____

_____

_____

_____

_____

_____

Exercise 5

Directions: Get a head start on an upcoming exam. Prepare a summary sheet for a chapter that you have completed and that will be included on the test. Follow these guidelines:

- Limit the summary to a maximum of two notebook pages.
- Use all sources of information related to the chapter.
- Select the most significant concepts and the best supporting facts and details.
- Use organizational patterns to logically arrange the information.
- Create headings for each section that can be used to cue self-quizzing.

CHECK YOUR PROGRESS

Directions: Put into action the test preparation strategies! After your next exam, use this checklist to evaluate your progress. Then use the space that follows to analyze your growth in at least two paragraphs.

PROGRESS CHECKLIST: Preparing for Tests

Yes   Usually   No

___ ___ ___ **1.** I focus on accomplishing my best on tests, rather than winning or losing.

___ ___ ___ **2.** I accept that problems and setbacks will occur.

___ ___ ___ **3.** I use stress management and other people to maintain a positive mental set.

___ ___ ___ **4.** I begin studying at least one week before an exam and follow a study schedule.

___ ___ ___ **5.** I make summary sheets to organize information for recall mastery.

___ ___ ___ **6.** I practice problems, case studies, and discussion questions to achieve analytical mastery.

___ ___ ___ **7.** I schedule a brief overall review session, emphasizing the areas that are most difficult for me.

___ ___ ___ **8.** I monitor my meals, sleep, and exercise to maintain good physical condition.

A. Discuss the test preparation strategies that are working well for you and how you have adapted them to your own needs.

B. Identify those strategies that have been less successful and why you feel they have been less useful. Explore ways you can use them better.

Don't Stop There! Do you sometimes think people overlook your best characteristics? Take a few lines to describe your three greatest strengths. How do you think these attributes help you with friends, on the job, and of course, at school? Don't be modest!

CHAPTER

11

Taking Tests

THE SKILL THAT GETS THE JOB

Executive Assistant.
For medical electronics company. Duties include convention planning and advertising. A quick-paced environment. Applicant must know how to keep cool under pressure.

WHAT'S YOUR EXPERIENCE?

When the heat is on, it's time to be cool, but that's not always easy to do. What skills or attitudes do you think are necessary for coping under pressure? How well do you cope when a test is difficult? What would you like to learn about this very important skill? Use the space below to explore your skill, your knowledge, and your questions about this chapter's topic.

_____

_____

_____

_____

_____

_____

_____

_____

_____

_____

_____

_____

In this chapter you will learn to

»»»   **Avoid panic with your positive mental set.**

»»»   **Relax your mind and body with exercise.**

»»»   **Be in charge of a test with a plan of action.**

»»»   **Make reasonable guesses when necessary.**

»»»   **Plan and write focused essay answers.**

TAKING TESTS

_____   _____
Name   Date

Circle the SMART test strategies.

A. Focus on a positive mental set.

B. Plan how you will complete the exam.

C. Make reasonable guesses.

D. Plan and organize essay answers.

E. All of the above.

In the previous chapter you focused your efforts on being prepared for exams in three vital areas. This chapter will again focus on stress management, academic knowledge, and your physical condition. Now, however, you will concentrate on controlling these factors under the pressure of taking the exam. You can extend your test coping strategies into other areas of performance as well: giving a speech, competing in a sport, or interviewing for a job. All situations in which you must perform under pressure require you to apply your knowledge and skill while maintaining your physical and mental balance.

CONTROL TEST ANXIETY WITH STRESS MANAGEMENT

imperceptibly

Sweaty palms, dry mouth, weak knees, knotted stomach. Have you experienced these physical signs of stress? Even when you are well prepared for performance, unchecked stress can command the body and shut down the mind. Most people have experienced at least once in their lives panic at the moment they are about to perform. Stress begins to build imperceptibly or suddenly grabs you in response to some stimulus. Panic takes over and performance becomes a struggle. Even diligent preparation is of little help.

Extreme anxiety and panic grow from fear. When facing a test most people fear failure, the negative reactions of others, and perhaps most of all, their own disappointment and sense of shame. In reaction, the body triggers what is called the fight-or-flight response. This reaction prepares the body for *physical danger,* sending extra oxygen to the muscles for combat or top speed running. Thus, your body is not prepared for the complex task of answering questions. To avoid panic and its symptoms, you must establish control over the negative feelings that trigger the fight-or-flight response. There are two times when you can place yourself in control, immediately prior to the exam and as you are taking the test.

Before the Exam: Reinforce Your Positive Mental Set

neutralize

As an exam approaches, keep focused on the important elements of your mental set. Be sure to address any negative feelings as they develop. This is an excellent time to use journal writing. If you don't keep a regular journal, scribble your thoughts down on anything at anytime. Neutralize your doubts on paper before they become fears. Keep these positive attitudes operating:

- **Your commitment to do your best.** Remember that you have set out not to win or to be the best in the class, but to strive for your personal best.

evoke

- **Your strong areas of preparation.** Build your confidence on the skill and knowledge you have gained during your week of study. Despite diligent study, most people worry about weak areas of knowledge and skill. Don't slip into negative thinking about any shortcomings. Instead of worrying about possible mistakes, focus on reminding yourself of behaviors that will prevent errors. Read the paired statements in Figure 11−1. Those on the left are vague, powerless thoughts that evoke anxiety. On the right are positive strategies that you can use to keep control and avoid mistakes.

FIGURE 11–1   *Forming Positive Thoughts*

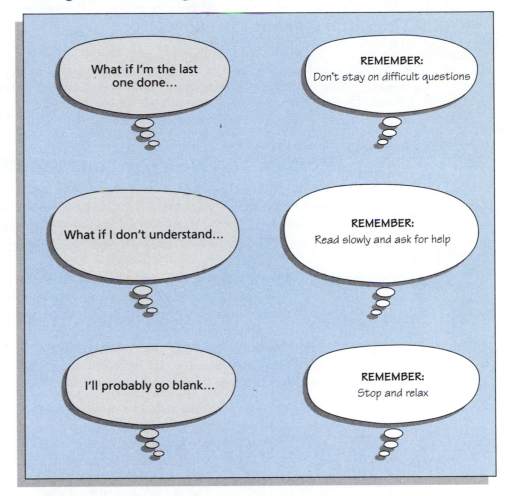

- **Your belief that errors can be overcome.** Remember that some mistakes will occur and that they provide an opportunity for new learning. If you dwell on mistakes and dread the time immediately after an exam, prearrange to spend time after the exam with a friend or mentor.

STRESSBUSTER

If you think negatively about yourself long enough, those ideas become part of your self-concept. If you think positively about yourself, those ideas can become part of your self-concept too. To build a stronger positive self-concept, target one of your strong points and repeat it to yourself at least four times during the day. Sell yourself to yourself.

Develop Relaxation Techniques

If the stress you experience is very strong and more difficult to control, you also need to use relaxation techniques. Most relaxation programs clear the mind while regulating breathing and relaxing muscles, thus avoiding the fight-or-flight

INFORMATION FILE: LEARNING THE ROPES

Experience Wanted

Would you like to relax and watch a video? Probably not if the video were an employment test. Some companies are now using interactive video tests to screen applicants for managerial positions. These tests use actors to dramatize work situations the applicants must solve, such as scheduling conflicts, safety violations, and charges of sexual harassment. Test designers recommend that applicants be themselves and give answers based on their *own work experience.*

response. Because your anxiety patterns have formed over a long period of time, you will need to use the techniques consistently at least several days in advance of your exam. Try these activities to establish control of your mind and body.

1. **Create a pleasant mental image.** This is your chance to run away from your studies for just a bit. Visualize a scene you find pleasurable and calm. You can place yourself in the setting, if you like. Perhaps you see yourself in your favorite chair with headphones on listening to all your favorite discs. Maybe you envision an empty beach with the water lapping up on the sand. Try to choose one visual image and use it regularly so that its familiarity automatically brings comfort.

2. **Become aware of your breathing, establishing a slow, steady rhythm.** Regulating your breathing is a key to preventing the fight-or-flight response from taking over. Begin with deep inhalations followed by long exhalations to slow your breathing pattern. Then set a calming tempo for the rest of your relaxation exercise.

3. **Relax your muscles.** The weariness you feel in your neck, around your eyes, and along your spine can be relieved by relaxing muscle groups. Start with your head, then progress to your shoulders, arms, and your back, then along your thighs to your toes. You will receive maximum relief if you first tense the group of muscles and then release them. Does this sound strange? Probably you already use some muscle relaxation—when you clench your fist, then extend each finger or when you tightly close your eyes then open them slowly. Try to match the tensing of a muscle group with a deep inhalation of breath and the relaxation of the muscles with your long, steady exhalation. Gradually you will feel a calm coordination between your mind and body.

You won't build an effective relaxation routine over a few days. But with consistent practice, your mind and body will begin to respond positively to certain activities. Then you can develop your own style and routine by quietly listening to your mind and body. If you want additional help, check your library for books and audiotapes on the subject or see your campus counseling staff.

Take Care of Your Body

A heightened stress level immediately before an exam sometimes causes students to neglect their basic physical requirements. Take these steps to counteract that tendency:

1. Go to bed about a half hour earlier the evening before the exam so that you have adequate time to relax and fall asleep.

2. The morning of the exam, have a nutritious breakfast, monitoring your intake of caffeine and sugar.

3. Instead of an extra cup of coffee or tea, exercise briefly, being sure to stretch and relax.

Keep Control

Having established control, you must also be prepared to maintain it if your stress begins to increase. Often students talk about times when panic overtakes them—encountering a difficult question, or someone finishing early. What are test situations that can trigger extreme stress for you? Briefly explain them here.

_____

_____

_____

_____

_____

Have these stress strategies ready for those difficult moments so you can regain control.

1. **Begin by arriving on time for the exam.** If you are running late, your stress level will rise.

2. **Concentrate on maintaining a positive mental set.** While you are waiting, avoid students who are overtly anxious and negative about the upcoming exam. Their negativity could trigger your own anxiety. If these people are difficult to avoid, block them out by focusing on your own positive mental set.

3. **If panic does begin, STOP and use relaxation techniques to regain control.** Take action by turning over your test paper. *Don't* continue with the test. Then use your relaxation strategies to calm your mind and body. At this point the most effective approaches are brief and direct:

   • Count slowly to reestablish rhythmic breathing.
   • Visualize your positive mental image to dispel negative thoughts.

- Recite the lyrics of a favorite song that combines positive thoughts with a soothing rhythm.

Do you think too much time would be lost using this approach? Usually students need just a minute or two to regain their composure. Without that break you would not be able to think clearly, perhaps wasting more than two minutes struggling with easy questions and even selecting wrong answers.

4. **Ask your instructor for help.** Many instructors are very supportive and can help you if you become anxious or confused during a test.

Avoid statements such as "My mind went blank." "I can't believe the stupid mistakes I made." Use your positive mental set and relaxation techniques to establish and maintain control in exam situations.

During the Test: Being Test-Wise

You can also have a great deal of control over the testing situation itself. If you have a specific plan of action for completing the test and each type of question, *you* are in charge, not that white sheet of paper. First you must know how you will approach the test itself. The biggest mistake students make is blindly beginning to answer questions without gaining background information and devising a plan. Follow these general test guidelines to make the most of your time and your academic knowledge.

1. **Listen carefully to any directions given by the instructor.** Even if she or he reads the directions from the test, pay attention. You do not know when an instructor might give a valuable tip, correct typographical errors, or indicate questions to be skipped.

2. **Look over the entire exam.** Pay attention to the types of questions in each section and the point values assigned. By looking over the test at first, you will know just what is ahead of you, and you won't be get an unpleasant surprise when you turn a page.

3. **Make a plan of action.** You don't have to begin with item 1 and work straight through the test to item 50. Decide how you can get the best score by first completing the sections of the test that are easiest and carry high point values. Sometimes people begin with the most difficult material, reasoning that they will need as much time as possible. This is not a good strategy for two reasons. Answering the hardest questions first could take too much time, robbing you of valuable time you'll need for easier questions. In addition, you will not be building confidence at the outset so you will be more susceptible to increased stress. Look at the simple plan devised by a student and his reasoning for this approach.

rationale

PLAN	RATIONALE
1st—section 3, multiple choice 40 points	easiest type of question & highest point value
2nd—section 1, true and false 15 points	usually quite easy

> *3rd—section 4, 3 essay questions   hard, but high point value*
> *   30 points*
> *4th—section 2, fill-in the blanks   usually very difficult*
> *   25 points*

Leaving essays and sentence completion items until later in the allotted time is a good strategy, because while working on other questions, you may acquire helpful facts for answering these more difficult types of questions. However, leaving essays until the very end is not wise, because you will need time to plan and write the longer answers that are required.

4. **Read the directions to each section carefully.** In an effort to save time, students sometimes skip directions when they see a familiar type of question. Consequently, they can miss important specific directions: to use their own paper, to underline the correct answer. Such oversights can be disastrous. Take the time to understand exactly what is expected.

5. **Read each question slowly for full understanding.** Many test questions are designed to catch the careless reader. If you tend to read rapidly because you are keyed up, slow yourself down by moving your pencil from word to word so you can "hear" the words in your head. Watch for **absolute words** and **conditional words** in multiple choice and true-false questions. **Absolute words** restrict the meaning of an answer and allow for no exceptions. Consequently, they usually make an answer incorrect or false. The following statement might seem true at first, but can you think of any exceptions?

All advertising is designed to influence the purchaser.

This statement is false because advertising that is designed to sell toys is often directed to children who do not purchase the items themselves but who do influence adults who make the purchases. Study these most common absolutes so you can readily spot them on an exam.

never	**every**	**everybody**
none	**always**	**everyone**
all	**only**	**no one**

Always be ready to use your logic, however, because some statements containing absolutes *are* true. Consider this statement.

None of America's presidents has been foreign born.

This statement is true because native birth is a Constitutional requirement for the presidency. Watch for absolutes, but always apply reason and knowledge to the answer you choose.

Conditional words are broad in meaning and expand the circumstances of the statement. Statements with conditional words are usually true or correct. Which is the best answer in this multiple choice question?

Vitamin C is
    A.   beneficial only in its natural forms.
    B.   not found in vegetables.

C.   never harmful.
D.   often used to treat the common cold.

Choice *D* is the best answer because it makes a broadly accurate statement whereas the other statements are narrowly set by absolutes. This is a list of the most common conditional terms. Be ready to recognize them in your test questions.

some	many
most	usually
often	few
sometimes	frequently

levied

6. **Guess on difficult questions if no penalty is levied.** Test makers sometimes deduct more points for wrong answers than for skipped items to discourage guessing. Most college instructors do not use this approach. For the average college exam, guessing will yield you more points and help to keep you in a positive frame of mind. When you *do* guess on a question, put a mark next to it so you can come back to it if you think of the correct answer.

7. **Do not choose answers based on patterns that emerge in your answers.** Often students become nervous when an odd pattern, such as four consecutive *D* answers, occurs. In a panic, they change the fourth answer. Rely on your knowledge instead of trying to second-guess the instructor. Sometimes teachers do create odd patterns in the answers. Also by changing that fourth answer, you are assuming it is the incorrect answer. Perhaps the error is in the first answer or maybe the third. Don't put chance in charge of the test. Put your mind and knowledge in charge.

8. **Disregard the pace and activities of those around you.** Often students become flustered when someone around them turns the page faster or gets up to leave. Usually they fear being the last to leave. Although production time is a consideration in some testing situations, such as dictation, it is almost always coupled with an accuracy factor as well. You cannot assume someone's achievement based merely on her or his speed. Have confidence in your own abilities—both in speed and accuracy.

9. **Pace yourself, and do not linger over difficult questions.** Avoid getting bogged down with a question or a particular section of the exam. You will lose valuable time needed for answering other questions. Also, remember that your first answer is probably the correct answer, and additional debate will only undermine your self-confidence. If you consistently have difficulty finishing exams, set specific time limits for each section of the test so you are sure to cover as much of the material as possible. Do not fall into the trap of constantly checking the clock. Worrying wastes time; answering questions uses your time constructively.

constructively

10. **Use any remaining time to look over the entire test.** For your best possible performance, check your work by

   • Rereading each set of directions for anything you might have overlooked.

   • Rereading questions to confirm your understanding.

STRESSBUSTER

Turn off station W-O-R-R-Y. Constant worrying about a problem will only make the situation worse, but turning off those thoughts can be difficult. Try visualizing the destruction of your worries:

- Crush them in a trash compactor.
- Send them off in a hot air balloon.
- Zap them with a computer virus.

When you've had some fun and your mind is clearer, take action to solve the problem one step at a time.

- Looking for clerical errors you might have made such as recording two *B*s consecutively instead of a *B* and an *A* or inverting 38 to 83.
- Editing to correct spelling errors and omitted words.

If you are *certain* that an answer is incorrect when you reread it, perhaps because of information gained in the rest of the test, then of course change the answer. However, do not begin changing answers because you are becoming doubtful of your choices. If you begin to find your anxiety level rising, then submit your exam with the confidence that you tried your best.

Be in control of the exam from the first minute to the last by establishing a plan, reading carefully, and checking for accuracy.

TYPES OF TEST QUESTIONS: HOW TO HANDLE THEM

You can also improve your testing advantage by understanding the best way to answer common types of questions. Do you feel comfortable with one type of question but dread another type? The tips in this section will give you confidence in answering the most common types of test questions.

Multiple Choice Questions

prevalent

Probably the most prevalent type of test question is the multiple choice item. These questions are actually incomplete statements followed by three to five choices for completion. The student must either recognize the correct choice or eliminate the incorrect ones. Follow these guidelines for doing your best on multiple choice questions.

1. **Carefully read the question and supply an answer from your head without looking at the choices.** Then read the choices and select the one closest to your mental answer. This will help you avoid a mental tug-of-war between two answers.

2. **If you cannot think of an answer on your own, read through the choices and use the process of elimination to choose the best answer.** Usually it is quite easy to eliminate two of the choices as inaccurate or not directly related to the question. With two choices eliminated, you have a 50 percent chance and can simply pick one of the remaining two choices. Rely on your hunches and do not look for patterns in the answers. Try the process of elimination with this typical multiple choice question.

INFORMATION FILE: LEARNING THE ROPES

To Tell the Truth. . .

Many types of employment tests are used to learn more about prospective employees. One controversial type is called the integrity or honesty test. Through a series of questions, employers try to determine the honesty of their applicants. Many critics of these tests say they are unfair because honesty is often difficult to measure. Researchers at the University of Iowa examined 40 integrity tests and found that test results matched very closely with supervisor's reports about test takers who had been hired. In addition, they found that employees with high integrity scores also demonstrated conscientious behavior such as low absenteeism and tardiness on the job.

Alaska and Hawaii
- A.   have nothing in common
- B.   both enjoy tropical climates
- C.   are both part of the North American continent
- D.   were the last territories to become states

Compare your reasoning for answering this question with the process of elimination that follows.

1. Choice A can be eliminated because the absolute *nothing* narrows the statement and excludes such similarities as language and statehood.
2. Choice B can be eliminated because Alaska does not have a tropical climate.
3. Choice C can also be eliminated because Hawaii is a series of islands and is not part of a continent.
4. D then remains as the only possible choice to accurately complete the statement.

3. **For questions requiring a combination of choices as the answer, treat each choice as a true or false item.** Students often find these confusing, so they blindly guess or skip the question. To simplify your task, treat each choice as a true and false item, placing a *t* or an *f* next to the corresponding letter. Continue in this manner through all the choices. Then "total" your responses. Examine how this method was used in the following example.

To prevent the transmission of sexual diseases, health specialists recommend
- *t* A. abstinence
- *t* B. using condoms
- *f* C. a high-fiber diet
- D. A and B
- E. all of the above

Because choice C is false, the correct answer is D.

4. **Use these guidelines when you must guess.**

   • **Select numbers in the middle of the range, not the extremes.**
   Usually instructors give incorrect choices that are higher and lower in value than the correct answer.

- **Choose an answer that is familiar, rather than one that is unknown.** Sometimes students pick the most difficult information, figuring the instructor has given a trick question. Usually the opposite is true. Instructors test information from lectures and the textbook. Therefore, most correct answers should be familiar to students who have studied and prepared.
- **Select long, descriptive answers rather than brief ones.** To be sure the correct choice is clear to readers, instructors often give full descriptions, and the choice stands out from the others because of its length.
- **Choose between two similar answers.** For example, if the correct answer to a question is *software,* most instructors would give *hardware* as one of the choices. By choosing between two similar answers, you usually have a 50–50 chance of being right.

True and False Questions

Students like the 50–50 odds of true and false questions. While this type of question does present fewer options, you should answer them carefully. Follow these guidelines for high marks on true and false questions:

1. **Determine the accuracy of all parts of the statement.** If one part of the statement is inaccurate, the entire statement is false. Decide if the following statement is true or false.

    Today nutritionists recommend a diet rich in high-fiber and high-fat foods.

    While health experts recommend high-fiber foods, they do not recommend foods with a high fat content; therefore, the statement is false.

2. **Take special note of negative words.** Obviously they reverse the meaning of the statement. Sometimes students confuse the negatives in the sentence with the negative choice of a false answer. A statement can contain a negative word or prefix and still be true or accurate. Look closely for negatives found in word parts such as *un, im, mis*. Is the following statement true or false?

    Prison overcrowding is undesirable.

    This statement is *accurate* because overcrowding leads to behavior problems; thus, the answer is *true*.

clarity
3. **Eliminate both negatives in a double negative statement for greater clarity.** Statements with two negatives are actually positive statements because the negatives cancel out each other. In this sentence, "Sexually transmitted diseases are not uncommon," the two negatives are *not* and *un*. When they are crossed out, the sentence is a positive statement.

    Sexually transmitted diseases are common.

    With the negatives removed, you can easily determine the accuracy of a statement.

4. **When you have no knowledge on which to base an answer, assume the statement is true.** Tests makers tend to emphasize accurate statements; therefore, most tests contain more true statements. For example, many students would skip the following test question because they were unfamiliar with the statistic cited. Rather than skip a question of this type, mark it true, knowing that you have a better than 50 percent chance of being correct.

> There are more than 3 million hotel rooms in the United States.

You can also answer matching exercises with greater skill if you put a few simple strategies into action.

Matching Questions

Instructors use this type of exercise to test recall knowledge when there is a large amount of terminology or basic facts to be mastered. Matching exercises consist of two lists, one providing specific descriptions; the other, general terms. Refer to this example as you read the following guidelines for answering matching test items.

Example:

Directions: Match each type of television program from column 1 with its correct definition from column II. Draw a line connecting each term with its definition.

I		II
1. docudrama	A.	program that examines news topics in segments of 15 to 30 minutes, often uncovering corruption or misconduct
2. investigative news stories	B.	program that presents a fictionalized story involving law enforcement
3. crime story	C.	program that retells a true event using actors to portray the people involved and their actions

---

1. **Be alert to any special conditions stated in the directions.** Sometimes directions indicate that choices from one list can be used more than once. Especially helpful are directions that explain the relationship between the lists. In the example above, the directions are very helpful because the relationship of terms and definitions is clearly stated.

2. **Analyze the relationship between the two lists if an explanation is not provided.** Here are some common relationships used:
   - Terminology and definitions.
   - People and their accomplishments.
   - Parts and their functions.
   - Places and their significance.

3. **Work consistently down one list.** An organized approach will help you avoid errors and poor choices. Usually working from the shorter, more general list is easier.

interdependent

4. **Skip items until you are *sure* of a match.** Guessing does not work for this type of question because all the choices are interdependent. Once you have used an answer, usually it cannot be used for later choices, and two errors can result from one incorrect guess. Therefore, don't stop at the first likely answer. Read the entire list until you find the best answer. In the example, the first definition might seem to match with *docudrama* until you read further in *both* lists. The key to matching items is patient, careful reasoning.

5. **Cross off choices as you use them.** This simple clerical step will help you avoid confusion and recording errors.

Now use the strategies to solve the example. The correct answers are *1-C, 2-A, 3-B*.

Sentence Completion Questions

You will see the value of a high mastery level when answering sentence completion or fill-in-the-blank questions because they require specific answers. When you don't know the desired answer, try these strategies.

1. **Look for contextual clues that will help you formulate an answer.** For example, when a plural verb is used, you know a plural subject is required. Pronouns may be indicators of gender, as in this statement:

    > The great expressionist artist _____ studied to be a minister like his father.

    The pronoun *his* indicates that a male artist is being sought.

2. **Pay special attention to the number of blanks used and the length of each.** In the example below, you quickly learn that two words are required, one considerably longer than the other.

    > Photosynthesis is the process by which plants collect _____ from _____ and release oxygen into the air.

    If you were unsure if energy was collected from chlorophyll or the reverse, the size of the blanks would help you determine the answer. Increasingly instructors are using blanks that are uniform in length to eliminate any unnecessary clues, however.

3. **Supply a general, descriptive answer when you do not have a specific answer.** Often such an answer will yield at least partial credit. In the completion question below, the correct answer is *double helix;* however, the student might receive partial credit for this less specific yet descriptive answer.

    > DNA is formed in the shape of <u>2 twisted spirals</u> that are joined by hydrogen bonds.

Short Answer and Essay Questions

Both these types of questions also require you to recall information and present it in a concise format. Usually essay questions ask more complex questions and are consequently worth more points. Use your analytical skills and the following strategies to accomplish your best on short answer and essay questions.

| FIGURE 11–2 | *Task Verbs in Essay Questions* |

VERB	TASK
Outline	**Generalize** major points and the most significant minor points, possibly in an informal outline form
List	Briefly **generalize** points
Summarize	Give a **generalized** review of the major concepts or facts
Define	Give a **specific** meaning
Describe	Give a **specific**, detailed picture
Identify	**Specify** points, giving descriptive details
Illustrate	Give a **specific** example or examples as explanation or proof
Compare	Show **similarities** with secondary differences
Contrast	Give **differences**
Distinguish	Show **contrasts**
Differentiate	Show **contrasts**
Trace	Give the **sequential** development or the steps of a process
Solve	Show the **steps** to solve a problem
Explain (why)	Give **causes and/or effects**
Explain (how)	Describe the **process**
Justify	Give proof or reasons (**cause and effects**)

1. **Select the question or questions you understand best, not those you feel you can write about the most.** Many students believe that the key to a good essay answer is length. Usually instructors prepare a set of key points that they want students to cover in their answers. If you are able to cover all the points adequately in 250 words, you will receive full credit, whereas someone who covers half the points in 500 words will probably receive just that—half credit.

2. **Focus on the task verbs to fully understand the requirements of the question.** Task verbs are the direction words used in the question. To complete the required task, you must understand these verbs. Figure 11–2 gives the most common task verbs and a brief explanation of the required task. Notice that the verbs have been grouped by their major organizational pattern. Be sure you circle each task verb so you can keep track of all the tasks you are to accomplish in your essay. For example, a typical essay question might be written like this:

   Trace the development of the personal computer, explaining why it became feasible as a consumer product in the 1970s.

How many tasks are required in this question? There are two tasks:

   1. The primary job of describing how the personal computer developed.

   2. Giving the reasons why personal computers became more practical in the 1970s.

FIGURE 11–3	*Student Brainstorming and Planning for an Essay Answer*

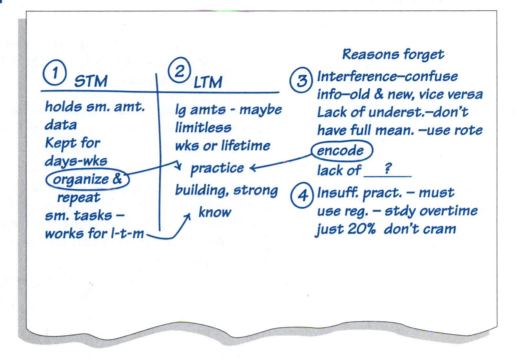

Now try finding the tasks in the next essay question:

> Identify the three main types of computers and compare the primary function of each, giving an example of each type's applications.

Did you find three tasks?

1. Specify and describe three types of computers.
2. Compare the jobs of each (give their differences too).
3. Give an example of how each type is used.

3. **Generate your ideas and the basic information required once you fully understand the question.** Use the reverse side of a test page to organize what you want to say. Remember to use your organizational patterns to logically arrange the information. If your mind goes blank and you cannot write, use brainstorming to trigger your thoughts. You can review the guidelines for brainstorming in Chapter 1. Figure 11–3 illustrates a student's brainstorming and plan for the essay. Figure 11–4 shows the finished product. Notice that the student's plan includes an introduction and a conclusion, which will give the essay a clear sense of purpose. Usually you can paraphrase the original question to create an introductory statement. Examine how the ideas of this question are recast into a general introductory statement.

recast

Question: Identify the **three main types** of computers and compare the **primary functions** of each, giving an example of each type's applications.

Introduction: *Computers can be classified into **three major types** according to their **primary uses.***

FIGURE 11–4   *Student Essay Answer*

Question: Describe two types of memory used in learning and identify two reasons people forget information. (list & describe)

In order to learn, people must use two types of memory and overcome the causes of forgetting.

The two types of memory are short-term and long-term memory. Short-term memory holds small amounts of information for a few hours or days. Usually the information has to be repeated so it can be retained. Short-term memory is used mostly for simple tasks and for holding information until it can be processed for long-term memory.

Long-term memory can hold large amounts of information for weeks, even a lifetime. For information to be retained, it must be organized or encoded and practiced. Long-term memory is used for building a body of knowledge.

Two factors in forgetting are interference and insufficient practice. Interference happens when information becomes confused with other information. Sometimes new information can not be recalled because it is confused with previous information, and old information can be lost when new information is introduced. People also forget when they do not use or practice information regularly. Often students wait until just before an exam to study. By then they probably remember just 20% of the information. Learning requires the use of short-term and long-term memory and strategies to over come the causes of forgetting.

You can recast the question one final time as a summarizing statement something like this:

Conclusion: The **three major types** of computers affect almost every part of peoples' daily lives from an airline reservation to a microwaved dinner.

If you are unable to write a good conclusion or an introduction, don't panic, simply give the main body of information. Although these features improve the cohesion of an essay, instructors do not deduct many points when they are lacking. Later on, you can practice developing introductions and conclusions using the discussion questions in your textbook.

INFORMATION FILE: LEARNING THE ROPES

A Hired Hand Is a Steady Hand

Even if you land a job, you might have to take a video test before you can come to work each day. Companies have begun to use a video test called Factor 1000 that measures eye-hand coordination. They are using this test in place of traditional drug testing for jobs that involve public safety such as driving a tour bus and handling poisonous gases. Before beginning work, the employee types in an ID code and completes several targeting tasks. The employee's performance is measured against his or her performance norm. If the employee falls below that level, he or she cannot work that day. Company officials say that below-average test performance is often due to extreme fatigue or illness rather than drug use. Removing unfit employees does pay off; one company reported a 67 percent drop in accidents and a 92 percent reduction in job errors.

4. **Give your own opinions and ideas only if they are required by the question.** Most essay questions are designed to test your knowledge of specific course material. Keep your focus there so you receive the highest grade possible.

5. **Use any remaining time to look over your essay.** First return to your circled task verbs and be sure you have fulfilled each one. Then read over your essay, using the 3-C criteria outlined in Chapter 1, to evaluate and improve your answer. Make any changes as neatly as possible because your overall organization and neatness will influence how the instructor grades your work.

At the time of an exam or any type of performance, the key word is control. To perform at your best, establish and maintain control of your stress level, testing skill, and knowledge of the information.

THE ASAP REWIND ‹‹ ‹‹ ‹‹

How can I avoid panicking just before a test?

Avoid panic by

- Maintaining a positive mental set.
- Using relaxation exercises.
- Seeking the instructor's help if needed.

What can I do to have control when I take a test?

Be in charge of a test by

1. Looking it over first.
2. Making a plan to complete each section of the test.
3. Reading *all* directions carefully.

How can I improve my overall test performance?

Follow these guidelines to maximize your test scores:

Read each question carefully.

Use the first answer you recall.

Make logical guesses when you don't know the answer.

Plan and **organize** essay answers.

WORD POWER

Exercise 1

Directions: Many words in this chapter can expand your vocabulary for improved reading and writing on exams. Define each word using the word meaning techniques: word parts, context, and dictionary. Then use it in an original sentence.

imperceptibly _____

_____

_____

neutralize _____

_____

_____

evoke _____

_____

_____

rationale _____

_____

_____

levied _____

_____

_____

constructively _____

_____

_____

prevalent _____

_____

_____

clarity _____

_____

_____

interdependent _____

_____

_____

recast _____

_____

_____

TAKE ACTION

Exercise 2

Directions: Help a friend who suffers from test anxiety. Dawn calls you one afternoon very worried about a major test she has the following day. She is an above average student but has had difficulty on exams in this course. Dawn says she cannot concentrate and has no appetite. Make four suggestions Dawn can use to control her anxiety. Remember, she is having trouble concentrating, so be specific and brief.

_____

_____

_____

_____

_____

_____

_____

_____

Exercise 3

Directions: Several students are discussing their approaches to taking exams. Read their statements and respond to each, explaining how they might have better control in testing situations.

1.   When I get an exam, I start right in at the beginning and don't look up until I'm done.

_____

_____

_____

2.   I work really fast too. I don't want to be the last one finished. That would be humiliating.

_____

_____

_____

3.   In sociology, I finish quickly because I leave so many blanks. I never seem to know the exact answers for those tests.

_____

_____

_____

4.   I've been told hunches are as good as a sure answer, so I just skim the questions and put down my first impression. If I don't, major panic takes over.

_____

_____

_____

5.   Yeah, I'm usually in a panic too. I can't think straight, and I keep wishing someone would help me out, but of course nothing can help you then.

_____

_____

_____

Exercise 4

Directions: This exercise gives you a chance to practice guessing on difficult multiple choice items. For many of the items, you probably will not have the specific knowledge required. Don't panic—guess, using the strategies from page 293–95. Underline the correct answer for each item. Use the answer key on page 308 to check your answers.

1. Reading readiness for preschool children includes
    A. a minimum height requirement
    B. the ability to distinguish basic shapes
    C. the ability to recall the alphabet
    D. A and B
    E. B and C

2. Demographics is
    A. a training video
    B. a three-dimensional diagram
    C. information about the size, distribution, and make-up of a population
    D. a type of textbook illustration

3. When answering a business phone
    A. never interrupt someone who is in conference
    B. usually give long-distance calls priority over local calls
    C. never place a caller on hold
    D. always assume that an executive wants calls screened

4. The average speaker says _____ words per minute.
    A. 50
    B. 100
    C. 150
    D. 300

5. Basic inherited characteristics are contained in
    A. genes
    B. ganglions
    C. cofactors
    D. gene locus

6. Interest that is computed on the sum of the original loan plus the accrued interest is called
    A. maturity value
    B. conversion period
    C. simple interest
    D. compound interest

7. Runner's knee refers to damage caused by repeated impact to _____ in the knee.
    A. cartilage
    B. ligaments
    C. tendons
    D. B and C
    E. all of the above

8. The typical top margin for the first page of a printed document is _____ inches.
    A. 1
    B. 1.5
    C. 2.5
    D. 3

9. A gestalt is a
    A. unified whole that cannot be reduced to its component parts
    B. small movement of the limbs
    C. period of embryonic development
    D. form of depression

10. Which of the following would be classified as an RNA virus?
    A. parvovirus
    B. papovirus
    C. adenovirus
    D. influenza virus

11. The agenda for a business meeting
    A. never includes a report by the presiding officer
    B. always includes a reading of the minutes of the previous meeting
    C. only lists scheduled speakers
    D. usually provides time for unfinished business

12. An analysis of an item across two or more financial statements is called
    A. vertical analysis
    B. horizontal analysis
    C. computing depreciation
    D. estimating inventory value

Exercise 5

Directions: Use the strategies for answering true and false questions to evaluate the accuracy of the following statements. Use the strategies from pages 295–96 to make logical guesses. Place a *T* or an *F* on the corresponding blank at the left. You can check your answers with the key on page 308.

____ 1. Preschool children do not show strong ownership tendencies.
____ 2. All adults have 32 teeth, 16 in the upper jawbone and 16 in the lower.
____ 3. OCR stands for optical character reader.
____ 4. A professional's personal appearance is not unimportant on the job.
____ 5. A well-constructed composition includes an introduction, a conclusion, a body of specific information, and good illustrations.
____ 6. Office romances are usually discouraged by supervisors.
____ 7. The first law of thermodynamics states that the total amount of energy in the universe remains constant.
____ 8. Preschool children do not benefit intellectually from play.
____ 9. Automobile insurance is based on the individual's age, marital status, religion, and driving record.
____ 10. Handouts and previous tests should not be overlooked when studying for a test.

Exercise 6

Directions: The following statements are based on the facts and ideas presented in Chapter 10. Don't refer to the chapter. Instead, use your strategies for sentence completion questions on page 297 to fill in each blank. Then check your answers with the answer key on page 308.

1. Study and review for an exam should begin approximately a _____ in advance of the test.

2. The three types of exam preparation are _____, _____ , and _____ .

3. Use a _____ _____ to plan your review activities for an exam.

4. Mastery for an exam should be at the _____ percent level.

5. _____ mastery is necessary for solving quantitative problems and case studies.

6. An _____ study session should conclude your practice before an exam.

7. To achieve analytical mastery, practice _____ and _____ from your textbook.

8. An _____ test question requires the student to combine and synthesize ideas in a short composition.

Exercise 7

Directions: Use the strategies for answering matching questions from pages 296–97 to complete the following exercise. Match each saying from column I on the left with its meaning from column II at the right. Place the corresponding letters on the blanks provided. Then check your answers on page 308.

	I		II.
___ 1.	A stitch in time saves nine.	A.	A lesson from experience is better than reasons in a book.
___ 2.	Pride goeth before the fall.		
___ 3.	He who laughs last, laughs best.	B.	Most people secretly feel hopeless.
___ 4.	Sleep that knits up the ravell'd sleave [*sic*] of care.[1]	C.	The person smiling in the end is the winner.
___ 5.	When man is wrapped up in himself, he makes a pretty small package.[2]	D.	Imperfect people shouldn't criticize others' faults.
___ 6.	A page of history is worth a volume of logic.[3]	E.	A night of rest takes away the worries of the day.
___ 7.	People who live in glass houses shouldn't throw stones.	F.	A timely repair avoids much work.
		G.	Don't take hasty action; think first.
___ 8.	A new broom sweeps clean.	H.	A selfish person is small in the eyes of others.
___ 9.	The mass of men lead lives of quiet desperation.[4]	I.	Conceit leads to failure.
___ 10.	Look before you leap.	J.	Novelty impresses.

[1]William Shakespeare.

[2]John Ruskin.

[3]Oliver Wendell Holmes.

[4]Henry David Thoreau.

Exercise 8

Directions: Use the steps for writing an essay question to answer one of the following questions. First, review each topic in your textbook. A chapter reference is given at the end of each question. Then choose the question you understand best. Do not refer to the text as you prepare your answer. Use your own paper for your brainstorming, plan, and essay. Ask your instructor for a key to the question you answered.

1. Explain two factors involved in setting a reading speed, and identify the three common pacing devices. (Chapter 7)

2. Describe the five steps in taking effective classroom notes. (Chapter 9)

3. Describe three common ineffective listening habits and give three reasons why ineffective habits develop. (Chapter 9)

CHECK YOUR PROGRESS

Directions: Put your strategies for coping with tests into action! After your next test, use this checklist to evaluate your progress. Then use the space that follows to analyze your growth in at least two paragraphs.

PROGRESS CHECKLIST: Coping with Tests

Yes   Usually   No

___ ___ ___   **1.** To avoid panic, I focus on my positive mental set and relaxation exercises.

___ ___ ___   **2.** When I receive a test, I listen to the instructor and make a plan of action.

___ ___ ___   **3.** I use the special question strategies to choose the best answers.

___ ___ ___   **4.** When a question is difficult, I make a reasonable guess and don't waste time.

___ ___ ___   **5.** For essay questions, I circle the task verbs and plan my answer.

___ ___ ___   **6.** When time remains, I check for obvious mistakes.

A. Discuss how the coping strategies for tests have worked for you. Give examples of changes you have been able to make and explain how they have been beneficial.

B. Identify those areas of test taking in which you are still having difficulties. Analyze why you think these difficulties still exist and explore ways you might overcome them.

Take Another Few Minutes. If you could eliminate tests from school completely, would you? Explain why you would take this position.

CHAPTER

12

Building on Experience

THE SKILL THAT GETS THE JOB

Architect's Technician.
Experienced CAD designer to develop projects. Salaried position with innovative firm. Must be a results-oriented person.

WHAT'S YOUR EXPERIENCE?

Most people would agree: Experience is the best teacher. How have you used the results of past experiences to create new plans or avoid old problems? What would you like to learn about developing through experience? Use the space below to explore your skill, your knowledge, and your questions about this chapter's topic.

_____

_____

_____

_____

_____

_____

_____

_____

_____

_____

_____

_____

_____

In this chapter you will learn to

»»» **Keep a grade record.**

»»» **Analyze your performance.**

»»» **Compute a grade point average.**

»»» **Set new goals.**

»»» **Use rewards for motivation.**

BUILDING ON EXPERIENCE

"Every end is a beginning" is a simple but wise saying. Whether you receive a graded test or hear about a job application, those results are only part of the picture. What you learn from the results and how you follow through with that knowledge is equally important. Many businesses recognize the importance of this process to productivity and encourage employees to make self-evaluations just as their supervisors evaluate them. This chapter presents simple steps you can use to grow from a variety of experiences, including tests, courses, or a school term.

MAKING THE MOST OF TEST RESULTS

Because emotions are intense when tests are returned, students sometimes respond with extreme feelings. Students who receive better-than-expected grades feel such a sense of relief that they become very relaxed and even overconfident. Soon their performance is as erratic as a roller-coaster ride. Enjoy your success, but remember that good grades rarely result from luck. Use your success to maintain or even improve your performance.

The low test grade—expected or unexpected—brings a flood of negative feelings. Usually anger dominates, and the student is unable to respond rationally. If you are disappointed by your test results, you are probably going to need a cooling-off period. Just be sure you don't tear up your test paper. With it go all the data about your strengths and weaknesses and consequently, the clues to how you can improve. File the test safely in your notebook. Then in a few days you can review it yourself or go over it with your instructor. You'll prolong your negative feelings if you handle them all alone. Talk with supportive friends and students. With the extreme feelings behind you, you can begin the important process of learning from your test.

Correcting Your Knowledge

First, be sure you have the correct answers to any questions you missed. If you are allowed to keep your test paper, write the correct answers on the test plus any explanations the instructor provides. If you must return your test paper, take notes in your lecture notebook. Be sure you focus on getting the correct information. If you do not, you are forming a weak foundation for future chapters and your final exam. Before you begin the next chapter, take some time to review those weak areas and bring them up to 90 percent mastery with practice. If you are working with a study group, schedule a session to review exam answers and correct your knowledge.

Keeping a Grade Record

Before you file away your test for safekeeping, make the grade part of a grade record you keep for that class. In each course you should keep a record of your grades for exams, quizzes, and any other assignment that will become part of your final average. With the grades recorded in one place, you can readily see your progress and you can estimate your average. Often students have only a vague idea of their current average in a course. As a result, they feel uneasy and unmotivated. If you haven't been recording your grades, begin compiling a list in each course today. If you do not have all your scores, consult with your instructors.

FIGURE 12–1   **Grade Record**

```
                                   Grades

        CMP 110 Computers

                        Tests                Grades

                    Chpt 1 & 2                C +
                    Chpt 3                    C
                    Chpt 4                    B–


        BUS 122 Intro to Bus

                Quizzes   Grades        Tests    Grades
                WK 1      A             Chpt 1   89
                WK 2      A             Chpt 2   93
                WK 3      B             Chpt 3   85
                WK 4      B             Chpt 4   90
                WK 5      A             Chpt 5   91
                                        (aver.)  89.6
```

The sample in Figure 12–1 shows a typical student grade record. You can make a section in your lecture notebook so your grades are handy for quick reference. With this overview of your progress, you can turn your attention to analyzing your performance on the last test and the goals you will set for the future.

ANALYZING YOUR PERFORMANCE

It is true that an exam doesn't always accurately reflect your knowledge or preparation. That's why it's important for *you* to analyze your performance. You, better than anyone, can point to the reasons for your successes and your shortcomings. After every exam or significant accomplishment, evaluate your abilities and efforts in these areas:

Focus and motivation.

Organization.

Active learning.

Stress management.

Always begin by identifying the areas in which you've done well. Since most people are quite critical of themselves, you could develop an unbalanced, negative picture of your performance. Let success breed success. Then you can use the suggestions of this chapter and your problem-solving skills to develop new strategies for improvement. Use these four steps to analyze your test performance.

1. **Double-check your ability to concentrate and your motivation level.** If you think these are important areas for improvement, review specific suggestions in Chapter 4.

2. **Analyze your organization.** How well did you plan for the exam by using your calendar and a study schedule? When you received the test, did you follow through with a plan of action? You can review these important strategies in Chapters 4, 10, and 11.

3. **Reevaluate your use of active learning strategies.** Which of these should become part of your improvement plan for the NEXT test?

   Class attendance

   Lecture note taking

   Paraphrasing and summarizing

   Self-quizzing

   Review Chapters 1, 8, and 9 or see your study skills instructor for additional help in employing and refining these learning strategies. They are your key to the in-depth learning that will make the difference on exams.

4. **Evaluate the impact of stress on your test performance.** If you experienced two or more of the following symptoms, test anxiety could have affected your performance on the last test.

   Insomnia.

   Lack of appetite.

   Lack of energy.

   General irritability.

   Inability to think.

   A pattern of obvious errors.

   To keep that balance of positive stress, consider these changes:

   Reduce your responsibilities so you can take more time for relaxation and for your studies.

   Obtain a tutor for one or more difficult courses.

   Use relaxation exercises daily, even when exams are not scheduled.

SETTING NEW GOALS

Now that you have fully analyzed your last test performance, you are ready to establish some new goals. The kind of goals you decide to set will depend on your overall performance in the course. Perhaps you are doing quite well, and your goal is simply to maintain your performance level so you can concentrate on other courses. Do you think it is unnecessary to set a goal if you want to maintain your performance level? Because people have a tendency to become lax and less focused when they are doing well, renewing goals when you're doing well is equally

INFORMATION FILE: THE YOU IN SUCCESS

Learning from a Winner . . .

Sekathia Smith was first put in a foster home at age two. By the time she was 16, two sets of foster parents and her birth mother had died. Finally living with her maternal grandparents, she worked at a small local college and a deli. She took courses at the college and found that the structure of school helped her to cope with the uncertainties of her life. At 26, she had not only earned a bachelor's degree, but also a degree in medicine. Looking back at her work, achievements, and her many college loans, Sekathia says, "I am my own investment, and I like what I see."

important as setting goals when you need to improve. For your goal to be effective, it must be specific. The following goal provides a specific focus and sufficient motivation to keep a student on target.

> *I intend to keep my B average in Business English, both in exams and class assignments.*

If you want to *improve* your performance in the course, your goals should aim at specific study and testing strategies that need improvement. First rank the four major factors that were discussed earlier according to their importance to your improvement. For example, a student who received a C− on his last test realizes that his study was not sufficiently in-depth and decides on this ranking:

> *2—Focus and motivation*
>
> *4—Organization*
>
> *1—Active mastery*
>
> *3—Stress management*

This student should not create a goal that covers all four factors because it would be unfocused. Here is a goal that will focus his energies on his two highest ranking study areas.

> *I intend to work for a C+ on my next test by using more active learning strategies and by working in a quieter area.*

As well as being specific, this goal provides a challenge and is realistically based on the student's past performance. Of course, any goal should be written down. Make it part of a journal entry or begin your new set of lecture notes with your new resolve. You can place it on the old exam as your personal conclusion or tape it up on your mirror. You can also use this evaluation process to evaluate your overall semester performance.

INFORMATION FILE: THE YOU IN SUCCESS

Challenging the Giant . . .

Apple Computer enjoyed years of popularity with consumers. Then came a challenge from the giant IBM who began making the same type of computer. Apple's chairman, Steve Jobs, did not confront the giant alone. He gathered together a group of talented programmers and designers and challenged them to build a technically superior computer that would be "Macbetter" and give consumers the "Macdifference." Together, Jobs and his team met those goals with the creation of the Macintosh Computer—a hit with computer users everywhere.

Making the Most of Your Semester Results

Most likely you will soon be receiving your course grades plus a term average, which is called the grade point average (G.P.A.) at many schools. Usually this average is calculated by computer, but you should understand how the calculations are done, since your G.P.A. is one measure of your academic success. As you read the following steps for calculating a grade point average, refer to the sample in Figure 12–2.

1. **Convert letter grades of A through F to point values.** Many schools use the following point system.

    A = 4.0
    B = 3.0
    C = 2.0
    D = 1.0
    F = 0

    Several variations of this system are used. Check your school catalog for the system used at your school.

2. **Multiply each point value by its corresponding number of course credits.** This step is important because it gives a greater value to an A earned in a four-credit course than to an A earned in a two-credit course. These numerical values are usually called grade points.

3. **Total your grade points and total your credits.** Be careful that you *do not total course grades* as you would if you were computing a simple average.

4. **Divide the total number of grade points by the total number of credits.** Be careful that you *do not total number of courses.* The answer from your division operation is your grade point average. Usually grade point averages are stated with no more than two decimal place values.

Knowing this simple computational process will give you confidence in setting semester academic goals and making plans for future semesters. Once you have completed the evaluation and planning process, it's time for a pat on the back.

FIGURE 12–2	*Computing a Grade Point Average*

	Grade Report	
Course	Grade	Course Credits
PHE 100	A	2
ENG 130	B	4
CMP 110	C	4
BUS 122	A	4

Step 1: Assign grade values

A = 4
B = 3
C = 2
A = 4

Step 2: Multiply grade values by credits

$4 \times 2 = 8$
$3 \times 4 = 12$
$2 \times 4 = 8$
$4 \times 4 = 16$

Step 3: Total credits and grade points

$2 = 8$
$4 = 12$
$4 = 8$
$4 = 16$
TOTALS = 14   44

Step 4: Divide total grade points by total credits

3.14 Grade Point Average

$$44 \div 14 = 14 \overline{)44.0}$$

42
─────
20
14
─────
60
56
─────
4

REWARDING YOURSELF

Taking time to relax and mark your accomplishments after each test and at the end of the semester is very important. If you do not, your schoolwork will become burdensome. One of the stressful aspects of student life is the lack of time for special activities and interests. Indulge yourself and enjoy your special interests in a way that you normally do not.

Another reward is to talk about your accomplishments. Having others recognize your efforts and your success will boost your confidence and motivation. Don't dismiss your efforts by deciding that your improvement was too small to share with others or to treat as significant.

As author of your textbook, I extend my congratulations to you. Most assuredly you are not the same student who first opened this book and attended your school's orientation sessions. Through hard work and belief in yourself, you have developed lifelong skills. Put CELEBRATION on your to-do list and make it a priority!

STRESSBUSTER

Pride, relief, sadness, regret—sometimes the conclusion of an activity can create a mix of feelings. They're all normal feelings in such a situation. Give yourself some time, then make plans for the future: how you'll keep in touch with important people and avoid old pitfalls. Soon you'll be on track again.

THE ASAP REWIND «« ««

What should I do when a test is returned?

Make the most of the results by correcting and mastering your mistakes and keeping a record of all test grades.

How can I use a test to improve my performance on future tests?

Analyze your concentration, organization, active learning, and stress management.

How can I motivate myself to achieve again?

Set new goals and reward yourself.

 WORD POWER

Exercise 1

Directions: The following words are typically associated with experience and are frequently used on job resumes because they convey action, strength, and skill. Define each word using your word parts and dictionary skills. Then give a brief example of how the word applies to **you** and your accomplishments. You can use examples from any part of your life.

accomplished (adjective) _____

_____

_____

autonomous _____

_____

_____

generate _____

_____

_____

implement _____

_____

_____

initiate _____

_____

_____

productive _____

_____

_____

resourceful _____

_____

_____

stability _____

_____

_____

versatile _____

_____

_____

vigorous _____

_____

_____

TAKE ACTION

Exercise 2

Directions: As a tutor, you are meeting with a new student, Doug. He is concerned about his progress in his course, but he can't give you any idea of his average. Explain to Doug the value of a grade record and how he can compile one.

_____

_____

_____

_____

_____

Exercise 3

Directions: At a recent work meeting, your supervisor asked for suggestions that would increase worker productivity and motivation. You suggested self-evaluations. Your boss thought it was a great idea, and now you must prepare an explanation for the next staff meeting. Write at least two paragraphs explaining why self-evaluation is beneficial and how it can be done. Be specific; the boss is counting on you.

_____

_____

_____

_____

_____

_____

_____

_____

_____

_____

Exercise 4

Directions: Apply the self-evaluation process to one of your recent exams. Complete each of the following steps.

1. Briefly describe your initial reactions to your score and how you coped with those feelings.

2. Record all the correct answers, if you have not already done so.

3. Add the grade to your grade record or compile one for the course that includes that test grade.

4. Select the two areas in which you feel you can make the greatest improvement on the next test and explain what specific changes you should make.

5. Write a specific goal that will lead you to the desired improvement in those areas.

_____

_____

_____

_____

_____

CHECK YOUR PROGRESS

Directions: Use the following survey to evaluate the foundation of study skills you have built throughout *ASAP*. Mark with an *X* your performance level for each of these study skills.

PROGRESS CHECKLIST

Yes Usually No

—— —— —— **1.** I accomplish most tasks that need to be done in a day.

—— —— —— **2.** I organize my materials and work area so items are accessible as needed.

—— —— —— **3.** I work in an area that allows me to concentrate on my goals.

—— —— —— **4.** To adapt to new situations, I familiarize myself with key people and available resources.

—— —— —— **5.** I practice important new information until it is memorized.

—— —— —— **6.** I analyze the organization and purpose of new information.

—— —— —— **7.** I adjust my reading strategies, depending on my purpose and the type of material I am reading.

—— —— —— **8.** I listen for a speaker's main point and record it if necessary.

—— —— —— **9.** If I become nervous in performance or testing situations, I use stress management techniques.

—— —— —— **10.** When my efforts aren't successful, I try to analyze the problem and find a solution.

A Handy Reference for Library Research

Developing good research skills is vital for your personal and professional development as well as your academic success. Today's libraries are dynamic, exciting centers filled with state-of-the-art technology that can unlock for you information from around the world. Indeed, as we enter the Information Age, your library is the place to be.

How can you make the most of this valuable resource? You need to carry out just three basic steps to establish your library research skills. To be successful in this process, give yourself adequate time to learn the organization of your library and be ready to ask questions. Because libraries have changed so greatly in the last decade, librarians regularly assist their patrons in using the equipment and materials that are available.

STEP 1:   KNOW YOUR LIBRARY'S RESOURCES

Today most libraries offer books, magazines, pamphlets and visual aids, audio tapes, and videocassettes. For organizational purposes, most materials are classified as fiction or nonfiction. So users can easily locate materials, libraries arrange their fiction materials by author and nonfiction materials by subjects or topics. Two classification systems are commonly used for nonfiction materials, the Dewey Decimal System and the Library of Congress system. Your librarian can acquaint you with the system used at your school. In addition, you should be acquainted with the following types of library materials.

Reference Materials

These works provide broad, summarized information on a wide range of topics and are usually housed in a separate part of a library called the reference section. Included in reference collections are encyclopedias, specialized dictionaries, almanacs, and handbooks. You may be particularly interested in the career handbooks that are typically available in school libraries. A special type of reference material is called the vertical file. This resource in most libraries is a collection of pamphlets, article reprints, and visual aids that cannot easily be bound. The material is usually filed in labeled folders or notebooks and is kept in regular file drawers.

Reference materials are often an excellent starting point for research, because they provide you with generalized information first so you can proceed to more detailed sources. Usually, reference materials cannot be removed or borrowed from a library. Therefore, when you plan to work in this area, be sure you have plenty of time to make notes or change to make photocopies. Larger libraries assign a librarian to the reference section so users can get special assistance in researching topics. Handy, isn't it?

Nonfiction Books

These resources are usually the largest part of a library collection. These books examine in greater depth fact-based topics. Nonfiction books will be very helpful to you when your research requires you to gather a great deal of information and examine it analytically. Most nonfiction books can be borrowed from a library for a specified period of time. When using a school library, however, you may find that some books have been placed on reserve by instructors. In this case, an instructor wants a book to be available for course reading assignments, and the library restricts use of the book so many students can use it. These restrictions vary from by-the-hour use in the library to overnight loans.

Fiction Books

These works include novels, plays, and collections of short stories. Probably you will use these books for work in English and literature classes and for your own pleasure reading.

The fiction and nonfiction books together make up what are often called the library stacks. The stacks are simply the rows and shelves of books. Stacks can be open or closed to users based on library policy. When stacks are open, you are able to walk through the rows, browse, and pick your selections from the shelves. When the stacks are closed, someone from the library staff gets books upon request. In addition to the stacks, many libraries provide an area for recreational reading that includes paperback books arranged on racks and chairs for casual reading. Check out this area in your library. It's a great place for a change of pace and new ideas.

Periodicals

This group of materials includes magazines, newspapers, and newsletters, which are excellent sources of current information. The type of periodicals available will depend on the type of library you use. At most postsecondary schools, libraries subscribe to some popular magazines such as *Time* and *People,* but they also offer more specialized magazines for the areas of study at that school, such as business and computer technology. Libraries also generally offer a broad range of newspapers, from local to international. Because storing and maintaining periodicals is difficult, back issues are often kept in a reduced form on microfilm. With a simple machine and the help of a librarian, you can enlarge, read, and even print a copy of a microfilm text.

Audiovisual Materials

Libraries offer a wide range of materials on audiotape, videocassette, slides, and various forms of film. The cataloging and arrangement of these materials vary greatly among libraries. Check with your librarian to learn what is available to you.

The wealth of knowledge available in a library is exciting. To access the information you want, you need to use certain tools and skills.

STEP 2: LOCATE USEFUL MATERIALS

A student locating information in a library is a bit like a detective solving a crime. You need patience, an eye for detail, and flexibility. Just as the detective has sources for leads, you need to be familiar with the tools for locating information in books and periodicals.

Books

Libraries list their books in a **card catalog,** either printed on file cards or stored in a computer. In either form, the catalog is an index of information. The books are classified in three ways: by author, title, or subject in an alphabetical arrangement. How you search for material depends on the information you already know. For example, if you are looking for a book recommended by a friend, you could search the catalog for either the title or the author of that specific book. When you do not have specific information, you can search the catalog for your general topic. For example, if you were interested in information about a career as a paralegal, you could search the catalog under the topic paralegal or paralegal studies.

Locating information by topics can be challenging. Students often complain that there is nothing on their topic. When you seem to hit a brick wall searching for a certain topic, don't give up. Try other related topics and synonyms. Paralegals are also called *legal assistants,* so you could try that term for a card catalog search. Be alert for the words *see* or *see also* in a catalog entry. This section will give you other topics to check out. The full catalog entry lists the author, title, publishing information, and most importantly, the classification number you can use to locate the book. Your librarian will be very helpful in teaching you how to read and fully use the valuable information in your school's cataloging system.

Periodicals

To tap into the rich information inside magazines and newspapers, you can use a variety of **indexes**: on computer, in books, or on microfilm. Indexes usually list information by author, subject, and title according to the year or month of publishing. Perhaps you have already used the *Reader's Guide to Periodical Literature.* This is an excellent source if you are looking for information in general, popular magazines. You can use other indexes such as the *Business Periodicals Index* or the *Social Sciences Index* when you look for information in specialized journals. You can locate newspaper articles by using the indexes for the papers available at your library. Many schools subscribe to the indexes for *The Wall Street Journal,* the *New York Times,* and the *Christian Science Monitor.* Some schools provide an indexing service for local papers as well.

Index entries give the author, the title, and publishing information for the article, and sometimes list additional topics to consult. Many abbreviations are used in listing this information—check the explanation of abbreviations given at the beginning of most indexes. You will have to check with the librarian for the availability and location of a particular magazine. Request systems differ among institutions.

RECORDING VITAL INFORMATION

Whenever you find a library source that you might use, you should carefully write down the significant information. Often students jot down just a partial entry. Then they find themselves wandering in the stacks, gazing at the books or double-checking an index for the full information. Be prepared to record information with the right supplies—notebook paper or index cards and a pen. Each time you locate a source, record the following bibliographic information:

BOOK	PERIODICAL
• author or editor	• author
• title	• article title
• publisher	• periodical title
• city of publishing	• volume number
• copyright date	• issue date
• catalog number	• page numbers

Not only will this information be important as you locate your sources, but also it will be important when taking notes.

Just as you label your lecture notes each day, you should carefully label any notes you make from a source. Use the author's last name and the first two words of the title if you have more than one work by the author. Be sure you list the pages the notes cover. For better understanding and to save time, paraphrase the author's words whenever possible. If you do directly quote the author, be sure to use quotation marks.

You will need your bibliographic information again if you are making a formal report, so file it away carefully. Using footnotes or creating a bibliography is called documentation. Your instructors will have specific documentation standards for their courses, but you can be ahead of the game if you *always* record the basic bibliographic information and fully label your notes.

BIBLIOGRAPHY

A

Axtel, Roger. *Gestures: The Do and Taboos of Body Language Around the World.* New York: John Wiley and Sons, 1991, pp. 113, 158, 184, 203.

B

Baig, Edward C. "Unlikely Treasures." *U.S. News and World Report* 113 (November 2, 1992), pp. 85–88.

Baig, Edward C. "Zap! Your Video Games Are Obsolete." *U.S. News and World Report* 110 (June 24, 1991), pp. 69–70.

Bjorklund, David F., and Barbara. "I Forget." *Parents,* August 1992, pp. 62–68.

Bower, Bruce. "Traumatic Memories: Lost and Found." *Science News* 139 (May 25, 1991), p. 333.

Braham, Barbara J. *Calm Down: How to Manage Stress at Work.* Glenview, Ill.: Scott, Foresman, 1990, pp. 62, 76.

Buhagiar, Marion, ed. *The Book of Secrets.* New York: Boardroom Reports, 1989, pp. 63, 179, 192, 198, 202, 232, 235, 241.

Burns, B. "In New Zealand, Good Reading and Writing Come 'Naturally'." *Newsweek* 118 (December 2, 1991), p. 118.

Burns, David D. "How to Conquer Anxiety." *Reader's Digest* 88, no. 524 (February 1991), p. 14.

C

Calonius, Erik. "How Top Managers Manage Their Time." *Forbes,* June 4, 1990, pp. 250–62.

Costley, Dan L., and Ralph Todd. *Human Relations in Organizations.* 4th ed. St. Paul: West Publishing, 1991, pp. 209–19, 235–38, 284, 313–16, 465.

D

Dickey, Thomas, ed. *The Wellness Encyclopedia.* Boston: Houghton Mifflin, 1991, p. 23.

Dobie, Kathie. "The New Volunteers." *Vogue* 181 (August 1991), p. 213.

E

Erickson, Deborah. "Lighten Up." *Scientific American* 264, no. 14 (June 1991), pp. 116–17.

F

Forbes, Malcolm S. "Fact and Comment." *Forbes,* May 29, 1989, pp. 19–21.

G

Gillispie, Charles, ed. *Dictionary of Scientific Biography.* Vol. 1. New York: Charles Scribner's Sons, 1970, pp. 354–56.

Gossage, Loyce C. *Business Mathematics: A College Course.* Cincinnati: South-Western, 1989, pp. 290, 543–44.

H

Haedekel, Peter. "Half of the Economy Is Collapsing, But There Are Some Pockets of Strength." *The Gazette* (Montreal, Canada), October 10, 1992, p. D-1.

Hamilton, Joan. "A Video Game That Tells if Employees Are Fit for Work." *Business Week,* June 3, 1991, p. 36.

Hawkins, Del I.; Roger J. Best; and Kenneth A. Coney. *Consumer Behavior: Implications for Marketing Strategy.* 5th ed. Homewood, Ill.: Richard D. Irwin, 1992, pp. 71, 132–33.

Horgan, John. "What if They Don't Have Radios?" *Scientific American* 268 (Fall 1993), p. 30.

J

Johnson, Otto, ed. *Information Please Almanac.* Boston: Houghton Mifflin, 1993, pp. 756, 890–91.

L

Larson, David E., ed. *Mayo Clinic Family Health Book.* New York: William Morrow, 1990, p. 350.

Lussier, Robert N. *Human Relations in Organizations: A Skill Building Approach.* Homewood, Ill.: Richard D. Irwin, 1993, p. 76.

M

Matthews, Peter, ed. *Guinness Book of World Records.* Middlesex, England: Guinness Publishing, 1993, pp. 61, 65, 157, 206–7.

May, Robert M. "How Many Species on Earth?" *Scientific American* 276 (October 1992), pp. 42–48.

McCauley, Jane R. *Dinnertime for Animals.* Washington, D.C.: National Geographic Society, 1991, p. 26.

McWhorter, Kathleen T. *Efficient and Flexible Reading.* Boston: Little Brown, 1983, p. 81.

Mitchell, Emily. "Look Who's Listening Too." *Time* 138 (September 30, 1991), p. 76.

Moseley, Maboth. *Irascible Genius: The Life of Charles Babbage.* Chicago: Regenery, 1964.

P

Panati, Charles. *Panati's Extraordinary Origins of Everyday Things.* New York: Harper & Row, 1987, pp. 3–9, 21, 25–26.

Pauk, Walter. *How to Study in College.* 3rd ed. Boston: Houghton Mifflin, 1984, pp. 127–34, 211–15.

Polley, Jane, ed. *Stories Behind Everyday Things.* Pleasantville, N.Y.: Reader's Digest, 1980, pp. 258–59, 367.

S

Satiman, Amy. "To Get Ahead, You Have to Put on an Act." *U.S. News and World Report* 110 (May 13, 1991), p. 90.

Schaun, George, and Virginia. *American Holidays and Special Days.* Lanham, Md.: Maryland Historical Press, 1986, pp. 44, 62, 99, 113, 123.

Segal, Troy. "When Johnny's Whole Family Can't Read." *Business Week,* July 20, 1992, p. 68.

Seidler, Horst; Wolfram Bernhard; Maria Teschler-Nicola; Werner Platzer; Dieter zur Neddlen; Rainer Henn; Andreas Oberhauser; and Thorstein Sjovold. "Some Anthropological Aspects of the Prehistoric Tyrolean Ice Man." *Science* 258 (October 16, 1992), pp. 455–57.

Seligman, Daniel. "Searching for Integrity." *Fortune* 127 (March 8, 1993), p. 140.

Sellers, Patricia. "I Am the Luckiest Person I've Ever Met." *Fortune* 126 (August 10, 1992), pp. 92–93.

"Snack to Attention." *Prevention,* August 1990, pp. 8–9.

Starr, Cecie, and Ralph Taggart. *Biology: The Unity and Diversity of Life.* 5th ed. Belmont, Calif.: Wadsworth, 1989, pp. 109–11, 318–19, 442, glossary.

Statford, Sherman P. "America Won't Win Till It Reads More." *Fortune,* 124 (November 18, 1991), p. 202.

Stix, Gary. "Human Spec Sheet." *Scientific American* 265 (November 1991), pp. 132–33.

Stone, Judith. "Wise Up, Sweetheart." *Discover* 13 (November 1992), pp. 36–40.

Symonds, Bill. "Blitz Your Way Through *War and Peace.*" *Business Week,* May 14, 1990, p. 162.

T

Tilton, Rita; J. Howard Jackson; and Sue Chappel Rigby. *The Electronic Office: Procedures and Administration.* Cincinnati: South-Western, 1991, pp. 31, 141–42.

Touflexis, A. "Drowsy America." *Time* 136 (December 17, 1990), pp. 78–81.

U

U.S. Bureau of the Census. *Statistical Abstracts of the United States 1991.* 11th ed. Washington, D.C.: Government Printing Office, p. 786.

W

Waldrop, Theresa. "They Are Engineered Like No Other Students in the World." *Newsweek* 118 (December 2, 1991), pp. 61–62.

West, Ann. *Newspaper Journalism.* Overland Park, Kans.: News Relief, Inc., 1992.

World Book Encyclopedia. 1992 ed., vol. 5, s.v. "Holmes, Sherlock," pp. 318–19.

World Book Encyclopedia. 1992 ed., vol. 9, s.v. "Doyle, Sir Arthur," p. 296.

World Book Encyclopedia. 1992 ed., vol. 11, s.v. "Journalism," p. 173.

World Book Encyclopedia. 1992 ed., vol. 14, s.v. "Newspapers," pp. 384, 390.

World Book Encyclopedia. 1992 ed., vol. 16, s.v. "Royal Household of Great Britain," p. 498.

Index